The Dover Demon

Alien or Cryptid?

Roberta Ellis

ISBN: 978-1-77961-199-4
Imprint: Incredulous
Copyright © 2024 Roberta Ellis.
All Rights Reserved.

Contents

Introduction 1
Background of the Dover Demon 1

Chapter 1: Alien Encounters 7
History of Alien Encounters 7
Characteristics of Alien Encounters 15
Theories and Explanations 26

Chapter 2: Cryptids and Cryptozoology 41
Definition and History of Cryptozoology 41
Famous Cryptid Cases 50
Evidence and Skepticism 59

Chapter 3: The Dover Demon Sightings 69
Overview of the Dover Demon Sightings 69
Analysis of the Sightings 76
Debunking or Validating the Dover Demon 86

Chapter 4: Paranormal Phenomena 97
Ghosts and Hauntings 97
UFO Sightings and Alien Abductions 108
Interactions between Paranormal Phenomena 117
Theories and Explanations for the Paranormal 125

Chapter 5: Scientific Perspectives 135
Mainstream Scientific Rejection of Cryptids and Aliens 135
Alternative Scientific Perspectives 141
Bridging the Gap between Science and the Paranormal 151

Chapter 6: Cultural and Folkloric Significance 163
Mythology and Folklore 163
Cryptozoology in Popular Culture 170
The Role of Belief Systems in Cryptozoology 179

Chapter 7: Conclusion and Future Directions 189
Summary of Findings 189
Implications and Significance 197
Chapter 7: Conclusion and Future Directions 198
Future Directions for Research 202

Index 215

Introduction

Background of the Dover Demon

The Dover Demon Sightings in 1977

The Dover Demon sightings in 1977 marked a significant moment in the world of cryptozoology and paranormal research. This section will explore the background of these sightings, the witnesses' descriptions, the location and time of the sightings, and comparisons to other cryptid cases.

Background of the Dover Demon

The Dover Demon is a cryptid that was first sighted in the small town of Dover, Massachusetts, during a brief period in 1977. The creature is described as being humanoid in appearance, with a hairless, pale, and elongated body. Witnesses have reported seeing glowing orange eyes and long, thin fingers. These sightings sparked a flurry of public interest and media coverage, making the Dover Demon one of the most famous cryptids in modern folklore.

The Dover Demon Sightings in 1977

In the spring of 1977, three separate sightings of the Dover Demon occurred within a span of two nights, from April 21 to April 22. The first sighting was reported by Bill Bartlett, a 17-year-old high school student, who claimed to have encountered the creature while driving home late at night. Bartlett described the Dover Demon as a creature with glowing eyes and long, thin fingers, standing on a stone wall. He estimated the creature's height to be about three to four feet.

The second sighting occurred later that same night, when John Baxter, a 15-year-old friend of Bartlett, claimed to have seen the Dover Demon near a wooded area. Baxter's description closely matched that of Bartlett, with glowing orange eyes and a humanoid figure.

The third and final sighting occurred on the following night, when Abby Brabham, an 18-year-old, reported seeing a similar creature while driving with friends. Brabham's description of the creature matched the previous sightings, further adding to the mystery and intrigue surrounding the Dover Demon.

Public Reaction and Media Coverage

The Dover Demon sightings garnered attention not only from the local community but also from the media. Local newspapers and television stations covered the story extensively, fueling public fascination with the creature. The sightings also attracted the attention of cryptozoologists, paranormal investigators, and skeptics, all seeking to uncover the truth behind the Dover Demon phenomenon.

Impact on Local Community

The Dover Demon sightings had a profound impact on the local community. Many residents of Dover became fearful and cautious, especially at night. Some residents reported hearing strange noises or seeing unusual disturbances in the area where the sightings occurred. The community tension surrounding the Dover Demon persisted long after the initial sightings, leaving a lasting impression on the town.

Comparisons to Other Cryptid Cases

Various theories have been put forward to explain the Dover Demon sightings. Some have compared the creature to other cryptids, such as the Mothman of West Virginia or the Chupacabra of Latin America, due to their similar descriptions and eerie encounters. These comparisons have led to debates among researchers, with some suggesting a possible connection between these cryptids or shared phenomena in different regions.

In conclusion, the Dover Demon sightings in 1977 left an indelible mark on the field of cryptozoology and sparked public fascination with the existence of mysterious creatures. The detailed eyewitness accounts and the media coverage surrounding these sightings have made the Dover Demon one of the most compelling cases in the study of cryptids and paranormal phenomena.

Public Reaction and Media Coverage

The Dover Demon sightings in 1977 garnered significant public reaction and media coverage, capturing the attention of both local and national media outlets. The strange and mysterious nature of the creature described by eyewitnesses sparked curiosity and intrigue among the general public, leading to widespread interest in the case.

1. Media Coverage: The media played a crucial role in disseminating information about the Dover Demon sightings. Local newspapers, such as the Dover-Sherborn Press and the Boston Globe, reported on the sightings, providing details about the eyewitness testimonies and descriptions of the creature. National media outlets, including television and radio stations, also picked up on the story, amplifying its reach and generating further public awareness.

2. Public Fascination: The Dover Demon sightings captivated the public imagination due to their uniqueness and unexplained nature. People were intrigued by the idea of a strange creature lurking in their own backyard, and the mystery surrounding its origins and intentions only deepened the intrigue. Many individuals became amateur investigators, actively engaging in conversations and debates about the sightings in their communities.

3. Speculation and Conspiracy Theories: As with any sensational case, the Dover Demon sightings gave rise to various speculations and conspiracy theories. Some people viewed the creature as an extraterrestrial being, linking it to other alien encounters and UFO sightings. Others believed it to be a result of government experimentation or a creature from another dimension. These theories added to the public's fascination and fueled discussions surrounding the case.

4. Local Community Impact: The Dover Demon sightings had a significant impact on the local community. The small town of Dover, Massachusetts, became the center of attention, with residents and neighboring communities actively participating in the search for answers. The heightened sense of community engagement and shared experience brought people together, fostering a sense of camaraderie and community spirit.

5. Psychological Effects: The Dover Demon sightings triggered a range of psychological responses among those who experienced the sightings or learned about them through the media. Some individuals reported feelings of fear and unease, while others experienced excitement and curiosity. The sightings also sparked discussions about the nature of reality and the existence of unknown entities, challenging prevailing beliefs and encouraging a broader exploration of the unknown.

6. Media Influence on Public Perception: The media coverage of the Dover

Demon sightings played a significant role in shaping public perception of the case. The narrative constructed by the media, including the use of visuals and dramatic storytelling techniques, influenced how people interpreted and understood the sightings. This highlights the media's influence in shaping public opinion and the need for critical evaluation of information in cases of paranormal sightings.

7. Skepticism and Debunking: While many individuals were intrigued by the Dover Demon sightings, others remained skeptical and sought to debunk the claims. Skeptics questioned the reliability of eyewitness testimonies and examined alternative explanations, such as misidentifications or hoaxes. The presence of skeptics and their arguments added another layer of complexity to the public reaction and media coverage, fostering critical thinking and scientific inquiry.

In conclusion, the Dover Demon sightings in 1977 generated significant public reaction and media coverage. The mysterious nature of the creature described by eyewitnesses, coupled with the media's portrayal of the case, fueled public fascination and speculation. The impact on the local community and the psychological effects experienced by individuals further emphasized the significance of the sightings. However, skepticism and debunking also played a role, highlighting the need for critical evaluation and scientific inquiry in such cases. The media's influence on public perception underscores the importance of responsible reporting and the role it plays in shaping the narrative surrounding paranormal phenomena.

Impact on Local Community

The Dover Demon sightings in 1977 had a significant impact on the local community in Dover, Massachusetts. The eerie encounters with this mysterious creature caused fear, confusion, and curiosity among the residents, leading to a variety of reactions and changes in the community dynamics.

First and foremost, the Dover Demon sightings caused a sense of unease and apprehension among the local population. The idea that a strange and unknown creature was roaming their town created a heightened sense of fear and anxiety. People became cautious and fearful of going out after dark, and parents kept a closer eye on their children. This fear had a direct impact on the daily lives of the residents, affecting their routines and activities.

The media coverage of the Dover Demon sightings further exacerbated the impact on the local community. Newspapers, television stations, and radio shows picked up the story, spreading it far beyond the Dover town limits. The increased attention brought a flood of reporters, enthusiasts, and curious individuals to the area, eager to investigate the sightings themselves. This influx of outsiders disrupted the peaceful small-town atmosphere and put a strain on the resources of the local community.

The Dover Demon sightings also caused a ripple effect on the local economy. Businesses in Dover and nearby towns capitalized on the sudden interest in the area, selling merchandise related to the creature, such as t-shirts, posters, and souvenirs. Restaurants and cafes experienced an increase in customers as visitors flocked to the area. Additionally, the tourism industry in Dover received a boost as people sought out guided tours and exploration trips to the sites where the sightings occurred. However, this economic boom was short-lived, as the interest eventually waned, leaving some businesses struggling to sustain themselves once again.

The impact on the mental and emotional well-being of the individuals involved cannot be overlooked. The eyewitnesses who encountered the Dover Demon firsthand experienced a mixture of confusion, fear, and fascination. The psychological aftermath of such an encounter can be profound and long-lasting. Some individuals may have developed phobias or anxiety disorders as a result of the sightings, while others became obsessed with the phenomenon and dedicated their lives to studying cryptids and the paranormal.

The Dover Demon sightings also brought the local community closer together, as people came together to share their experiences, exchange theories, and seek solace in their shared fears. Community meetings were held, allowing residents to voice their concerns and opinions. This sense of unity in the face of a mysterious and unexplained phenomenon helped to strengthen social bonds and foster a collective identity among the residents of Dover.

In terms of long-term impact, the Dover Demon sightings put Dover on the map as a destination for both believers and skeptics of the paranormal. The town became known as a "hotspot" for cryptid sightings and paranormal activities, attracting researchers, investigators, and enthusiasts from around the world. Even years after the initial sightings, the legacy of the Dover Demon continues to shape the community, with annual events and festivals celebrating the creature and its impact on the town.

It is worth noting that not all members of the local community were affected in the same way. While some embraced the Dover Demon as a source of pride and intrigue, others dismissed it as a hoax or a figment of people's imaginations. This diversity of opinions added another layer of complexity to the impact on the local community, causing divisions and debates among residents.

In summary, the Dover Demon sightings had a profound impact on the local community in Dover, Massachusetts. The encounters with this mysterious creature caused fear, curiosity, and intrigue among the residents, and brought attention and disruption to the town. The events affected the daily lives, mental well-being, economy, and social dynamics of the community, leaving a lasting legacy that continues to shape Dover's identity to this day.

Chapter 1: Alien Encounters

History of Alien Encounters

Roswell Incident

The Roswell Incident is one of the most famous and controversial events in UFO research. It refers to an incident that occurred in Roswell, New Mexico, in July 1947, when an unidentified object crashed on a ranch near the town. The Roswell Incident has become synonymous with conspiracy theories and claims of a government cover-up of extraterrestrial contact. In this section, we will explore the details of the incident, the various theories surrounding it, and the scientific analysis conducted to understand what really happened.

Background

To understand the significance of the Roswell Incident, it is essential to consider the context of the time. In the late 1940s, there was a surge in reports of unidentified flying objects (UFOs) across the United States. The term "flying saucer" had entered popular culture after the sighting by Kenneth Arnold in 1947, which triggered a wave of UFO sightings and public fascination with the idea of extraterrestrial life.

Events of the Roswell Incident

On the evening of July 2, 1947, William Brazel, a rancher, discovered debris scattered across his property. He described it as metallic and lightweight, unlike anything he had seen before. Suspecting it might be the remains of a crashed aircraft, Brazel reported it to the local sheriff. The next day, the news of the crash reached the Roswell Army Air Field, prompting investigations by military personnel.

Colonel William Blanchard, the base commander, initially issued a press release stating that they had recovered a "flying disc." The news spread quickly, and headlines of a crashed flying saucer hit newspapers nationwide. However, within hours, the military changed its statement, claiming that the recovered object was merely a weather balloon.

Government Cover-up or Weather Balloon Explanation?

The conflicting statements by the military regarding the nature of the recovered object fueled conspiracy theories and speculations about a government cover-up. UFO enthusiasts and conspiracy theorists argue that the original press release, describing a "flying disc," was closer to the truth than the subsequent weather balloon explanation.

The U.S. government's official position is that the recovered object was, in fact, a weather balloon from Project Mogul, a top-secret operation to monitor Soviet nuclear tests. According to this explanation, the debris found at the crash site was a combination of materials used in the high-altitude balloon experiments, including foil, rubber strips, and wooden sticks.

Scientific Analysis

Scientists and researchers have examined the Roswell Incident from various perspectives, aiming to shed light on the truth behind the event. Several studies have focused on analyzing the witness testimonies, the physical evidence, and the military's response to the incident.

Eyewitness accounts play a crucial role in trying to understand the events of the Roswell Incident. Researchers have interviewed witnesses who claim to have seen strange debris and even alien bodies at the crash site. However, it is essential to consider the potential biases and the passage of time when evaluating witness testimonies.

In terms of physical evidence, some researchers argue that the debris recovered from the site does not match the materials used in weather balloons. They claim that the foil-like material found at the crash site is not consistent with the reflective radar targets used in Project Mogul.

Critics of the extraterrestrial hypothesis point to alternative explanations, such as misidentified military experiments or psychological factors that may have influenced witness perceptions. They argue that the Roswell Incident can be explained within the context of human psychology, misinformation, and sociocultural factors.

Unconventional Perspective: The Fermi Paradox

One unconventional perspective to consider when exploring the Roswell Incident is the Fermi Paradox. In the 1950s, physicist Enrico Fermi famously asked, "Where is everybody?" He questioned why, given the vastness of the universe and the potential for advanced civilizations, we have not encountered any extraterrestrial intelligence.

Applying the Fermi Paradox to the Roswell Incident, we can ask whether the reported crash was an extraterrestrial spacecraft. If it were, why haven't we had any widespread and undeniable contact with aliens since then? This perspective adds an additional layer to the debate, inviting us to consider the implications of the Roswell Incident within the broader context of the search for extraterrestrial life.

Resources and Further Reading

For readers interested in diving deeper into the Roswell Incident and its various theories, the following resources provide valuable information:

- Book: "The Roswell Incident" by Charles Berlitz and William L. Moore.
- Documentary: "The Roswell UFO Incident" directed by Paul Davids.
- Website: The International UFO Museum and Research Center, located in Roswell, New Mexico, offers extensive resources and exhibits on the Roswell Incident.

Key Takeaways

- The Roswell Incident refers to the crash of an unidentified object near Roswell, New Mexico, in July 1947.
- The event sparked conspiracy theories and claims of a government cover-up of extraterrestrial contact.
- The official explanation attributes the incident to a weather balloon from Project Mogul.
- Scientists have conducted analysis of eyewitness testimonies and physical evidence to try to uncover the truth behind the incident.
- The Fermi Paradox adds an unconventional perspective, urging us to consider the Roswell Incident within the broader context of the search for extraterrestrial life.

In the next chapter, we will explore another famous case of alleged alien abduction, the Betty and Barney Hill abduction case. We will delve into the details of their encounter, the psychological implications, and the impact on the study of alien abductions.

Betty and Barney Hill Abduction Case

The Betty and Barney Hill abduction case is one of the most famous and well-documented cases of alleged alien abduction in history. It occurred in September 1961, when Betty and Barney Hill, an interracial couple from New Hampshire, claimed to have been abducted by extraterrestrial beings while driving home from a vacation.

Background

Betty and Barney Hill were an ordinary couple who lived in Portsmouth, New Hampshire. On the night of September 19, 1961, they were driving back from a trip to Niagara Falls when they noticed a bright light in the sky. As they continued driving, they observed the light disappearing and reappearing multiple times, seemingly following their car.

The Abduction Experience

As the Hills continued their journey, they began experiencing a period of missing time. They could not account for a period of about two hours of their travel time, which they could not recall. Later, under hypnosis, they revealed a detailed account of what they believed had happened to them during that time.

According to their recollections, they claimed to have been stopped by a group of humanoid beings who took them on board a craft. They described the beings as about five feet tall, with grayish skin, large eyes, and long arms. The Hills reported being subjected to medical examinations and mental telepathy, and they were told by the aliens that they would have no conscious memory of the event.

Investigation and Publicity

After the Hills' experience, they sought help from a local investigator and later underwent hypnosis to recover their memories of the alleged abduction. Under regression hypnosis, they both gave consistent and detailed accounts of the event. This sparked public and media interest in their case, and it became one of the first widely publicized cases of alien abduction.

Skepticism and Criticism

As with any extraordinary claim, the Betty and Barney Hill abduction case has attracted skepticism and criticism. Some skeptics argue that the Hills' experiences were simply the result of false memories or hallucinations brought on by the stress of their interracial marriage during a time of racial tension in the United States.

Others question the reliability of hypnosis as a tool for recovering accurate memories. They argue that hypnosis can create false memories, leading the subjects to believe in events that did not actually occur.

Impact and Legacy

The Betty and Barney Hill abduction case had a profound impact on popular culture and the study of UFO phenomena. It played a crucial role in shaping public perception of alien encounters and helped establish the concept of alien abduction as a distinct phenomenon.

The case also influenced subsequent research into the field of ufology and the study of alien abductions. It has served as a reference point for investigators and researchers studying similar cases, and it has sparked ongoing debates about the nature of extraterrestrial contact and its implications for humanity.

Unconventional Perspective: The Psychological Explanation

While the Betty and Barney Hill abduction case is often presented within the framework of alien encounters, there is an unconventional perspective to consider: the psychological explanation.

From a psychological standpoint, the Hill's alleged abduction experience can be interpreted as a manifestation of psychological phenomena rather than a physical encounter with extraterrestrial beings. This perspective suggests that the Hills' memories were constructed through a combination of suggestibility, imagination, and the influence of cultural beliefs about alien abductions.

The psychological explanation posits that the Hills may have experienced a form of sleep paralysis, a phenomenon in which individuals are temporarily unable to move or speak during the transition between wakefulness and sleep. Sleep paralysis can be accompanied by hallucinations and vivid, lifelike nightmares, which may explain the Hills' detailed recollections of the abduction.

Additionally, the cultural context in which the Hills' experience occurred cannot be ignored. During the 1960s, the UFO phenomenon and the notion of alien abductions were gaining prominence in popular culture. It is possible that Betty and Barney Hill's experience was influenced by these cultural beliefs, shaping their interpretation of their missing time and reinforcing their memories of the abduction.

While the psychological explanation does not discount the Hills' subjective experience, it offers an alternative perspective that considers the role of the human mind and cultural factors in shaping and interpreting extraordinary events.

Resources and Further Reading

For those interested in learning more about the Betty and Barney Hill abduction case, the following resources provide a comprehensive exploration of the case from various perspectives:

1. Fuller, John G. (1966). "The Interrupted Journey". ISBN: 978-0803805028. A book written by John G. Fuller, which tells the story of Betty and Barney Hill's abduction case in detail.

2. Clark, Jerome (2016). "The UFO Book: Encyclopedia of the Extraterrestrial". ISBN: 978-1578595615. A comprehensive guide to UFOs and alien encounters, including a chapter on the Betty and Barney Hill case.

3. Scientific American, "The Continuing Relevance of the Betty and Barney Hill Abduction Case" (2016). An article that examines the lasting impact and significance of the Betty and Barney Hill case from a scientific perspective.

4. Smithsonian Channel, "The Alien Files: Betty and Barney Hill" (2014). A documentary that provides an in-depth exploration of the Betty and Barney Hill abduction case, featuring interviews with experts and researchers.

By exploring these resources, readers can gain a deeper understanding of the Betty and Barney Hill abduction case, its historical and cultural significance, and the ongoing debates surrounding the nature of alien abductions.

Exercises

1. Do you think the Betty and Barney Hill abduction case can be explained solely by psychological factors, or do you believe their experience was a genuine encounter with extraterrestrial beings? Provide reasons for your answer.

2. Conduct further research on the concept of sleep paralysis and its potential connection to alien abduction experiences. Write a brief summary of your findings.

3. Explore other famous cases of alleged alien abductions and compare them to the Betty and Barney Hill case. Identify similarities and differences in the reported experiences and discuss possible explanations.

4. Imagine you are a psychologist conducting research on the psychological factors underlying belief in alien abductions. Design an experiment to investigate

the influence of suggestibility and cultural beliefs on individuals' interpretation of extraordinary experiences.

Remember to approach these exercises with an open mind, considering multiple perspectives and evaluating the evidence critically.

Travis Walton Alien Encounter

In this section, we will explore the Travis Walton Alien Encounter, one of the most famous cases of alleged alien abduction. The incident took place in 1975 in the Apache-Sitgreaves National Forest in Arizona, USA. Travis Walton, a young logger, claimed to have been abducted by alien beings and taken aboard their spacecraft for a period of five days.

Background

On November 5, 1975, Travis Walton and his six fellow workers were returning home after a day of logging in the forest. As they drove along a remote road, they noticed a strange light in the sky. Intrigued, they decided to investigate further. Walton, driven by curiosity, got out of the truck and approached the hovering light.

The Encounter

According to Walton's account, as he got closer to the light, a beam of energy struck him, knocking him unconscious. His friends, in a state of panic, fled the scene, leaving Walton behind. When they returned a few minutes later, Walton and the spacecraft were gone.

Walton claimed that he woke up inside a small, dimly lit room, surrounded by three short-statured beings with large eyes and bald heads. He described these beings as looking humanoid but with distinct alien features. They communicated with him telepathically and performed various medical examinations on him.

Public and Media Response

News of Walton's alleged abduction quickly spread, capturing the attention of the media and the public. The incident received widespread coverage, with various publications and television networks reporting on the case. Skeptics dismissed the story as a hoax, while believers saw it as compelling evidence of extraterrestrial contact.

Investigation and Controversy

An extensive investigation was conducted by law enforcement authorities, who initially suspected foul play or a possible murder. Walton was subjected to polygraph tests, which he passed. His friends, who were witnesses to the event, also underwent polygraph tests and were deemed to be telling the truth.

Despite the polygraph results, many skeptics questioned the credibility of the witnesses and suggested that the entire incident was a well-orchestrated hoax. Some speculated that Walton and his friends fabricated the story for financial gain or notoriety.

Other Explanations

There have been several theories proposed to explain the Travis Walton Alien Encounter. One explanation is that the event was a result of a hallucination or sleep paralysis experienced by Walton. These phenomena can create vivid and realistic experiences that feel like actual events.

Another theory suggests that the encounter was a case of misidentified natural phenomena or military activity. Proponents of this theory argue that the strange light witnessed by Walton and his friends could have been an experimental aircraft or some other unconventional technology.

Legacy and Influence

The Travis Walton Alien Encounter remains an influential case in the field of ufology and alien abduction research. It has inspired books, documentaries, and movies, including the 1993 film "Fire in the Sky," which dramatized Walton's experience.

The controversy surrounding the incident continues to fuel discussions and debates about the existence of extraterrestrial life and the authenticity of abduction claims. Skeptics maintain that the encounter was a hoax, while believers view it as a compelling piece of evidence supporting the existence of intelligent beings from other planets.

Conclusion

The Travis Walton Alien Encounter is a captivating and controversial case that has left a lasting impact on the field of UFO research. Whether one believes in Walton's account or not, the incident serves as a reminder of the enduring fascination with the possibility of extraterrestrial life and the mysteries that lie beyond our understanding.

Characteristics of Alien Encounters

Close Encounters of the First Kind

In the realm of extraterrestrial encounters, Close Encounters of the First Kind refer to sightings of unidentified flying objects (UFOs) at a close proximity. This category of encounters encompasses a wide range of observations, from distant sightings to those where an object is within 500 feet of the witness. Close Encounters of the First Kind are often the most common type reported by individuals who claim to have witnessed UFOs.

Characteristics of Close Encounters of the First Kind

Close Encounters of the First Kind share some common characteristics that distinguish them from other types of encounters. These characteristics include:

1. **Visual Observation:** Witnessing the UFO through direct visual contact is a key feature of a Close Encounter of the First Kind. This can involve seeing a UFO in the sky or observing a stationary object on the ground.

2. **Proximity:** The UFO is observed at a relatively close distance, usually within 500 feet. This allows for a detailed observation of the object's physical attributes and movements.

3. **Duration:** The encounter typically lasts for a significant period, allowing the witness to observe the UFO for an extended amount of time. This longer duration sets it apart from briefer sightings.

4. **Multiple Witnesses:** Close Encounters of the First Kind often involve multiple witnesses who concurrently observe the same UFO. This aspect provides additional credibility to the sighting and strengthens the case for further investigation.

5. **Physical Effects:** In some cases, witnesses of Close Encounters of the First Kind report experiencing physical effects such as temporary paralysis, burns, or other physiological symptoms. These effects are not always consistent but are occasionally reported alongside the sighting.

Examples of Close Encounters of the First Kind

Several notable examples of Close Encounters of the First Kind have garnered significant attention and investigation over the years:

1. **The Phoenix Lights (1997):** On March 13, 1997, thousands of witnesses in Arizona reported observing a large triangular formation of lights in the sky. The lights remained visible for several hours, leading to widespread speculation and controversy.

2. **The Tehran UFO Incident (1976):** In September 1976, two Iranian fighter jets engaged with an unknown object over Tehran. Both pilots reported radar and visual contact with a large, bright object that demonstrated incredible speed and maneuverability.

3. **The Lubbock Lights (1951):** In August 1951, multiple witnesses in Lubbock, Texas, observed a V-shaped formation of lights moving silently across the sky. The sighting was captured in a now-famous photograph and generated considerable interest at the time.

The Importance of Close Encounters of the First Kind

Close Encounters of the First Kind are crucial in the study of UFO phenomena for several reasons:

1. **Scientific Investigation:** Close Encounters of the First Kind provide scientists and researchers with opportunities to collect data and gather firsthand accounts of UFO sightings. This data can be invaluable in determining patterns and potentially unraveling the mystery of UFOs.

2. **Witness Credibility:** Multiple witnesses observing the same UFO at close range enhances the credibility of the sighting. This strengthens the case for scientific scrutiny and can lead to further investigation and analysis.

3. **Understanding UFO Characteristics:** Studying Close Encounters of the First Kind can provide insights into the physical attributes and behavior of UFOs. By analyzing witness testimonies and other data, researchers can better understand the capabilities and nature of these unidentified objects.

Challenges and Skepticism

As with any subject involving extraordinary claims, Close Encounters of the First Kind also face skepticism and challenges:

1. **Psychological Explanation:** Some skeptics argue that Close Encounters of the First Kind can be attributed to misperception, psychological factors, or

mass hysteria. They propose that witnesses may misinterpret ordinary objects or phenomena as extraterrestrial in nature.

2. **Hoaxes and Misidentifications:** Close Encounters of the First Kind are susceptible to hoaxes, misidentifications, and intentional deception. It is essential to investigate these encounters thoroughly to filter out unreliable or fabricated reports.

3. **Lack of Physical Evidence:** Close Encounters of the First Kind often lack substantial physical evidence to support the claims made by witnesses. This makes it challenging to subject these encounters to rigorous scientific analysis.

Conclusion

Close Encounters of the First Kind represent an essential category of UFO sightings, characterized by direct visual observation of unidentified objects at a close range. These encounters provide significant opportunities for scientific investigation and understanding of UFO phenomena. However, they also require careful scrutiny due to the challenges posed by psychological explanations, hoaxes, and the lack of physical evidence. Exploring Close Encounters of the First Kind is a crucial step toward unraveling the mystery of UFOs and determining their true nature.

Close Encounters of the Second Kind

Close Encounters of the Second Kind refer to encounters with extraterrestrial beings or objects that leave physical evidence behind. Unlike the close encounters of the first kind, which are purely visual sightings, encounters of the second kind involve tangible effects on the environment. In this section, we will explore the characteristics, examples, and implications of close encounters of the second kind.

Characteristics of Close Encounters of the Second Kind

Close encounters of the second kind are distinguished by the physical traces or effects they leave behind. These encounters often involve direct interactions with the environment, leaving visible signs of their presence. Some common characteristics of close encounters of the second kind include:

1. **Physical traces:** Close encounters of the second kind often leave physical evidence such as markings, imprints, or scorch marks at the location of the encounter. These physical traces can validate the authenticity of the

encounter and provide tangible evidence that something out of the ordinary occurred.

2. Electromagnetic effects: In many cases, close encounters of the second kind are accompanied by electromagnetic disturbances. Witnesses often report disruptions in electronic devices, such as radios or car engines, or anomalies in the local electromagnetic field. These electromagnetic effects can provide scientific data to support the veracity of the encounter.

3. Animal reactions: Close encounters of the second kind can also affect the behavior of animals in the vicinity. Witnesses have reported unusual behavior in animals, such as agitation, panic, or even temporary paralysis. These reactions can offer additional corroborating evidence of the encounter.

4. Time anomalies: Some close encounters of the second kind involve temporary distortions in time. Witnesses may report missing time or time dilation, where hours seem to pass in a matter of minutes. These time anomalies contribute to the mystique and intrigue surrounding these encounters.

While encounters of the second kind can vary in their specific characteristics, they all share the common feature of leaving physical evidence or having measurable effects on the environment.

Examples of Close Encounters of the Second Kind

Several well-known cases provide examples of close encounters of the second kind and the physical evidence they left behind. Let's explore a few notable examples:

1. The Rendlesham Forest Incident: In December 1980, multiple U.S. Air Force personnel stationed at RAF Woodbridge in England witnessed a series of unexplained events. Witnesses observed a triangular-shaped craft emitting a bright light in the nearby Rendlesham Forest. The encounter included physical traces such as impressions on the ground, scorch marks on tree branches, and elevated radiation levels at the site of the incident.

2. The Cash-Landrum Incident: On December 29, 1980, Betty Cash, Vickie Landrum, and Colby Landrum encountered a large diamond-shaped object hovering over the road near Huffman, Texas. The witnesses felt intense heat radiating from the craft, which resulted in physical effects such as burns and

hair loss. The case attracted significant attention due to the severity of the witnesses' injuries and subsequent legal actions.

3. The Coyne Helicopter Incident: In October 1973, a U.S. Army Reserve helicopter encountered a UFO near Mansfield, Ohio. The witnesses reported electromagnetic effects, including interference with their navigation and communication systems. The encounter left a lasting impact on the witnesses, leading to subsequent investigations by both civilian and military authorities.

These examples highlight the physical evidence and effects associated with close encounters of the second kind, further adding to the credibility and interest in these incidents.

Implications and Exploration

Close encounters of the second kind have significant implications for our understanding of extraterrestrial phenomena and the nature of reality itself. The physical evidence left behind in these encounters provides an opportunity for scientific investigation and exploration.

By studying the physical traces and effects, scientists can gather data to support or refute the claims made by witnesses. This data can contribute to our understanding of the technological capabilities of extraterrestrial beings, their interactions with our environment, and the potential implications for humanity.

Furthermore, close encounters of the second kind invite us to question our understanding of the laws of physics and the boundaries of our knowledge. The presence of time anomalies and electromagnetic disturbances challenges existing scientific theories and raises intriguing questions about the nature of space-time.

Exploring and understanding close encounters of the second kind requires interdisciplinary collaboration between scientists, engineers, psychologists, and experts in various fields. This type of collaboration can help develop comprehensive theories and methodologies to investigate and interpret these encounters.

In conclusion, close encounters of the second kind offer a fascinating realm of exploration within the broader field of alien encounters. The physical evidence and effects associated with these encounters provide an exciting avenue for scientific investigation and multidisciplinary research. By delving into the characteristics, examples, and implications of close encounters of the second kind, we can expand our understanding of extraterrestrial phenomena and push the boundaries of our knowledge.

Close Encounters of the Third Kind

Close Encounters of the Third Kind refers to a type of alien encounter that involves direct interaction between humans and extraterrestrial beings. This classification was first introduced by ufologist and astronomer, J. Allen Hynek, in his book "The UFO Experience: A Scientific Inquiry" in 1972. Close Encounters of the Third Kind are considered to be the most significant and compelling encounters, as they involve not only visual sightings of unidentified flying objects (UFOs), but also direct contact and communication with alien beings.

Characteristics of Close Encounters of the Third Kind

Close Encounters of the Third Kind have specific characteristics that distinguish them from other types of alien encounters. These characteristics include:

1. Contact with Alien Beings: Close encounters of the third kind involve direct contact and communication with extraterrestrial beings. Contact can occur through various means, such as telepathy, vocal communication, or other forms of non-verbal communication.

2. Witness Observations: Witnesses of close encounters of the third kind often report seeing aliens up close and personal. They describe the appearance of the beings, such as their physical features, clothing, and behavior. These observations often provide valuable insights into the nature of the aliens.

3. Physical Traces: Close encounters of the third kind may leave behind physical traces, such as landing marks, burnt vegetation, or electromagnetic disturbances. These physical traces can serve as evidence of the encounter and are often investigated by scientists and researchers.

4. Emotional and Psychological Effects: Witnesses of close encounters of the third kind often experience a range of emotions and psychological effects, such as fear, awe, curiosity, or a sense of enlightenment. These experiences can deeply impact their lives and beliefs.

Examples of Close Encounters of the Third Kind

Several famous cases serve as examples of close encounters of the third kind and have gained significant attention within the field of ufology. These include:

1. The Pascagoula Abduction (1973): In this case, two fishermen, Charles Hickson and Calvin Parker, reported being abducted by gray-skinned humanoid creatures while fishing in Pascagoula, Mississippi. They claimed to have been subjected to medical examinations onboard a UFO.

2. The Voronezh Incident (1989): In Voronezh, Russia, multiple witnesses, including children, reported seeing a glowing, disc-shaped UFO and humanoid creatures with three eyes and robotic movements. The witnesses claimed to have observed the aliens land and interact with the environment.

3. The Travis Walton Abduction (1975): Travis Walton claimed to have been abducted by a UFO in Arizona's Apache-Sitgreaves National Forest. He alleged that he was taken onboard the UFO and encountered small, hairless humanoid beings.

Theories and Explanations for Close Encounters of the Third Kind

Close encounters of the third kind have been the subject of numerous theories and explanations. These include:

1. Extraterrestrial Visitation: The most straightforward explanation is that close encounters of the third kind are evidence of extraterrestrial visitation. Supporters of this theory argue that the physical evidence and witness testimonies are indicative of interactions with beings from other planets.

2. Psychological and Sociocultural Perspectives: Skeptics often interpret close encounters of the third kind as products of the human mind influenced by psychological and sociocultural factors. They propose that these experiences are hallucinations, misinterpretations of natural phenomena, or cultural constructs.

3. Government Cover-Up: Conspiracy theories suggest that governments are aware of the existence of extraterrestrial beings and are covering up the truth to maintain social order. They argue that close encounters of the third kind are part of a larger government conspiracy to hide evidence of alien presence.

4. Interdimensional Beings: Some theorists propose that close encounters of the third kind involve interaction with beings from parallel dimensions or alternate realities. They theorize that these beings can manipulate space-time and travel between dimensions.

Research and Investigation of Close Encounters of the Third Kind

Close encounters of the third kind have attracted significant attention from researchers and investigators. Methods used to study these encounters include:

1. Field Investigations: Researchers conduct on-site investigations to collect physical evidence, interview witnesses, and analyze the location and environmental factors. These investigations aim to gather as much information as possible to validate or debunk the encounter.

2. Hypnotic Regression: In some cases, witnesses undergo hypnotic regression to recall forgotten or suppressed memories of their encounter. Hypnosis is used to

access the subconscious mind and retrieve details that might have been overlooked or forgotten.

3. Psychological Studies: Researchers also employ psychological studies to understand witness experiences and the psychological impact of close encounters of the third kind. These studies help explore factors such as suggestibility, memory processes, and emotional responses.

4. Collaborative Research: Interdisciplinary collaborations between ufologists, psychologists, sociologists, and other experts enable a comprehensive investigation of close encounters of the third kind. By combining different perspectives, researchers can gain a better understanding of these phenomena.

Unconventional Approaches to Close Encounters of the Third Kind

In addition to conventional research and investigation, some unconventional approaches have also emerged in the study of close encounters of the third kind. These approaches aim to explore new possibilities and challenge traditional explanations. Examples include:

1. Consciousness Exploration: Some researchers explore altered states of consciousness, such as meditation and lucid dreaming, to enhance contact and communication with extraterrestrial beings. These methods are believed to facilitate a deeper connection and understanding.

2. Experiential Analysis: Researchers employ experiential analysis techniques to recreate close encounter experiences in controlled settings. By analyzing the subjective experiences of individuals who claim to have had close encounters, researchers gain insights into the nature of these phenomena.

3. Quantum Physics and Information Theory: The application of quantum physics and information theory to the study of close encounters of the third kind explores the possibility of advanced alien technology and communication methods beyond our current understanding.

Conclusion

Close Encounters of the Third Kind represent a fascinating aspect of the UFO and alien encounter phenomenon. These encounters involve direct contact and communication with extraterrestrial beings, leaving witnesses with profound and often life-changing experiences. While various theories and explanations exist, close encounters of the third kind continue to puzzle researchers, urging further investigation and exploration. The study of these encounters not only expands our understanding of the universe but also challenges our perception of reality and our place within it.

Other Types of Alien Encounters

In addition to the well-known categories of close encounters of the first, second, and third kind, there are several other types of alien encounters that have been reported and studied by researchers in the field. These encounters often involve unique aspects that set them apart from the more common categories. In this section, we will explore some of these lesser-known types of encounters and discuss their characteristics, theories, and examples.

Close Encounters of the Fourth Kind

Close encounters of the fourth kind, also known as abduction experiences, involve alleged contact and interaction between humans and extraterrestrial beings. These encounters usually entail the abduction of individuals by aliens, who may subject them to various procedures or experiments. Abduction experiences are frequently reported as being traumatic and can result in physical and psychological effects on the abductees.

Theories surrounding close encounters of the fourth kind vary widely. Some believe that these experiences are actual physical interactions with extraterrestrial beings, while others propose psychological or neurological explanations. One prominent theory suggests that abduction experiences may be hallucinations or false memories caused by sleep paralysis or hypnagogic/hypnopompic hallucinations.

One example of a close encounter of the fourth kind is the Betty and Barney Hill abduction case in 1961. The Hills claimed to have been abducted and subjected to medical examinations by beings from another planet. Their detailed recollections of the event, obtained through hypnosis, have made this case one of the most well-known and studied abduction cases in history.

Close Encounters of the Fifth Kind

Close encounters of the fifth kind involve voluntary human-initiated contact with extraterrestrial beings. Unlike other types of encounters, which are typically unplanned or unexpected, close encounters of the fifth kind are deliberately sought out by humans through various means such as meditation, remote viewing, or arranging specific conditions to attract contact.

Contactees, individuals who claim to have had close encounters of the fifth kind, often report telepathic communication with alien beings and the exchange of information or teachings. These encounters are believed by some to provide insights into the nature of consciousness, spirituality, and humanity's place in the universe.

Critics of close encounters of the fifth kind argue that these experiences are primarily subjective and can be attributed to psychological factors such as suggestion, imagination, or wishful thinking. However, proponents argue that there have been documented cases of multiple witnesses experiencing similar encounters, suggesting that there may be an objective component to these experiences.

One notable example of a close encounter of the fifth kind is the case of the Friendship Case in Italy. A group of individuals claimed to have established contact with extraterrestrial beings through telepathic communication, which allegedly included the exchange of advanced scientific knowledge. This case has sparked ongoing debates within the UFO research community.

Close Encounters of the Sixth Kind

Close encounters of the sixth kind, also known as hybridization encounters, involve alleged reproductive interactions between humans and extraterrestrial beings. These encounters typically involve claims of alien-human hybrid offspring or instances where humans are used as hosts for alien fetuses.

Reports of close encounters of the sixth kind often intersect with theories of genetic manipulation and the creation of a hybrid race. Some theories suggest that extraterrestrial beings may be conducting crossbreeding experiments to create a mixed species that combines human and alien traits.

The validity and scientific plausibility of close encounters of the sixth kind have been highly debated. Skeptics argue that these claims are unfounded and lack empirical evidence. However, proponents believe that these encounters may be indicative of an alien agenda to integrate with or supplant the human race.

It is important to note that close encounters of the fourth, fifth, and sixth kinds are considered to be more controversial and less widely accepted within the scientific community compared to the first, second, and third kinds. These encounters often rely heavily on subjective accounts and lack verifiable evidence.

In conclusion, while close encounters of the first, second, and third kind are the most commonly recognized types of alien encounters, there are other categories that involve unique aspects of contact and interaction with extraterrestrial beings. Close encounters of the fourth, fifth, and sixth kind encompass a range of experiences from alleged abductions to voluntary contact and reproductive interactions. While the scientific community remains divided on the validity of these encounters, they continue to be a subject of interest and study within the field of ufology.

Theories and Explanations

Extraterrestrial Hypothesis

The extraterrestrial hypothesis is a theory that proposes that unidentified flying objects (UFOs) and their occupants are of extraterrestrial origin. According to this hypothesis, UFO sightings and encounters are evidence of visitation by intelligent beings from other planets or star systems.

Background

The concept of extraterrestrial life has fascinated humanity for centuries. Ancient civilizations believed in the existence of gods and beings from other worlds. However, it was only in the mid-20th century, with the advent of modern UFO sightings, that the idea of extraterrestrial visitation gained significant attention.

The 1947 Roswell incident, where an alleged UFO crash occurred in New Mexico, is often considered a turning point in the popularization of the extraterrestrial hypothesis. Since then, numerous UFO sightings, abduction cases, and alleged contact experiences have been reported worldwide.

Principles of the Extraterrestrial Hypothesis

The extraterrestrial hypothesis is based on several key principles:

1. Advanced Technology: Proponents argue that the extraordinary capabilities exhibited by UFOs, such as high-speed maneuvers, instantaneous acceleration, and absence of visible propulsion systems, suggest the involvement of advanced extraterrestrial civilizations.

2. Interstellar Travel: The extraterrestrial hypothesis posits that UFOs travel vast interstellar distances to reach Earth. This assumes either faster-than-light travel or the utilization of advanced propulsion systems beyond our current understanding of physics.

3. Abduction Phenomena: Many UFO abduction cases involve alleged interaction between humans and extraterrestrial beings. Proponents of the extraterrestrial hypothesis argue that these encounters imply a deliberate study of the human species by extraterrestrial visitors.

Problems and Solutions

The extraterrestrial hypothesis faces several challenges and questions:

1. Lack of Conclusive Evidence: Skeptics argue that despite decades of UFO sightings and reports, no definitive proof of extraterrestrial visitation has been obtained. The absence of tangible evidence, such as an intact UFO or artifacts of extraterrestrial origin, has led many scientists to dismiss the hypothesis.

2. Distance and Time Constraints: Critics highlight the vast distances between stars and the immense time required for interstellar travel. The nearest potentially habitable exoplanets are many light-years away, making it unlikely that extraterrestrial civilizations would choose Earth as their primary destination.

3. Interpretation Bias: Skeptics suggest that UFO sightings are often misinterpretations of natural or man-made phenomena, psychological experiences, or hoaxes. The human tendency to ascribe unidentified objects to extraterrestrial origins without sufficient evidence is seen as a potential flaw in the extraterrestrial hypothesis.

However, proponents of the extraterrestrial hypothesis offer possible solutions to these challenges:

1. Unexplained Sightings: The existence of numerous unidentified aerial phenomena, witnessed by credible observers such as pilots and military personnel, supports the argument that some UFOs may indeed be of extraterrestrial origin. These sightings cannot be easily dismissed as mere misidentifications or hoaxes.

2. Advanced Technology: Proponents believe that advanced extraterrestrial civilizations could possess technologies far beyond our current understanding. Hypothetical concepts like wormholes or advanced propulsion systems, based on theoretical physics, may allow for rapid interstellar travel.

3. Incomplete Scientific Understanding: Proponents argue that our limited knowledge of the universe and the laws of physics may hinder our ability to fully comprehend the nature of extraterrestrial visitation. They advocate for continued scientific research and investigation into UFO phenomena.

Examples and Resources

There are several well-known UFO cases that support the extraterrestrial hypothesis:

1. The Betty and Barney Hill Abduction: In 1961, the Hills reported an abduction experience with detailed recollections of extraterrestrial beings and a medical examination on board a UFO. Their case is often cited as one of the earliest and most compelling abduction cases.

2. The Phoenix Lights: In 1997, thousands of witnesses in Phoenix, Arizona, reported a massive V-shaped craft silently hovering over the city. The event remains unexplained, fueling speculation about extraterrestrial involvement.

For further exploration of the extraterrestrial hypothesis, the following resources are recommended:

1. "The UFO Enigma: A New Review of the Physical Evidence" by Peter A. Sturrock: This book presents an analysis of UFO sightings and physical evidence, examining the scientific aspects of the extraterrestrial hypothesis.

2. The Mutual UFO Network (MUFON): MUFON is a leading organization dedicated to the scientific investigation of UFO phenomena. Their website provides access to case studies, reports, and research articles.

Tricks and Caveats

When discussing the extraterrestrial hypothesis, it is important to maintain a balanced perspective and consider alternative explanations for UFO sightings. It is crucial to differentiate between anecdotal evidence and scientific data. Careful scrutiny of witness testimonies, analysis of physical evidence, and cross-referencing with multiple sources are essential to avoid jumping to unsupported conclusions.

It is also important to be mindful of cultural biases and the influence of media in shaping public perception of UFO phenomena. Critical thinking and a skeptical approach must be applied when evaluating claims related to extraterrestrial visitation.

Exercises

1. Research and analyze a well-known UFO sighting case that supports the extraterrestrial hypothesis, such as the Roswell incident or the Rendlesham Forest incident. Present the key evidence and counterarguments for the extraterrestrial explanation.

2. Interview individuals who claim to have had UFO encounters. Evaluate their testimonies critically, considering alternative explanations and psychological factors that may influence their perceptions.

3. Conduct a statistical analysis of UFO sighting reports in your region, comparing the number of unexplained sightings to known natural or man-made phenomena. Discuss the implications of these findings for the extraterrestrial hypothesis.

Unconventional Perspective

One unconventional perspective related to the extraterrestrial hypothesis is the concept of "ancient astronauts." This hypothesis suggests that extraterrestrial beings may have visited Earth in the distant past and influenced human civilization. Proponents of this idea point to ancient religious texts, archaeological anomalies, and unexplained structures as potential evidence of extraterrestrial intervention in human history.

While this perspective lacks substantial scientific evidence, it highlights the multidisciplinary nature of the extraterrestrial hypothesis, incorporating elements of archaeology, anthropology, and comparative mythology. It serves as a reminder that exploring the existence of extraterrestrial life requires an open mind and a willingness to think beyond conventional boundaries.

Psychological Hypothesis

The psychological hypothesis is a theory that seeks to explain alien encounters and paranormal phenomena from a psychological perspective. It suggests that these experiences are not actual interactions with extraterrestrial beings or supernatural entities, but rather manifestations of human psychology. This hypothesis is based on the idea that the mind can project its own beliefs, fears, and desires into the external world, creating illusions or hallucinations that are interpreted as encounters with aliens, ghosts, or cryptids.

One key aspect of the psychological hypothesis is the role of perception and cognitive processes in shaping our experiences. Our brains are constantly processing information from our senses and constructing our perception of reality. However, sometimes our perception can be influenced by various factors, such as expectations, biases, and cultural conditioning. These perceptual biases can lead us to interpret ambiguous or unusual sensory inputs as encounters with aliens or paranormal entities.

For example, in the case of alien encounters, individuals who believe in extraterrestrial life may interpret unusual lights in the sky as alien spacecraft, while skeptics may attribute the same phenomenon to natural or man-made causes. Similarly, in the case of ghost sightings, people who believe in the existence of spirits may interpret strange noises or shadows as evidence of a haunting, while others may explain these phenomena as mere coincidences or products of their imagination.

Another important aspect of the psychological hypothesis is the role of belief systems and cultural influences. Our beliefs, values, and cultural background shape how we interpret and make sense of our experiences. In certain cultures, belief in supernatural entities is deeply ingrained, which can increase the likelihood of interpreting unusual experiences as encounters with ghosts, cryptids, or aliens. Additionally, media representations, such as movies, books, and television shows, can also influence our beliefs and expectations, further shaping our interpretation of paranormal phenomena.

The psychological hypothesis suggests that some individuals may be more prone to experiencing and interpreting paranormal phenomena due to certain psychological factors. For instance, individuals with a high level of suggestibility, fantasy-proneness, or a tendency to dissociate from reality may be more likely to report encounters with aliens, ghosts, or cryptids. Furthermore, individuals who have experienced trauma, have a history of mental illness, or are undergoing stressful life events may be more likely to interpret their experiences in a paranormal context.

While the psychological hypothesis provides a compelling explanation for alien encounters and paranormal phenomena, it is important to recognize its limitations. It does not dismiss the subjective experiences of individuals, but rather seeks to understand the psychological processes underlying these experiences. Additionally, the psychological hypothesis does not necessarily rule out the existence of supernatural entities or extraterrestrial life, but rather suggests that psychological factors can play a significant role in shaping our interpretation of these phenomena.

In order to support or refute the psychological hypothesis, researchers have conducted numerous studies on the cognitive and psychological factors related to paranormal experiences. These studies have explored the role of suggestibility, cognitive biases, memory distortions, and emotional factors in shaping our perception of paranormal phenomena. Additionally, researchers have also investigated the effectiveness of various therapeutic approaches, such as cognitive-behavioral therapy and hypnosis, in helping individuals who believe they have had paranormal experiences.

Overall, the psychological hypothesis offers valuable insights into the complex nature of alien encounters and paranormal phenomena. By understanding the role of perception, cognition, and belief systems, we can gain a deeper understanding of why individuals have these experiences and how they interpret them. However, further research is needed to fully explore the psychological mechanisms underlying these phenomena and to determine the extent to which psychological factors can account for reported encounters with aliens, ghosts, and cryptids.

Case Study: The Betty and Barney Hill Abduction

One well-known case often cited in relation to the psychological hypothesis is the Betty and Barney Hill abduction case. In 1961, the Hills reported being abducted by aliens and subjected to various medical examinations aboard a UFO. Their story gained significant media attention and became one of the most famous cases of alien abduction.

From a psychological perspective, the Hill case can be analyzed in terms of the role of suggestion and memory distortion. It is believed that the Hills' experiences may have been influenced by their exposure to science fiction literature and media at the time, which could have shaped their expectations and beliefs about aliens and abduction scenarios. Furthermore, the hypnosis sessions that the Hills underwent to recover suppressed memories may have inadvertently created false memories or confabulations.

Research on false memories has shown that memory is malleable and can be easily influenced by external factors, such as suggestive questioning or leading statements. Hypnosis, in particular, has been shown to be a powerful tool for altering memories and creating false narratives. Therefore, it is possible that the Hills' memories of the abduction were influenced by the suggestions of their hypnotist and the cultural expectations surrounding alien encounters.

While the psychological hypothesis does not discount the possibility that the Hills genuinely believed they were abducted by aliens, it suggests that their experiences may have been the result of a combination of psychological factors, including suggestibility, imagination, and cultural influences. This case highlights the complex interplay between perception, memory, and belief systems in shaping our experiences of the paranormal.

Further Reading:
- Irwin, H. J., & Watt, C. A. (2007). An introduction to parapsychology (5th ed.). McFarland. - French, C. C., & Stone, A. (2014). Anomalistic psychology: Exploring paranormal belief and experience. Macmillan International Higher Education. - Radford, B. (2017). Investigating Ghosts: The Scientific Search for Spirits. Rhino Books.

Exercise: Exploring Belief Systems
Consider your own beliefs and experiences related to paranormal phenomena. Reflect on how your cultural background, media influences, and personal beliefs have shaped your interpretation of these experiences. Write a short essay discussing the role of belief systems in shaping our perception and interpretation of the paranormal. Consider alternative explanations for your experiences and reflect on how psychological factors may have influenced your beliefs.

Government Conspiracy Theories

Government conspiracy theories have long been a significant aspect of the study of paranormal phenomena and unexplained mysteries. These theories propose that governments, often operating clandestinely, are involved in covering up evidence of extraterrestrial life or cryptid sightings, withholding information from the public, and manipulating events to preserve their own agendas. While some may dismiss government conspiracy theories as mere speculation or paranoia, others view them as plausible explanations for unexplained phenomena.

Historical Background

Government conspiracy theories have a rich history that stretches back several decades. One of the most well-known conspiracy theories is the Roswell Incident. In 1947, an unidentified object crashed near Roswell, New Mexico, sparking rumors of a crashed UFO. The U.S. military initially claimed it was a weather balloon, but many believe it was a cover-up for a genuine extraterrestrial event. The Roswell Incident fueled suspicions of government involvement in hiding evidence of alien life.

Another prominent conspiracy theory is the alleged government cover-up surrounding the assassination of President John F. Kennedy. Many believe that the true perpetrators of the assassination were never revealed, and that powerful entities within the government orchestrated the event to conceal a deeper conspiracy. This theory points to the involvement of clandestine organizations like the CIA or the military-industrial complex.

Motives for Conspiracy

One question that arises when considering government conspiracy theories is the motive behind the cover-up. Why would the government go to such lengths to hide the truth about aliens or cryptids? Several theories attempt to answer this question:

1. **National Security:** Some argue that the government keeps information classified to protect national security interests. If the existence of extraterrestrial life or cryptids were confirmed, it could lead to panic and destabilization of society. The government may see it as their duty to shield the public from this knowledge for fear of widespread chaos.

2. **Technological Advantages:** Another motive often proposed is that governments are keeping advanced technologies and scientific discoveries hidden from the public. If the existence of aliens or cryptids were acknowledged, it could imply the existence of revolutionary technologies that could be weaponized or used for competitive advantage by other nations.

3. **Control and Power:** Conspiracy theorists argue that governments use secrecy to maintain control and consolidate power. By withholding

information about aliens or cryptids, they maintain a monopoly over knowledge and keep the public in a state of ignorance, making it easier to manipulate and control societal narratives.

Evidence and Criticisms

Supporters of government conspiracy theories often cite certain events and evidence as proof of their claims. For example, the release of classified government documents through the Freedom of Information Act (FOIA) has revealed instances where the government has deliberately withheld information from the public. This has fueled suspicions of broader cover-ups, including those related to aliens and cryptids.

Critics, on the other hand, argue that government conspiracy theories often lack substantial evidence and are driven by a mistrust of authority rather than solid proof. They claim that the secrecy surrounding classified information can be attributed to legitimate national security concerns, rather than a cover-up of paranormal phenomena.

The Role of Whistleblowers

One aspect of government conspiracy theories is the role of whistleblowers – individuals who claim to have insider knowledge or firsthand experience of government cover-ups. These whistleblowers play a critical role in popularizing and validating conspiracy theories. One notable example is Edward Snowden, a former National Security Agency (NSA) contractor who leaked classified information about government surveillance programs. While Snowden's case does not directly relate to aliens or cryptids, it highlights the potential for government secrecy and the credibility of insiders who come forward.

Caveats and Controversies

It is important to approach government conspiracy theories with a critical mindset and consider alternative explanations. While it is true that governments have engaged in secrecy and cover-ups in the past, this does not necessarily confirm the existence of extraterrestrial life or cryptids.

Conspiracy theories can also be easily manipulated and exploited, leading to the spread of misinformation. The internet, in particular, has facilitated the rapid dissemination of conspiracy theories, making it vital to verify sources and critically evaluate information before accepting it as truth.

Nevertheless, government conspiracy theories persist, fueled by a general distrust of authority and a desire to unearth hidden truths. They continue to captivate and intrigue those who are fascinated by the unknown, pushing the boundaries of scientific inquiry and challenging conventional wisdom.

Summary

Government conspiracy theories provide an alternative lens through which to view unexplained phenomena. While they are often dismissed by mainstream society, these theories inspire debate and critical thinking about the role of governments in shaping our understanding of the world. Whether they hold any truth or not, government conspiracy theories serve as a reminder to question authority, seek evidence, and explore the realms of possibility beyond the confines of conventional knowledge.

Exercises

1. Reflect on the potential consequences of government conspiracy theories on society. How can these theories impact public trust in government institutions and scientific research?

2. Research a well-known government conspiracy theory and critically analyze the evidence and counterarguments presented by proponents and skeptics. Write a short essay outlining your findings.

3. Consider a recent event or phenomenon that has garnered conspiracy theories involving government cover-ups. Identify the underlying motive behind the conspiracy theory and assess its plausibility based on available evidence.

4. Conduct a group discussion on the ethical implications of government secrecy. Debate whether governments have a responsibility to disclose information about aliens or cryptids, considering potential consequences for national security and public perception.

5. Design an educational campaign aimed at promoting critical thinking and media literacy to combat the spread of misinformation related to government conspiracy theories. Develop strategies to inspire skepticism and encourage evidence-based reasoning among the general public.

Additional Resources

- Brotherton, R. (2015). *Suspicious Minds: Why We Believe Conspiracy Theories*. Bloomsbury Sigma.

- Coady, D. (2012). *Conspiracy Theories: The Philosophical Debate*. Ashgate.

- Goertzel, T. (2010). *Conspiracy Theories in American History: An Encyclopedia*. ABC-CLIO.

- Keeley, B. L. (2019). *Conspiracy Theories in the United States and the Middle East: A Comparative Approach*. University of California Press.

- Lewandowsky, S., et al. (Eds.). (2015). *The Conspiracy Theory Handbook*. University of Western Australia.

Key Terms

- Government conspiracy theories

- Cover-up

- National security
- Technological advantages
- Control and power
- Whistleblowers
- Misinformation
- Media literacy

Note: The exercises, additional resources, key terms, and other elements of this section are intended to supplement the main content and encourage further exploration and critical thinking. They are not necessary for understanding the core concepts presented in the section, but rather serve as optional extensions for interested readers.

Cultural and Sociological Perspectives

Cultural and sociological perspectives play a significant role in understanding the phenomenon of cryptids and aliens. These perspectives help us explore how beliefs, values, and social interactions influence the perception and interpretation of such encounters. In this section, we will delve into the cultural and sociological dimensions of cryptids and aliens, examining their impact on society, belief systems, and collective consciousness.

Cultural Influences on Perceptions

Culture shapes our perspectives on the world and influences how we interpret and perceive phenomena. When it comes to cryptids and aliens, cultural factors can significantly impact the way people understand and relate to these creatures.

For example, let's consider the belief in the Loch Ness Monster. The legend of Nessie has become deeply ingrained in Scottish culture and folklore. The monster's image is featured on various merchandise, and the legend is celebrated in festivals and events. This cultural celebration of the Loch Ness Monster creates a sense of collective identity for the local community and reinforces the belief in its existence.

Similarly, cultural influences can shape perceptions of aliens. Science fiction films, literature, and popular culture have presented various depictions of extraterrestrial beings, ranging from friendly visitors to hostile invaders. These portrayals shape public imagination and contribute to the cultural construction of beliefs and expectations regarding alien encounters.

Social Constructs and Cryptid Beliefs

Sociological perspectives play a crucial role in understanding why some individuals believe in the existence of cryptids like Bigfoot, Chupacabra, or the Jersey Devil. These beliefs often arise within specific social and cultural contexts and are shaped by various factors.

One sociological theory that can shed light on cryptid beliefs is social constructivism. According to this theory, reality is socially constructed through shared meanings and interpretations. In the case of cryptids, belief systems and local folklore can contribute to the creation and perpetuation of these creatures' existence.

For example, the belief in Bigfoot is deeply intertwined with the cultural heritage and indigenous traditions of certain Native American tribes. These tribes have long-held stories and legends about wild, hairy giants that inhabit the forests. As such, the belief in Bigfoot becomes part of their cultural identity and is passed down through generations.

Furthermore, social factors such as group dynamics and social networks can influence belief in cryptids. People often form communities around these beliefs, with shared experiences and a sense of belonging. These communities validate and reinforce each other's beliefs, creating a social context that strengthens the conviction in cryptid encounters.

Mass Media and Belief Formation

Mass media plays a significant role in shaping public perceptions and belief systems, including those related to cryptids and aliens. Media coverage of cryptid sightings and alien encounters can influence public opinion and either validate or challenge existing beliefs.

In the case of the Dover Demon, media coverage played a crucial role in popularizing the sightings and generating public interest. News articles, television reports, and online discussions contributed to the dissemination of information and shaped public opinions about the creature's existence.

However, media can also contribute to skepticism and debunking of cryptid claims. Skeptical investigations and critical analysis of evidence are often covered by the media, which can shift public opinion and challenge deeply held beliefs.

It is essential to critically examine the relationship between mass media and belief formation regarding cryptids and aliens. While media can provide a platform for sharing information and experiences, it is important to approach these presentations with a critical mindset and consider alternative perspectives.

Belief Systems and the Paranormal

Belief systems, including religious and spiritual beliefs, often intersect with the paranormal, including beliefs in cryptids and aliens. Different belief systems provide frameworks for interpreting and explaining these phenomena.

For example, religious interpretations may link cryptid encounters to spiritual or divine entities. In some cultures, cryptids are believed to be guardian spirits or omens, adding a layer of religious significance to such encounters.

Psychological and sociological perspectives also provide insights into belief systems surrounding cryptids and aliens. The need for meaning, control, and a sense of wonder can drive individuals to embrace these beliefs. Additionally, collective belief systems can provide solace and a sense of community for individuals who have had paranormal experiences.

Cultural Significance and Cryptozoology

Cryptozoology, as an interdisciplinary field, bridges science, folklore, and cultural heritage. The study of cryptids holds cultural significance as it preserves and investigates local legends and traditions. It allows communities to maintain a connection with their cultural heritage and keep alive the stories and beliefs associated with cryptid sightings.

Cryptozoological research also contributes to the understanding of cultural and social dynamics. By examining the origins and variations of cryptid legends, researchers can gain insights into the historical and cultural contexts that shape these belief systems. Furthermore, the study of cryptids can shed light on the human imagination, collective consciousness, and the power of belief.

Example: The Influence of Cultural Perspectives on Cryptid Sightings

To illustrate the influence of cultural perspectives on cryptid sightings, let's consider the case of the Chupacabra. The Chupacabra is a creature from Latin American folklore, often described as a vampire-like being that attacks livestock and drains their blood.

The belief in the Chupacabra has spread beyond its cultural origins and gained international recognition. However, the description of the creature varies across regions, with different cultural interpretations shaping its appearance and behavior.

In Puerto Rico, where the Chupacabra myth originated, it is often described as a reptile-like creature with spikes on its back. In other countries, such as Mexico and the United States, the Chupacabra is depicted as a more canine-like creature.

These variations reflect the cultural lenses through which people perceive and interpret cryptid encounters.

The cultural significance of the Chupacabra is evident in the impact it has had on local communities. The belief in the creature has led to fear, livestock losses, and even attempts to capture or kill the alleged Chupacabras. As such, the cultural perspectives surrounding the Chupacabra have tangible consequences in people's lives and livelihoods.

Conclusion

Cultural and sociological perspectives provide valuable insights into the complex interplay between belief systems, social constructs, and the phenomenon of cryptids and aliens. These perspectives help us understand how culture shapes perceptions, beliefs, and experiences related to these creatures. By examining the cultural and sociological dimensions of cryptids and aliens, we can gain a deeper appreciation for the role they play in our collective consciousness and the broader societal impact they have.

Chapter 2: Cryptids and Cryptozoology

Definition and History of Cryptozoology

Origins of Cryptozoology as a Field of Study

The study of cryptozoology, which focuses on the investigation and search for creatures whose existence is disputed or unproven by mainstream science, has its origins in various cultural, historical, and scientific factors. To understand the development of cryptozoology as a field of study, we need to delve into its origins and the key events and individuals that propelled its growth.

Cultural Fascination with Unknown Creatures

Humans have always been fascinated by creatures that defy conventional understanding and challenge the boundaries of our knowledge. Throughout history, myths, legends, and folk tales featuring strange and elusive creatures have been passed down through generations. These stories have sparked the human imagination and nurtured a curiosity about the existence of such creatures. The cultural fascination with unknown creatures played a significant role in the emergence of cryptozoology as a separate scientific discipline.

Explorer's Tales and Natural History

In the 19th and early 20th centuries, explorers and naturalists began traveling to remote and unexplored regions of the world. Their extensive expeditions yielded exciting discoveries, providing evidence for the existence of creatures previously deemed mythical or extinct. For instance, the discovery of the coelacanth in 1938, a fish believed to have gone extinct 65 million years ago, highlighted the possibility of finding other presumed extinct creatures. These explorers' tales and the advancements in natural history laid the foundation for the study of creatures that do not fit neatly into established taxonomies.

Ivan T. Sanderson and the Coining of the Term "Cryptozoology"

One of the key figures responsible for establishing cryptozoology as a distinct field of study was Ivan T. Sanderson, an influential British-American naturalist and writer. In the 1940s, Sanderson began cataloging and investigating reports of unknown creatures from around the world. He was particularly interested in creatures like Bigfoot and the Loch Ness Monster. In 1959, Sanderson introduced the term "cryptozoology" in his book "Abominable Snowmen: Legend Comes to Life." This term, derived from the Greek words "kryptos" meaning hidden and "zoology" meaning the study of animals, encapsulated the essence of the field — the study of hidden animals.

Bernard Heuvelmans and Species Survival Theory

Another significant figure in the founding of cryptozoology was Bernard Heuvelmans, a Belgian-French scientist and writer. Heuvelmans expanded upon Sanderson's work, formulating the concept of "cryptozoology proper" and introducing the influential theory of "species survival." According to Heuvelmans, many mythical creatures could be unidentified or undiscovered species that managed to survive against the odds. Heuvelmans' works, notably his book "On the Track of Unknown Animals" published in 1955, provided a scientific framework for the study of cryptids and further popularized cryptozoology.

The Loch Ness Monster and Other Famous Cryptid Cases

The Loch Ness Monster, a cryptid believed to inhabit the Scottish Loch Ness, garnered widespread attention and became a focal point for cryptozoologists. Numerous sightings and photographs created a sensation, triggering public interest and debate. The Loch Ness Monster case, along with other famous cryptid cases such as the Yeti and the Chupacabra, captured the imagination of the public and generated significant media coverage. These high-profile cases played a pivotal role in raising public awareness about the existence of enigmatic creatures and fueling the growth of cryptozoology as a distinct discipline.

Enthusiast Organizations and Cryptozoology Journals

Enthusiast organizations dedicated to cryptozoological research and investigation have played a crucial role in the development of the field. The International Society of Cryptozoology (ISC), founded in 1982 by Mark A. Hall, provided a platform for cryptozoologists to exchange ideas, share research findings, and collaborate on investigations. The ISC also published the journal "Cryptozoology," featuring scholarly articles on various cryptids and related topics. The establishment of such organizations and dedicated journals provided legitimacy and a sense of community for cryptozoologists, fostering the growth and development of the field.

Advancements in Technology and Data Collection

Technological advancements have played a significant role in advancing cryptozoology as a scientific discipline. Advancements in camera technology and the widespread use of smartphones have made it easier for eyewitnesses to capture potential evidence of cryptids. Additionally, advancements in DNA analysis and other scientific techniques have allowed for more rigorous examination of alleged physical evidence attributed to cryptids. These technological advancements have provided cryptozoologists with new tools and methodologies to investigate and analyze cryptid sightings and evidence.

The Popularity of Popular Culture

Cryptozoology's prominence in popular culture has undeniably contributed to its growth and recognition. The inclusion of cryptids in literature, movies, television shows, and documentaries has fascinated audiences worldwide. Cryptozoological phenomena have become part of the cultural fabric, merging entertainment with serious scientific investigation. This cross-pollination between popular culture and cryptozoology has drawn in new enthusiasts, expanded public interest, and encouraged further research and exploration.

In conclusion, the origins of cryptozoology as a field of study can be traced back to cultural fascination, the explorer's tales, and the natural history discoveries. The contributions of influential figures like Ivan T. Sanderson and Bernard Heuvelmans, along with famous cryptid cases, enthusiast organizations, technological advancements, and the influence of popular culture, have all shaped cryptozoology into a distinct and interdisciplinary scientific discipline. By understanding its origins, we can appreciate the complexity and depth of the field and its potential for further scientific exploration and discovery.

Notable Cryptozoologists and their Work

In the field of cryptozoology, several researchers have dedicated their lives to the study of unknown and elusive creatures. Their work has contributed significantly to the understanding and exploration of cryptids. In this section, we will explore the lives and contributions of some of the most notable cryptozoologists.

Bernard Heuvelmans

One of the pioneers of cryptozoology, Bernard Heuvelmans (1916-2001), played a crucial role in establishing the field as a legitimate area of scientific inquiry. Heuvelmans coined the term "cryptozoology" and wrote the seminal work "On the Track of Unknown Animals" in 1955. His extensive research and writings focused on cataloging and documenting various cryptids from around the world. Heuvelmans' work provided a framework for future researchers and helped legitimize the study of unknown animals.

Ivan T. Sanderson

Ivan T. Sanderson (1911-1973) was a British zoologist and writer known for his investigations into various cryptozoological phenomena. He traveled extensively to collect eyewitness accounts and physical evidence of cryptids. Sanderson's notable contributions include his research on the Loch Ness Monster, Yeti, and Mothman. He also established the Society for the Investigation of the Unexplained (SITU), which promoted the scientific study of cryptozoology and other anomalous phenomena.

Loren Coleman

Loren Coleman (born 1947) is an American cryptozoologist and author who has made significant contributions to the field. He has written numerous books on cryptozoology, including "The Field Guide to Bigfoot, Yeti, and Other Mystery Primates Worldwide." Coleman has also conducted field investigations and collected eyewitness accounts of various cryptids, including Bigfoot, Champ, and the Dover Demon. He played a crucial role in popularizing cryptozoology and bringing it to the mainstream.

Karl Shuker

Karl Shuker (born 1959) is a British zoologist, cryptozoologist, and author known for his scientific approach to the study of cryptozoology. He has written extensively on various cryptids, including sea serpents, lake monsters, and mystery cats. Shuker's work combines his zoological knowledge with cryptozoological investigations, aiming to bridge the gap between mainstream science and cryptozoology. He has contributed significantly to the understanding and classification of cryptids.

David J. P. Cootes

David J. P. Cootes (1963-2012) was a Malaysian cryptozoologist who specialized in the study of unknown primates, especially the Orang Pendek in Sumatra. Cootes conducted several expeditions to search for evidence of the creature and brought international attention to the plight of endangered primates. His work highlighted the importance of conservation efforts in protecting these elusive and often endangered cryptids.

Cryptozoology Today

Today, many dedicated researchers continue to explore the mysteries of cryptozoology. While some skeptics dismiss the field as pseudoscience, notable cryptozoologists strive to collect reliable evidence and apply scientific methods to their investigations. The work of these researchers is essential in expanding our knowledge of the natural world and preserving biodiversity.

Challenges and Future Directions

The study of cryptozoology faces several challenges, primarily due to the elusive nature of cryptids and the lack of mainstream scientific recognition. However, advancements in technology and collaboration between scientists and cryptozoologists offer promising avenues for future research.

One major challenge in cryptozoology is the scarcity of physical evidence. Eyewitness testimonies and footprint casts are often the primary sources of data, making it difficult to conduct rigorous scientific analysis. Future research could focus on developing innovative techniques for collecting physical evidence, such as advanced DNA analysis and remote sensing technologies.

Another challenge is the need for interdisciplinary collaboration. Cryptozoology draws on various fields, including biology, anthropology, and cultural studies. By fostering collaborations between experts from different disciplines, a more comprehensive and cohesive understanding of cryptids can be achieved.

Longitudinal studies and case histories are also crucial for advancing the field. By studying cryptid sightings and encounters over extended periods, researchers can identify patterns and gain insights into the behavior and ecology of these creatures. Gathering such data requires long-term funding and sustained efforts from both professional scientists and citizen scientists.

Education and public awareness play a vital role in the future of cryptozoology. By engaging with the public and promoting critical thinking, researchers can encourage interest in the field and combat misinformation. Public involvement in data collection and analysis, through initiatives like citizen science, can expand the scope of cryptozoological research.

In conclusion, notable cryptozoologists have made significant contributions to the field, paving the way for future investigations. Despite the challenges faced by cryptozoology, the field holds immense potential for scientific discovery and conservation efforts. By adopting rigorous scientific methodologies, fostering interdisciplinary collaborations, and increasing public awareness, the study of cryptozoology can continue to evolve and shed light on the mysteries of unknown animals.

The Cryptozoology Society and its Contributions

The field of cryptozoology, the study of hidden or unknown animals, has been furthered by the efforts of various organizations and individuals dedicated to the pursuit of understanding and cataloging these elusive creatures. One such organization is the Cryptozoology Society, which has played a significant role in the advancement of cryptozoological research and the dissemination of knowledge in this field. In this section, we will explore the history, accomplishments, and contributions of the Cryptozoology Society.

History of the Cryptozoology Society

The Cryptozoology Society was founded in 1965 by renowned cryptozoologist Loren Coleman. Coleman, having a deep fascination with mysterious creatures and a desire to investigate reports of unknown animals, recognized the need for a formal organization in the field of cryptozoology. The society was established as a platform for cryptozoologists to connect, share information, and collaborate on research projects.

Since its inception, the Cryptozoology Society has grown into an international organization with a diverse membership composed of researchers, scientists, enthusiasts, and skeptics. The society acts as a hub for the exchange of ideas and fosters cooperative efforts amongst experts in the field.

Objectives and Purpose

The Cryptozoology Society operates with the primary objective of advancing the scientific study of hidden or unknown animals. Its purpose lies in the systematic investigation of cryptozoological reports, the collection of evidence, and the dissemination of knowledge to the wider scientific community and the public.

To achieve these objectives, the society engages in several key activities:

1. Field Investigations Members of the Cryptozoology Society actively conduct field investigations into reported sightings and encounters with cryptids. These investigations involve on-site exploration, rigorous data collection, documentation of eyewitness testimonies, and analysis of physical evidence, if available. The society encourages collaboration between its members and other researchers, providing a platform for coordinated efforts in the field.

2. Archival Research The society also recognizes the importance of historical research in cryptozoological studies. Members engage in archival research, unearthing old newspaper articles, letters, and other primary sources to identify historical accounts, folklore, and cultural references to cryptids. By understanding the cultural context and the evolution of these stories, researchers can gain insights into the possible existence and origins of elusive creatures.

3. Scientific Collaboration Collaboration with other scientific disciplines is a cornerstone of the Cryptozoology Society's approach. By collaborating with experts in fields such as zoology, botany, ecology, and genetics, the society aims to integrate cryptozoology into mainstream scientific research. This interdisciplinary approach allows for the application of rigorous scientific methodologies and enhances the credibility of cryptozoological studies.

Contributions of the Cryptozoology Society

The Cryptozoology Society has made significant contributions to the field of cryptozoology. Here are a few notable examples:

1. **Cataloging Cryptids**   One of the primary contributions of the society is the comprehensive cataloging of cryptids from around the world. Through extensive research and collaboration, the society has compiled a database containing information about various reported species, including their descriptions, reported behaviors, alleged habitats, and historical sightings. This catalog serves as a valuable resource for researchers and enthusiasts interested in exploring the world of hidden animals.

2. **Education and Public Outreach**   Recognizing the importance of public awareness and education, the Cryptozoology Society actively engages in outreach programs. These programs aim to dispel misconceptions about cryptozoology, promote scientific inquiry, and encourage critical thinking in the public. The society organizes lectures, workshops, and conferences, where members and invited experts share their knowledge and findings. Additionally, the society publishes a quarterly journal that features research articles, case studies, and updates on ongoing projects.

3. **Collaborative Publications**   The Cryptozoology Society has produced several groundbreaking publications in the field. These publications include comprehensive studies, monographs, and field guides on various cryptids. By encouraging collaboration and inviting contributions from experts worldwide, the society ensures that these publications contain the most up-to-date information and reflect diverse perspectives. These publications serve as important reference works for both researchers and cryptozoology enthusiasts.

4. **Peer-Reviewed Research**   To promote scientific rigor and credibility, the Cryptozoology Society has established a peer-review process for scientific publications in the field. Researchers are encouraged to submit their findings to the society's journal, where they undergo rigorous peer-review by experts in relevant disciplines. This ensures that the research is subjected to critical evaluation, improving the quality of published works and contributing to the scientific dialogue surrounding cryptozoology.

Challenges and Future Directions

Despite its contributions, the Cryptozoology Society faces several challenges in its pursuit of understanding hidden or unknown animals. Skepticism from mainstream science, the lack of funding, and the scarcity of physical evidence are some of the hurdles that cryptozoologists encounter. To address these challenges and further advance the field, the society has outlined the following future directions:

1. **Collaboration with Mainstream Science** Building bridges between cryptozoology and mainstream science is critical for overcoming skepticism and increasing acceptance. The Cryptozoology Society aims to foster stronger collaborations with established scientific institutions and researchers by sharing data, methodologies, and research findings. By integrating cryptozoology into broader scientific conversations, the society seeks to legitimize the field and encourage further investigation.

2. **Technological Advancements** Advancements in technology have the potential to revolutionize cryptozoological research. The society calls for increased use of advanced tools such as DNA analysis, remote sensing techniques, and unmanned aerial vehicles (drones) in the study of hidden animals. These technologies can aid in the collection of more reliable evidence, expand the scope of investigations, and enhance the credibility of cryptozoological studies.

3. **Citizen Science Initiatives** To expand the reach of research efforts, the Cryptozoology Society encourages citizen science initiatives. Citizen scientists, often enthusiastic amateurs, can contribute to data collection, assist in field investigations, and provide valuable insights and observations. The society aims to develop guidelines and platforms that enable meaningful contributions from citizen scientists while maintaining scientific rigor.

4. **Long-Term Studies** Longitudinal studies focusing on specific cryptids can provide valuable information about their behavior, population dynamics, and ecological interactions. The Cryptozoology Society advocates for long-term studies that involve regular monitoring, data collection, and analysis over extended periods. These studies offer a more comprehensive understanding of cryptids and can help establish their conservation status, if necessary.

In conclusion, the Cryptozoology Society serves as a dedicated organization that advances the scientific study of hidden or unknown animals. Through field investigations, archival research, scientific collaborations, and educational outreach, the society contributes to the growing body of knowledge in cryptozoology. Despite challenges, the society remains committed to bridging the gap between mainstream science and cryptozoology, promoting interdisciplinary research, and engaging the public in scientific exploration.

Famous Cryptid Cases

Loch Ness Monster

The Loch Ness Monster is perhaps one of the most well-known and enduring cryptids in the world. Located in the Scottish Highlands, Loch Ness is a large, deep freshwater lake famous for its mysterious creature. Reports of the Loch Ness Monster, affectionately known as "Nessie," date back centuries, with numerous sightings and alleged encounters captivating the imagination of both locals and tourists alike.

Historical Background

The history of the Loch Ness Monster can be traced back to ancient times, with tales and legends of a large water-dwelling creature lurking in the depths of Loch Ness. The first modern sighting of Nessie occurred in the early 20th century, sparking widespread interest and curiosity. Since then, there have been countless eyewitness accounts, photographs, and even sonar readings claiming to provide evidence of the creature's existence.

Eyewitness Accounts

Eyewitness accounts play a crucial role in shaping our understanding of the Loch Ness Monster. Many people from all walks of life have reported seeing a large, serpent-like creature swimming in the waters of Loch Ness. These eyewitnesses describe Nessie as having a long neck, a humped back, and a large body, often likening its appearance to that of a plesiosaur, an ancient marine reptile.

For example, in 1933, the first modern photograph purportedly showing the Loch Ness Monster was taken by Hugh Gray. The photograph, known as the "Gray's Photo," depicted a dark mass with what appeared to be a long neck emerging from the water. While some considered it definitive proof of Nessie's existence, others dismissed it as a hoax or a misidentification.

Scientific Investigations

Over the years, several scientific investigations have been conducted in an attempt to unravel the mystery of the Loch Ness Monster. These investigations have employed various technologies, including sonar scanning, underwater cameras, and DNA analysis, to search for evidence of Nessie's presence in the Loch.

In 2003, a team of researchers led by Dr. Neil Gemmell embarked on a groundbreaking project to collect and analyze water samples from Loch Ness. This study aimed to uncover any traces of DNA that may belong to unknown or unidentified species. While the results did not provide definitive proof of the Loch Ness Monster's existence, they did yield a rich biodiversity within the Loch, including a range of fish species and microorganisms.

Exploring Explanations

Numerous theories and explanations have been put forth to explain the Loch Ness Monster phenomenon. One popular hypothesis is that Nessie is a surviving plesiosaur, a prehistoric reptile thought to have gone extinct millions of years ago. Proponents of this theory argue that Loch Ness provides the ideal environment for a creature like Nessie to live undetected.

However, this hypothesis faces significant challenges. The Loch Ness ecosystem, with its limited food supply and harsh conditions, would make it highly unlikely for a large creature to sustain itself unnoticed for such a long time. Additionally, no conclusive physical evidence, such as skeletal remains, has ever been found to support the existence of a plesiosaur in Loch Ness.

Psychological Perspectives

Psychological explanations have also been proposed to account for the Loch Ness Monster sightings. The phenomena of pareidolia, misperception, and misidentification play a significant role in how we interpret visual stimuli, especially when presented with unfamiliar or ambiguous shapes in the environment.

In the case of Nessie, some argue that eyewitnesses may have experienced pareidolia when perceiving patterns or shapes in the water that resembled a large creature. The influence of preconceived beliefs and expectations can also contribute to the misinterpretation of natural phenomena as something paranormal or extraordinary.

The Cultural Significance

The Loch Ness Monster holds great cultural significance, not only for the local communities surrounding Loch Ness but also for Scotland as a whole. Nessie has become an iconic symbol of Scottish folklore and attracts millions of tourists each year. The creature's image is widely used in marketing campaigns, ranging from souvenirs to promotional materials, contributing to the region's tourism industry.

The legend of Nessie also serves as a source of inspiration for artists, writers, and filmmakers. Numerous books, documentaries, and movies have been produced, further fueling public fascination and keeping the Loch Ness Monster firmly rooted in popular culture.

Conclusion

The mystery of the Loch Ness Monster persists to this day, captivating the minds and imaginations of millions around the world. While scientific investigations have not provided definitive proof of the creature's existence, the cultural significance and the enduring allure of Nessie continue to fuel public interest. Whether real or mythical, the legend of the Loch Ness Monster serves as a reminder of the wonder and mystery that still exists in our world.

Bigfoot

In the field of cryptozoology, one of the most famous and enduring cryptid legends is that of Bigfoot. Also known as Sasquatch, this creature is believed to be a large, hairy humanoid inhabiting the remote forests of North America. The mystery and fascination surrounding Bigfoot have captured the imaginations of people from all walks of life, leading to numerous reports, sightings, and investigations.

Origins and Legends

The origins of the Bigfoot legend can be traced back to various Native American tribes who have long held beliefs in the existence of a giant, ape-like creature lurking in the wilderness. In fact, the term "Sasquatch" itself derives from the Halkomelem word used by indigenous peoples in the Pacific Northwest, meaning "wild man" or "hairy man."

The legend of Bigfoot gained wider prominence in the 20th century, primarily through anecdotal accounts and alleged sightings. Tales of encounters with a large, bipedal creature with enormous footprints and a foul odor spread across North America, captivating the public's attention and fueling a desire to uncover the truth behind this elusive creature.

Physical Characteristics

Described as a massive creature standing between 7 to 10 feet tall, Bigfoot is believed to possess a muscular build covered in dark brown or reddish-brown hair. Its enormous footprints, often measuring around 24 inches in length, have become a distinguishing feature and a subject of much fascination. The footprints are frequently cited as evidence of Bigfoot's existence, with numerous plaster casts and photographs being collected over the years.

Although no definitive proof of Bigfoot's existence has been obtained, the wide range of reported sightings suggests a consistent biological profile. Witnesses typically describe the creature as having a conical head, a prominent brow ridge, and a robust, ape-like appearance. These physical characteristics align with the general depiction of Bigfoot in popular culture and have contributed to its enduring image.

Sightings and Investigations

Countless sightings of Bigfoot have been reported across North America, with notable clusters occurring in regions such as the Pacific Northwest, the Appalachian Mountains, and the Great Lakes. These sightings have varied in terms of witness credibility, ranging from ordinary citizens to trained professionals such as park rangers and law enforcement officers.

Despite the abundance of alleged encounters, the scientific community remains skeptical about the existence of Bigfoot. Critics argue that the lack of concrete physical evidence, such as DNA samples or captured specimens, undermines the credibility of these claims. However, cryptozoologists and enthusiasts continue to conduct investigations, hoping to gather evidence that supports the presence of this elusive creature.

Explanations and Debunking

Various theories have been proposed to explain the Bigfoot phenomenon. One hypothesis suggests that Bigfoot could be a surviving relic population of Gigantopithecus, an extinct ape species that inhabited the forests of Asia over a million years ago. According to this theory, Bigfoot would be the North American equivalent of the Asian ape, albeit with certain adaptations to its environment.

Another explanation posits that Bigfoot sightings could be attributed to misidentifications of known animals, such as black bears or large primates. Factors such as poor lighting conditions, distance, and the fleeting nature of the encounters often make it difficult for witnesses to accurately assess the creature they have encountered. Additionally, some skeptics argue that hoaxes and pranks perpetrated by individuals seeking attention or perpetuating the myth of Bigfoot have further clouded the credibility of the phenomenon.

Scientific Exploration and Challenges

The search for evidence of Bigfoot's existence continues to captivate the interest of scientists and enthusiasts alike. However, conducting scientific studies on such an elusive creature presents numerous challenges. The vast and rugged terrain where Bigfoot is believed to reside, coupled with the rarity and elusiveness of the creature, poses logistical difficulties for field research.

Furthermore, the ambiguous nature of Bigfoot evidence, such as inconclusive footprint casts or blurry photographs, makes it challenging to obtain definitive scientific conclusions. The lack of verified DNA samples or physical remains further complicates the task of establishing a scientific basis for the existence of Bigfoot.

Pop Culture and Influence

Bigfoot has undeniably left an indelible mark on popular culture. The creature has been featured in numerous books, movies, and television shows, fueling the public's fascination with cryptozoology and the unknown. From documentaries exploring alleged sightings to fictional accounts of encounters with these mysterious creatures, Bigfoot's legend continues to captivate audiences around the world.

Furthermore, Bigfoot's cultural significance extends beyond entertainment media. The creature has become a symbol of wilderness and the unknown, representing the unexplored depths of our natural world. It has also sparked debates about the limits of scientific knowledge and the existence of hidden mysteries waiting to be discovered.

Conclusion

The legend of Bigfoot remains one of the most enduring mysteries in the realm of cryptozoology. While skeptics argue that the lack of definitive evidence undermines its credibility, the continued reports and public interest in this creature keep the debate alive. Whether Bigfoot represents a real, undiscovered species or a mix of misidentifications and hoaxes, the allure of unraveling the truth behind this legendary creature continues to captivate the hearts and minds of believers and skeptics alike.

In the next chapter, we will explore another captivating paranormal phenomena - ghost sightings and hauntings. Stay tuned for a journey into the realm of the supernatural.

Chupacabra

The Chupacabra is a legendary creature that is said to reside in the Americas, particularly in regions such as Mexico, Puerto Rico, and parts of the southern United States. The name "Chupacabra" translates to "goat-sucker" in Spanish, which reflects its alleged habit of attacking and draining the blood of livestock, especially goats and sheep. The sightings and reports of the Chupacabra have sparked both curiosity and fear, often associated with paranormal and cryptid phenomena.

Origins and Description

The Chupacabra first gained attention in the mid-1990s when a series of animal attacks occurred in Puerto Rico. The creatures responsible for these attacks were described as having a reptile-like appearance with spines or quills running down their backs. They were reported to be about the size of a small bear or large dog, standing on two legs, with glowing red eyes and sharp fangs. Subsequent sightings of the Chupacabra in the Americas have described similar features, with some variations depending on the region.

Sightings and Incidents

Numerous reports of Chupacabra sightings have emerged over the years, often accompanied by claims of mysterious livestock deaths. Many eyewitnesses have described encounters with a creature matching the iconic Chupacabra description, leading to a widespread belief in its existence.

One notable incident occurred in 2004 in Calama, Chile, where several goats were found dead with puncture wounds on their necks and their blood completely drained. The local community attributed these killings to the Chupacabra. However, scientific investigations revealed that the deaths were likely caused by dog attacks instead of a mythical creature.

Explanations and Skepticism

The Chupacabra has generated significant debate and skepticism among scientists, cryptozoologists, and skeptics alike. Several theories have been proposed to explain the Chupacabra sightings and alleged livestock killings.

Biological Explanations: 1. Canid or Coyote with Mange: Some skeptics argue that the Chupacabra sightings could be attributed to wild canids or coyotes suffering from mange, a skin disease caused by parasitic mites. The hair loss, scaly skin, and unusual appearance of the animals affected by mange could create a vampire-like image, leading to the Chupacabra legend. 2. Feral Dogs: Others suggest that feral dogs or stray dogs may be responsible for the animal attacks attributed to the Chupacabra. These dogs could exhibit predatory behavior, such as attacking livestock, leading to the belief in the existence of a mysterious creature.

Cultural and Psychological Explanations: 1. Folklore and Urban Legends: Some researchers propose that the Chupacabra phenomenon is primarily driven by folklore, urban legends, and mass hysteria. The power of storytelling, combined with media exposure and cultural beliefs, can shape perceptions and create a shared belief in supernatural creatures. 2. Misidentification and Exaggeration: Skeptics argue that many Chupacabra sightings can be attributed to misidentification of known animals or exaggeration of their characteristics. In dim lighting or stressful situations, it is possible for witnesses to mistake common animals, such as coyotes, dogs, or sick animals, for the Chupacabra.

Cryptozoological Significance

The Chupacabra has become a prominent figure in cryptozoology, the study of hidden animals. Although skeptics dismiss the creature as a result of folklore and misidentifications, cryptozoologists continue to investigate the possibility of unknown or undiscovered species.

The Chupacabra phenomenon highlights the importance of critical thinking and skepticism in investigating such claims. Cryptozoologists must approach each sighting with a scientific mindset, considering alternative explanations and carefully examining available evidence.

Unconventional Example: Animal DNA Analysis

To shed more light on the Chupacabra mystery, some researchers have applied modern DNA analysis techniques to identify the possible origins of alleged Chupacabra samples. In a notable example, a Texas-based veterinarian analyzed DNA from several carcasses purportedly belonging to Chupacabras.

The analysis revealed that the samples primarily came from canids, including coyotes, foxes, and domestic dogs. Some samples also showed genetic traces of raccoons and wolves. These findings suggest that the Chupacabra myth may stem from misidentified or distorted features of known animals rather than from an entirely new species.

While DNA analysis provides valuable insights, it also poses challenges in dealing with degraded or contaminated samples. Researchers must ensure proper sample collection and employ rigorous laboratory techniques to obtain reliable and conclusive results.

Conclusion

The Chupacabra legend demonstrates how cultural beliefs, folklore, mass hysteria, and misidentifications can contribute to the creation and persistence of cryptids. While the Chupacabra remains a fascinating legend, scientific investigations and critical analysis suggest that the creature is likely a product of human imagination and the misinterpretation of actual animal sightings.

Cryptozoologists and scientists continue to explore the possibility of unknown species, but they emphasize the importance of evidence-based approaches and skepticism in evaluating claims related to cryptids like the Chupacabra. By applying scientific principles and rigorous methodologies, researchers aim to uncover the truth behind the mysteries that capture our imagination and curiosity.

Jersey Devil

The Jersey Devil is a legendary creature said to inhabit the Pine Barrens of southern New Jersey. Also known as the Leeds Devil, it has fascinated locals and intrigued cryptozoologists for centuries. In this section, we will explore the history, sightings, and cultural significance of the Jersey Devil.

Origin and Folklore

The origins of the Jersey Devil legend date back to the early 18th century. According to folklore, Mrs. Leeds, a resident of the Pine Barrens, was pregnant with her thirteenth child. In frustration, she reportedly exclaimed, "Let it be a devil!" during childbirth. The child was then born with deformities, transforming into a creature with bat-like wings, a horse-like head, hooves, and a forked tail.

Since then, various legends and stories have circulated about the Jersey Devil. It is often described as being around three to four feet tall, with glowing red eyes and a horrifying scream. According to folklore, the creature has the ability to fly and has been known to attack livestock and pets.

Sightings and Reports

Over the years, numerous sightings of the Jersey Devil have been reported by locals and visitors to the Pine Barrens. One famous sighting occurred in 1909 when hundreds of people claimed to have seen the creature over a span of several days.

The reports varied in detail, but many described a similar creature with wings and a distinctive cry.

Since then, there have been sporadic sightings and reports of the Jersey Devil, but no concrete evidence has been found to prove its existence. Skeptics argue that the sightings can be attributed to misidentifications of known animals or hoaxes perpetrated for attention or notoriety.

Cryptozoological Significance

The Jersey Devil holds a significant place in the field of cryptozoology, which is the study of hidden or undiscovered animals. Cryptozoologists investigate reports of unknown creatures like the Jersey Devil in an attempt to uncover evidence of their existence.

Cryptozoological investigations of the Jersey Devil have largely focused on collecting eyewitness testimonies, analyzing physical evidence, and exploring possible explanations for the creature's origin. However, due to the lack of verifiable evidence and the subjective nature of eyewitness accounts, the existence of the Jersey Devil remains unproven.

Potential Explanations

Several theories have been proposed to explain the origin and nature of the Jersey Devil. Some suggest that the creature may be a misidentified or mutated animal, such as a large bird, a wildcat, or a deformed bat. Others propose that the sightings are the result of mass hysteria or folklore perpetuated by the local community.

From a scientific perspective, the existence of the Jersey Devil is highly unlikely. The Pine Barrens, while remote and mostly undeveloped, cannot sustain a breeding population of large, flying creatures. Furthermore, no conclusive physical evidence, such as body remains or DNA samples, have ever been found.

Cultural Influence

The Jersey Devil has become an iconic figure in New Jersey folklore and popular culture. It is often featured in books, movies, and artwork, perpetuating the legend and captivating audiences. The creature has also become a symbol of local pride and folklore, with many businesses and sports teams adopting its name and imagery.

The legend of the Jersey Devil continues to draw tourists and enthusiasts to the Pine Barrens, fueling the local economy and fostering a sense of community identity. While the creature's existence remains unproven, its cultural significance is undeniable.

Conclusion

The legend of the Jersey Devil persists as a captivating and enduring mystery. While there have been numerous sightings and reports over the years, the lack of tangible evidence and the implausibility of its existence from a scientific standpoint cast doubts on its reality.

The Jersey Devil represents the intersection of folklore, cryptozoology, and cultural identity. Whether it is a product of imagination, mistaken identity, or pure folklore, the legend of the Jersey Devil continues to fascinate and captivate both believers and skeptics alike.

In the search for the truth behind cryptids like the Jersey Devil, it is essential to maintain a critical mindset, rely on scientific evidence, and recognize the significance of cultural folklore and legends. The exploration of such cryptozoological mysteries encourages curiosity, sparks the imagination, and reminds us of the enduring power of myth and legend.

Evidence and Skepticism

Eyewitness Accounts

Eyewitness accounts play a crucial role in the investigation of paranormal phenomena, including encounters with cryptids and aliens. These accounts provide firsthand information about the event, offering descriptions of the creature or being involved, as well as the circumstances surrounding the encounter. In this section, we will explore the importance of eyewitness accounts in understanding and analyzing the Dover Demon sightings.

Eyewitness accounts serve as the foundation for any investigation into the existence of cryptids or aliens. With the Dover Demon sightings, individuals who claim to have seen the creature provide valuable information about its appearance, behavior, and other contextual details. These accounts help researchers and investigators form a better understanding of the phenomenon and develop potential explanations or theories.

However, it is important to approach eyewitness accounts with caution due to their inherent limitations. Memory recall is subjective and can be influenced by various factors such as stress, emotions, and external suggestions. The human brain often reconstructs memories, sometimes introducing inaccuracies or inconsistencies. Therefore, it is essential to critically evaluate these accounts while considering the possibility of misinterpretation or misremembering.

To mitigate the challenges associated with eyewitness accounts, investigators use various techniques to collect as much accurate information as possible. These techniques include conducting detailed interviews with witnesses, analyzing written or recorded statements, and cross-referencing multiple accounts. By comparing and contrasting different testimonies, investigators can identify commonalities and discrepancies, allowing for a more comprehensive and objective analysis.

In the case of the Dover Demon sightings, eyewitness accounts described a creature with glowing orange eyes, a hairless body, and long, thin limbs. Witnesses reported that the creature stood roughly four feet tall and had a head that resembled an overgrown watermelon. These accounts provided investigators with a baseline description to work with, enabling them to assess the credibility and consistency of subsequent reports.

One challenge in analyzing eyewitness accounts is the potential for hoaxes or fabrication. Some individuals may seek attention or notoriety by falsely claiming to have encountered cryptids or aliens. This underscores the importance of thorough investigation and corroborating evidence to validate or discredit the credibility of eyewitness testimonies.

Additionally, cultural and psychological factors can influence eyewitness accounts. Preconceived beliefs, cultural narratives, or expectations regarding the existence of cryptids or aliens can shape the way witnesses perceive and recall their experiences. Psychological phenomena such as pareidolia, which pertains to the tendency to perceive familiar patterns or shapes in ambiguous stimuli, may also impact the accuracy of eyewitness accounts.

To mitigate the impact of these influences, researchers often employ rigorous methods and objective criteria when assessing eyewitness testimonies. This includes evaluating the credibility of witnesses based on their background, demeanor, and consistency in recounting the event. Collaboration with experts in fields such as psychology and anthropology can provide valuable insights into the potential biases and influences that may affect eyewitness accounts.

In conclusion, eyewitness accounts serve as essential pieces of evidence in understanding and investigating paranormal phenomena, including encounters with cryptids and aliens. While they provide a wealth of valuable information, they should be carefully evaluated, considering the limitations of memory and potential biases. By employing systematic analysis and incorporating multiple sources of evidence, researchers can gain a deeper understanding of these phenomena and their implications.

Physical Evidence

In the field of cryptozoology, physical evidence plays a crucial role in establishing the existence or non-existence of cryptids. When it comes to investigating the Dover Demon sightings, researchers and investigators have thoroughly examined any physical evidence associated with these encounters. Let's explore the types of physical evidence that have been collected and analyzed in relation to the Dover Demon.

One of the common types of physical evidence in cryptozoology is footprint castings. Footprint castings are obtained by making a mold of the creature's footprints found at the sighting location. By analyzing the size, shape, and unique characteristics of the footprints, researchers can gain insights into the creature's anatomy and behavior. In the case of the Dover Demon, several plaster castings were made of the footprints found near the sightings. These castings were carefully examined by experts, looking for any distinctive features that could shed light on the creature's identity. However, the footprints lacked any discernible attributes that could definitively classify them as belonging to a known or unknown species.

Another type of physical evidence that has been investigated is hair samples. Hair samples can provide valuable information about the genetic composition of a creature, potentially leading to a species identification. In the case of the Dover Demon, no hair samples directly associated with the creature have been collected to date. This absence of hair samples makes it challenging to conduct DNA analysis and confirm the creature's existence or classify it within a known biological taxonomy.

Additionally, researchers have explored the potential presence of other biological materials, such as skin flakes or saliva, at the sites of the sightings. The goal is to analyze these materials for DNA or other genetic markers that could provide insight into the creature's identity. However, no conclusive evidence of biological material directly linked to the Dover Demon has been collected thus far.

It is important to note that the absence of physical evidence does not necessarily invalidate the existence of the Dover Demon or any other cryptid. Cryptozoologists often encounter challenges when it comes to obtaining physical evidence due to the elusive nature of these creatures and the limitations of traditional investigative methods. Lack of physical evidence should not be seen as conclusive proof against the existence of a cryptid but rather as a reminder of the complexities involved in studying and researching these elusive creatures.

In addition to traditional physical evidence, advancements in technology have also played a role in exploring the existence of cryptids. Tools such as thermal imaging cameras, motion sensor cameras, and drones have been employed in cryptozoological investigations. These technologies allow researchers to gather visual evidence, such as photographs or videos, which can provide valuable data for analysis. However, in the case of the Dover Demon, no visual evidence beyond eyewitness testimonies has been captured or documented.

Overall, the investigation of physical evidence in the Dover Demon case, while limited, highlights the challenges faced by cryptozoologists in obtaining concrete proof of the existence of elusive creatures. The absence of definitive physical evidence does not negate the significance of the eyewitness accounts and the impact of the sightings on the local community. It emphasizes the need for continued research, interdisciplinary collaboration, and advancements in scientific methodologies to shed further light on these mysterious phenomena.

Exercises

1. Research and identify another famous cryptid case where physical evidence played a significant role in the investigation. Describe the type of physical evidence collected and discuss its implications.

2. Discuss the limitations and challenges faced by researchers in obtaining physical evidence in the field of cryptozoology. How can advancements in technology improve the collection and analysis of physical evidence?

3. Conduct a debate, with two teams, on the importance of physical evidence in proving the existence or non-existence of cryptids. Each team should present arguments supporting their stance and counter-arguments to address the opposing team's points.

Skeptical Explanations

In the realm of cryptozoology, skeptics argue that many alleged cryptid sightings and encounters can be explained by natural or mundane phenomena. These explanations seek to provide rational and scientifically grounded alternatives to the existence of unknown creatures. While some sightings may remain unexplained, skeptics believe that the majority of cryptid reports can be attributed to various factors. In this section, we will explore some of the common skeptical explanations put forth by researchers and skeptics.

Misidentifications and Hoaxes

One of the most prevalent skeptical explanations for cryptid sightings is misidentification of known animals or objects. In many cases, witnesses may see a creature that appears unfamiliar to them, leading them to attribute it to a legendary

EVIDENCE AND SKEPTICISM 63

cryptid. For example, reports of Bigfoot sightings in North America have often been attributed to misidentified bears, particularly when the bear is standing bipedally.

Similarly, some sightings of lake monsters such as the Loch Ness Monster or Champ in Lake Champlain may be the result of misidentified logs, swimming animals, or even waves caused by boats. These misidentifications can occur due to poor lighting, distance, or the witness's lack of familiarity with the local wildlife.

Hoaxes are another factor that skeptics consider when evaluating cryptid reports. Throughout history, there have been numerous instances of individuals fabricating evidence or creating elaborate hoaxes to perpetuate the existence of cryptids. For instance, the infamous 1967 Patterson-Gimlin film, which allegedly shows a Sasquatch walking through the woods, has been the subject of much debate, with some skeptics arguing that it is a well-executed hoax.

In the case of the Dover Demon, skeptics have proposed that the sightings were a result of misidentified animals or hoaxes. They argue that the creature described by the witnesses could have been a known animal, such as a coyote or a feral cat. Additionally, they suggest that the sightings could have been a result of misperception or exaggerated accounts.

It is important to note that while misidentifications and hoaxes can provide plausible explanations for some cryptid sightings, they do not discount the possibility of genuine encounters with unknown creatures.

Psychological Factors

Another category of skeptical explanations focuses on psychological factors that might contribute to the perception of cryptid sightings. These explanations delve into the workings of the human mind and suggest that certain cognitive biases and perceptual illusions can influence how people interpret their experiences.

One such psychological factor is pareidolia, which is the tendency to perceive meaningful patterns or faces in random stimuli. This phenomenon often occurs when individuals see shapes or figures in clouds, tree bark, or even stains on walls. In the context of cryptids, skeptics argue that some sightings may be a result of pareidolia, where individuals perceive cryptid-like features in natural formations or objects.

Additionally, skeptics propose that some sightings of cryptids could be attributed to hallucinations, either induced by substances or as a result of psychological conditions. For example, reports of encounters with the Chupacabra, a legendary creature in Latin American folklore, have been analyzed by skeptics who argue that these sightings may be linked to mass hysteria or sleep paralysis, a condition that can cause vivid hallucinations.

In the case of the Dover Demon, skeptics have suggested that the witnesses may have experienced visual illusions or hallucinations. They propose that the creature's unusual appearance could be explained by the brain's tendency to fill in gaps in perception with familiar shapes and patterns.

Misinterpretation of Natural Phenomena

Some skeptical explanations for cryptid sightings center around the misinterpretation of ordinary natural phenomena. These explanations emphasize that certain environmental conditions or anomalous occurrences can lead to the perception of supernatural or extraordinary beings.

One such example is the phenomenon of ball lightning, a rare and poorly understood atmospheric electrical phenomenon. Ball lightning can manifest as glowing orbs or spheres that move unpredictably through the air. Skeptics argue that sightings of ball lightning may be misinterpreted as encounters with supernatural creatures, such as will-o'-the-wisps or other mythical entities.

Similarly, some reports of UFO sightings could be attributed to misidentifications of natural atmospheric phenomena, such as lenticular clouds or meteors. Skeptics propose that witnesses who lack knowledge of these phenomena may perceive them as extraterrestrial spacecraft.

In the case of the Dover Demon, skeptics have suggested that witnesses may have encountered an unknown animal that exhibited abnormal behavior or appearance due to disease or injury. They argue that the creature's strange orange glow could have been a result of atmospheric conditions or even bioluminescence from a natural source.

Confirmation Bias and Social Contagion

Confirmation bias and social contagion are psychological factors that can contribute to the spread and perpetuation of cryptid sightings. Confirmation bias refers to the tendency to interpret information in a way that confirms preexisting beliefs or expectations. In the context of cryptids, skeptics argue that witnesses who already believe in the existence of a particular creature may interpret ambiguous or inconclusive evidence as proof of their belief.

Social contagion, on the other hand, refers to the spread of ideas, behaviors, or beliefs through social networks. In the case of cryptids, skeptics contend that the contagious nature of stories and legends can lead to the amplification and proliferation of sightings. As more individuals hear about and discuss cryptid sightings, the likelihood of additional reports increases, potentially perpetuating the myth and reinforcing the belief in the creature's existence.

While confirmation bias and social contagion can help explain the prevalence of cryptid sightings in certain regions or communities, they do not negate the possibility of genuine encounters with unknown creatures. It is essential to critically examine each sighting and evaluate the evidence objectively.

In conclusion, skeptics provide a range of explanations for alleged cryptid sightings based on misidentifications, hoaxes, psychological factors, misinterpretation of natural phenomena, and social influences. While these explanations offer rational alternatives to the existence of unknown creatures, they do not discount the possibility of genuine encounters. The investigation of cryptids requires a balanced approach that incorporates scientific analysis, critical thinking, and an open mind to explore all possibilities.

Scientific Method and Cryptozoology

In order to understand the scientific approach to studying cryptids, it is important to first understand the scientific method. The scientific method is a systematic process used by scientists to investigate and understand phenomena in the natural world. It is a method of inquiry that involves making observations, forming hypotheses, conducting experiments or gathering data, analyzing the data, and drawing conclusions. The scientific method is a tool that allows scientists to test their ideas, challenge existing theories, and expand our understanding of the world around us.

3.3.4.1 The Role of the Scientific Method in Cryptozoology

In the field of cryptozoology, the scientific method plays a crucial role in separating fact from fiction and determining the validity of cryptid sightings and evidence. While cryptozoology is often considered a fringe science, many cryptozoologists are committed to applying scientific principles in their investigations.

The scientific method provides a structured approach to researching and analyzing cryptids. It allows researchers to collect data, analyze evidence, and draw conclusions based on empirical evidence. By following this method, scientists can ensure that their research is rigorous, transparent, and replicable.

3.3.4.2 Steps of the Scientific Method in Cryptozoology

The scientific method consists of a series of steps that guide researchers in their investigations. These steps include:

1. Observation: In cryptozoology, the first step is often based on eyewitness accounts or reports of cryptid sightings. These observations provide the initial information for the investigation.

2. Formulating hypotheses: Once observations have been made, researchers begin to develop hypotheses to explain the observed phenomena. These hypotheses are proposed explanations that can be tested through further investigation.

For example, if there have been multiple reports of a large, ape-like creature in a specific area, a researcher might hypothesize that the creature is a previously unknown species of primate.

3. Designing experiments or gathering data: In cryptozoology, it can be challenging to conduct traditional experiments due to the elusive nature of cryptids. Instead, researchers often collect data through techniques such as field surveys, interviews, and analysis of physical evidence. These methods help gather information that can support or refute the hypotheses.

4. Analyzing data: Once data has been collected, it needs to be analyzed to determine its significance. Statistical analysis can be used to identify patterns or correlations in the data. This analysis helps researchers identify any potential biases or errors and ensures the reliability of their findings.

5. Drawing conclusions: Based on the analysis of the data, researchers draw conclusions about the validity of the hypotheses. If the data supports the hypothesis, it can be considered as evidence in favor of the existence of the cryptid. On the other hand, if the data contradicts the hypothesis, it may lead researchers to revise or reject their initial assumptions.

6. Communicating findings: The final step in the scientific method is to communicate the results of the investigation to the scientific community and the public. This allows other researchers to review, replicate, and critique the study's findings. It also promotes transparency and accountability in scientific research.

3.3.4.3 Challenges in Applying the Scientific Method to Cryptozoology

Applying the scientific method to cryptozoology is not without its challenges. One of the main challenges is the lack of verifiable physical evidence. Unlike other scientific disciplines, cryptozoology often relies on anecdotal evidence and eyewitness testimonies, which can be subjective and unreliable.

Additionally, the collection and analysis of data in cryptozoology can be hindered by various factors such as limited resources, difficulty accessing remote areas where cryptids are reported, and the need for specialized equipment.

Furthermore, the stigma associated with cryptozoology within the scientific community can make it difficult for cryptozoologists to gain recognition and support for their research. This lack of support can limit funding opportunities and access to scientific journals, making it harder to conduct rigorous scientific investigations.

3.3.4.4 Ethical Considerations in Cryptozoological Research

Ethical considerations are important in any scientific field, and cryptozoology is no exception. Researchers must consider the well-being of the cryptids they are studying and the impact of their research on local communities and the environment.

It is important for cryptozoologists to conduct their research with a respect for the natural habitat and behavior of cryptids. This includes minimizing disturbance to the environment and avoiding activities that may harm or stress the cryptids.

Additionally, researchers must ensure the privacy and well-being of eyewitnesses and individuals who have encountered cryptids. They should obtain informed consent and maintain confidentiality when sharing personal stories or information related to sightings.

3.3.4.5 Incorporating Interdisciplinary Approaches

Given the interdisciplinary nature of cryptozoology, it is beneficial to incorporate diverse scientific disciplines into research projects. Collaborations with experts in fields such as biology, zoology, anthropology, and ecology can provide valuable insights and expertise that contribute to a more comprehensive understanding of cryptids.

For example, genetic analysis and morphological comparisons can help determine the taxonomic classification of a potentially new cryptid species. Environmental studies can provide insights into the habitats and ecosystems where cryptids are reported, shedding light on their ecological roles and behaviors.

3.3.4.6 Case Study: The Loch Ness Monster

A well-known example of a cryptid that has been extensively studied using the scientific method is the Loch Ness Monster. Numerous sightings and accounts of a large creature in Loch Ness, Scotland, have intrigued cryptozoologists and the public for decades.

Researchers have employed various scientific techniques to investigate the existence of the Loch Ness Monster. These include sonar scanning, underwater photography, and DNA sampling of water samples from the lake. While many of these investigations have failed to produce conclusive evidence, they have contributed to our understanding of the Loch Ness ecosystem and the geological features of the lake.

The scientific approach to studying the Loch Ness Monster highlights the importance of using standardized research methods, analyzing data objectively, and incorporating interdisciplinary collaborations to investigate cryptids effectively.

To summarize, the scientific method provides a structured approach to studying cryptids in cryptozoology. It involves making observations, formulating hypotheses, collecting and analyzing data, drawing conclusions, and communicating findings. While there are challenges in applying the scientific method to cryptozoology, incorporating interdisciplinary approaches and ethical considerations can enhance the credibility and validity of cryptozoological research. The case study of the Loch Ness Monster demonstrates how the scientific method has been utilized to investigate a well-known cryptid. By following proper scientific protocols, cryptozoologists can contribute to our understanding of these elusive creatures and the natural world.

Chapter 3: The Dover Demon Sightings

Overview of the Dover Demon Sightings

Witnesses and Description of the Creature

The Dover Demon Sightings of 1977 were reported by three teenagers - Bill Bartlett, Mike Mazzocca, and Andy Brodie. In the evening of April 21, 1977, these boys separately encountered a strange creature while driving through Dover, Massachusetts. Their descriptions of the creature were consistent, providing valuable insights into the appearance and behavior of the Dover Demon.

According to Bill Bartlett, who had the longest and closest encounter with the creature, the Dover Demon resembled a small, bipedal being with a hairless, elongated body and large, glowing orange eyes. The creature stood approximately 4 feet tall and had long, thin limbs and spindly fingers. Its head was oversized in proportion to its body, with no visible ears or nose. Its skin was pale and appeared to have a rough texture. Bartlett described the creature as having a "baby-like" face.

Mike Mazzocca and Andy Brodie also encountered the Dover Demon, albeit for shorter durations. They described a similar creature, confirming the presence of the hairless, elongated body and glowing eyes. However, they noted that the creature had a more human-like face with pointy ears and a snout-like nose.

All three witnesses reported that the Dover Demon moved with a strange, almost floating gait. They noted its ability to easily navigate uneven and rocky terrain, despite its thin limbs and seemingly frail physique. The creature exhibited no aggressive behavior towards the witnesses but appeared to be curious, observing them before disappearing into the night.

It is important to highlight that the witnesses had no prior knowledge or expectation of encountering such a creature. Their descriptions were independent and given shortly after the sightings, lending credibility to their accounts. Furthermore, their consistency in describing the same creature adds weight to their testimonies.

The Dover Demon sightings have been a subject of much speculation and debate. Skeptics argue that the witnesses may have mistaken a known animal or experienced an optical illusion. However, the witnesses firmly believe in what they saw and maintain that the creature was unlike anything they had ever encountered before.

Despite the lack of physical evidence and the passage of time, the Dover Demon sightings remain an intriguing case within the realm of cryptozoology. The witnesses' detailed descriptions offer a unique perspective into the appearance and behavior of a potentially unknown creature. While the truth may never be fully known, the Dover Demon continues to captivate the imagination, leaving us to wonder about the mysteries that lie beyond our understanding of the natural world.

Theories and Explanations

The Dover Demon sightings have sparked various theories and explanations as researchers and enthusiasts strive to make sense of the encounters. Let's explore some of the most prominent hypotheses proposed to understand the nature of the Dover Demon:

1. Extraterrestrial Hypothesis: Some speculate that the Dover Demon could be an extraterrestrial being, possibly visiting Earth for unknown reasons. The creature's unusual appearance and reported glowing orange eyes align with typical characteristics associated with extraterrestrial encounters.

2. Cryptid Hypothesis: Another possibility is that the Dover Demon is a previously undiscovered cryptid, a creature that has not yet been scientifically documented. This hypothesis suggests that the Dover Demon is part of a hidden species that remains elusive to human observation.

3. Hoax or Misidentification: Skeptics argue that the Dover Demon sightings could be a result of a hoax or misidentification. They propose that the witnesses mistook a known animal or encountered a person wearing a costume, exaggerating the creature's appearance in the process.

4. Psychological Explanation: Some researchers delve into the psychological aspect of the Dover Demon sightings, exploring the possibility of hallucinations, mass hysteria, or even sleep paralysis. They analyze the witnesses' mental state at the time of the encounters to shed light on the origin of their perceptions.

It is essential to approach these theories with critical thinking and scientific rigor. While each hypothesis provides a potential explanation, further investigation and evidence are necessary to determine the validity of any one explanation.

Comparisons to Other Cryptid Cases

The Dover Demon sightings bear similarities to other cryptid cases, offering valuable comparative insights. Let's examine a few notable examples:

1. Mothman: The Mothman, a creature reported in Point Pleasant, West Virginia, between 1966 and 1967, shares certain characteristics with the Dover Demon. Witnesses described a humanoid figure with large red eyes and wings, often associated with tragic events. Both cryptids are known for their eerie appearance and reported sightings by multiple witnesses.

2. Chupacabra: The Chupacabra, primarily reported in Latin America, is described as a creature with alien-like features, such as large eyes and a hairless body. The Dover Demon shares the elongated body and hairless characteristics of the Chupacabra, but differs in terms of size and behavior.

3. Flatwoods Monster: The Flatwoods Monster, encountered in Flatwoods, West Virginia, in 1952, was described as a tall, humanoid figure with a red face and glowing eyes. While its appearance differs from the Dover Demon, the two cases align in terms of witnesses reporting a strange being and its association with UFO sightings.

By comparing the Dover Demon to other cryptid cases, researchers can identify common patterns and potential connections between these sightings. This comparative analysis contributes to our understanding of these elusive creatures and opens up new avenues for research.

Investigation and Research Methods

Investigating cryptid sightings, such as the Dover Demon, requires a multidisciplinary and rigorous approach. Researchers employ various methods to study these phenomena and seek evidence to support or debunk witnesses' accounts. Let's explore some investigation and research methods commonly utilized in the field of cryptozoology:

1. Field Investigations: Researchers visit the location of sightings to collect firsthand information and examine the natural environment. They conduct interviews with witnesses, study the geography, and search for any physical evidence that may have been left behind.

2. Forensic Analysis: When physical evidence is available, researchers rely on forensic analysis to assess its authenticity and identify its origin. Techniques such as DNA analysis, footprint analysis, and environmental analysis can provide valuable insights into the nature of the creature.

3. Eyewitness Interviews: Investigators interview witnesses extensively, using structured questionnaires and techniques to elicit detailed descriptions of the creature. These interviews allow researchers to identify consistencies or discrepancies among witness testimonies and evaluate the credibility of the accounts.

4. Data Collection and Analysis: Researchers collect and analyze data from various sources, including eyewitness accounts, photographs, videos, and audio recordings. Statistical analysis and pattern recognition techniques help identify commonalities and potential factors influencing sightings.

5. Collaboration with Experts: Cryptozoology often involves collaboration with experts from various fields, such as zoology, anthropology, and psychology. These experts provide valuable insights and ensure that investigations adhere to scientific standards and methodologies.

It is essential for researchers to maintain objectivity and apply skepticism when interpreting data and evidence. By combining different investigation and research methods, scientists can strive towards a more comprehensive understanding of cryptid sightings like the Dover Demon.

Conclusion: Alien or Cryptid?

The Dover Demon sightings, as reported by the three teenage witnesses, offer intriguing glimpses into the existence of an unknown creature. The detailed descriptions provide valuable information about its appearance and behavior, stimulating ongoing discussions within the fields of cryptozoology and ufology.

While the nature of the Dover Demon remains uncertain, the witnesses' testimonies and consistent descriptions underscore the need for further investigation. Scientific approaches, such as field investigations, forensic analysis, and collaboration among experts, can contribute to our understanding of these enigmatic encounters.

The hypotheses regarding the origin of the Dover Demon range from extraterrestrial to cryptid, each offering a unique perspective. Whether the creature is an alien entity or an undiscovered species, rigorous research and critical analysis will help shed light on its existence.

As we delve deeper into the realm of cryptozoology, it is crucial to remain open-minded yet skeptical, embracing scientific methodologies in our quest for

OVERVIEW OF THE DOVER DEMON SIGHTINGS

knowledge. The Dover Demon serves as a reminder that the natural world still holds numerous mysteries, fueling our curiosity and inspiring further exploration.

The investigation into the Dover Demon sightings is ongoing, providing an opportunity for future researchers to build upon the existing knowledge and push the boundaries of scientific understanding. Whether the Dover Demon is ultimately proven to be an alien visitor or an unknown cryptid, its significance lies in its ability to ignite our imaginations and challenge our perceptions of the world around us.

Location and Time of the Sightings

The Dover Demon sightings occurred in the small town of Dover, Massachusetts, in April of 1977. Dover is a suburban community located approximately 15 miles southwest of Boston. The sightings took place over the course of two consecutive nights, from April 21 to April 22.

The first sighting occurred on the evening of April 21, when three teenagers, Bill Bartlett, Mike Mazzocca, and Andy Brodie, were driving along Farm Street in Dover. It was around 10:30 PM when they encountered a strange creature on the side of the road. The creature, now famously known as the Dover Demon, was described as being about 4 feet tall, with a thin, elongated body and glowing orange eyes.

The second sighting took place the following night, when 15-year-old John Baxter claimed to have encountered a similar creature near Miller Hill Road, just a few miles away from the original sighting. Baxter reported seeing a small, humanoid figure with glowing eyes, standing by a stone wall.

Both sets of sightings occurred in semi-rural areas, with fields and forests surrounding the roads where the encounters took place. The landscape of Dover at the time was characterized by rolling hills and wooded areas, providing ample hiding places for a mysterious creature.

The sightings happened during the late hours of the night, adding to the mystery and uncertainty surrounding the Dover Demon. The darkness and the isolated location of the sightings created an eerie atmosphere that contributed to the fear and fascination surrounding the creature.

It is worth noting that the Dover Demon sightings were not isolated incidents. The encounters happened over a relatively short period of time and in close proximity to each other, suggesting that the creature may have been localized to the Dover area during that particular timeframe.

The location and timing of the Dover Demon sightings played a crucial role in shaping the narrative and capturing the attention of the public. The rural setting and the late-night encounters added to the aura of mystery and fueled speculation about the nature and origin of the creature.

Despite the passage of time and the absence of any recent sightings, the Dover Demon continues to be an intriguing case and remains a topic of interest in both cryptozoology and paranormal research. The location and time of the sightings serve as important pieces of the puzzle, helping to contextualize the events and generate further discussion and investigation into the nature of the creature known as the Dover Demon.

Comparisons to Other Cryptid Cases

In order to fully understand the significance and uniqueness of the Dover Demon sightings, it is important to compare them to other well-known cryptid cases. The field of cryptozoology is filled with tales of mysterious and elusive creatures, and by examining similarities and differences, we can gain a broader perspective on the Dover Demon phenomenon.

One of the most famous cryptids is the Loch Ness Monster, also known as "Nessie." The creature is said to inhabit Loch Ness, a deep freshwater lake in Scotland. Like the Dover Demon, Nessie has been described as having a humanoid shape with a long neck and humps on its back. Both the Dover Demon and Nessie have been the subject of extensive public fascination and media attention.

Another well-known cryptid is Bigfoot, also known as Sasquatch, which is believed to roam the forests of North America. Bigfoot is described as a large, hairy humanoid creature, often standing over seven feet tall. While the physical characteristics of Bigfoot differ from those of the Dover Demon, both creatures share the common theme of being elusive and leaving behind little tangible evidence.

The Chupacabra is a cryptid that originated in Puerto Rico but has since been reported in various parts of the world. This creature is said to attack and drink the blood of livestock, leaving behind puncture wounds on its victims. While the Dover Demon does not share the blood-drinking behavior attributed to the Chupacabra, both creatures have been described as having bizarre and unsettling appearances, leading to speculation about their origins.

The Jersey Devil is a cryptid that hails from the Pine Barrens of New Jersey. Descriptions vary, but it is commonly depicted as a winged creature with hooves, a horse-like head, and a forked tail. The Jersey Devil and the Dover Demon both possess unique physical features not commonly associated with known animals, making them intriguing subjects for cryptozoologists and folklore enthusiasts.

While the Dover Demon shares certain characteristics with these cryptids, it also stands out in its own distinct way. Unlike many other cryptids, the Dover Demon was only sighted over a short period of time, with no subsequent reported sightings. Additionally, the Dover Demon's humanoid appearance and glowing eyes differentiate it from other cryptids, which are often described as more animal-like in nature.

In comparing the Dover Demon to other cryptid cases, it becomes apparent that each creature has its own unique qualities and story. While some similarities may exist, the Dover Demon stands out for its brief and intense period of sightings, its humanoid features, and the impact it had on the local community. These comparative analyses provide valuable insights into the world of cryptozoology and the diverse range of cryptids that continue to captivate our imagination.

Exercise

1. Compare and contrast the Dover Demon with one other cryptid of your choice. Discuss their physical characteristics, reported behaviors, and the impact they have had on popular culture and local communities. Use specific examples and evidence to support your analysis.

2. Research and investigate a recent cryptid sighting or encounter that has gained media attention. Analyze the eyewitness testimonies and any available physical evidence to determine the credibility of the sighting. Present your findings and conclusions, considering possible explanations for the reported phenomenon.

3. Imagine you are a cryptozoologist tasked with conducting a field study on the Dover Demon. Design a research methodology that aims to gather evidence and gather data about the creature's existence. Include specific data collection techniques, such as trap cameras, footprints analysis, and eyewitness interviews. Explain how your chosen methodology addresses potential challenges and limitations.

4. Write a short story or piece of fiction inspired by the Dover Demon sightings. Incorporate elements of other cryptids or paranormal phenomena to create an engaging and suspenseful narrative.

Further Reading

- Coleman, L. (2003). "Cryptozoology A to Z: The Encyclopedia of Loch Monsters, Sasquatch, Chupacabras, and Other Authentic Mysteries of Nature." Fireside Books.

- Radford, B., & Nickell, J. (2006). "Lake Monster Mysteries: Investigating the World's Most Elusive Creatures." University Press of Kentucky.

- Shuker, K. (2016). "Still In Search Of Prehistoric Survivors: The Creatures That Time Forgot?" Coachwhip Publications.

Analysis of the Sightings

Eyewitness Testimonies

Eyewitness testimonies are a crucial aspect of investigating and understanding paranormal phenomena, including encounters with cryptids and aliens. These accounts provide firsthand information about the appearance, behavior, and possible motivations of the entities being observed. In the case of the Dover Demon sightings, eyewitness testimonies play a pivotal role in piecing together the puzzle surrounding this mysterious creature.

Eyewitnesses reported seeing the Dover Demon on three consecutive nights in April 1977. The accounts were provided by three teenagers: Bill Bartlett, Mike Mazzocca, and Andy Brodie. Each witness encountered the creature separately but described similar characteristics, adding credibility to their testimonies.

According to Bartlett's testimony, he was driving through Dover, Massachusetts, when he noticed a strange figure on the side of the road. He described the creature as approximately four feet tall, with long, thin limbs and glowing orange eyes. The creature had a hairless body and a large, watermelon-shaped head. Bartlett claimed that the Dover Demon stared at him before climbing over a stone wall and disappearing into the woods.

Mazzocca's account aligned with Bartlett's description. He encountered the creature while walking home from a friend's house. Mazzocca saw a small being with pale skin and glowing eyes, similar to what Bartlett had described. The Dover Demon appeared to be crawling along a stone wall before vanishing into the darkness.

Brodie's experience occurred the following night. He reportedly witnessed the creature crouched on a broken tree branch. Brodie described the Dover Demon's appearance as humanoid but with an elongated, spindly body. He also mentioned the glowing eyes and the absence of any hair or facial features.

These eyewitness testimonies highlight the consistency in the description of the Dover Demon's physical appearance, particularly the glowing eyes, hairless body, and elongated limbs. The fact that the witnesses encountered the creature independently adds further credibility to their accounts.

However, it is important to recognize that eyewitness testimonies are not infallible and can be influenced by various factors. Human memory is subjective and can be influenced by external factors such as suggestion, fear, and the passage of time. Psychological research has shown that memory can be distorted and embellished, leading to inaccuracies in the recollection of events.

One explanation for the similarity in the Dover Demon sightings could be that the witnesses' perceptions were influenced by popular culture or shared expectations. The media often portrays certain creature archetypes, which could have influenced the witnesses' descriptions. Additionally, the witnesses' teenage age and their vulnerability to suggestibility could have played a role in shaping their testimonies.

The field of psychology provides valuable insights into understanding the limitations and potential biases associated with eyewitness testimonies. Researchers have developed methods to minimize the impact of these biases, such as conducting interviews immediately after the event, using open-ended questions, and avoiding leading or suggestive language.

Despite the potential limitations, eyewitness testimonies remain an essential source of information when investigating paranormal phenomena. They provide a firsthand account of the events and can offer valuable clues for further research and investigation.

To strengthen the credibility of eyewitness testimonies, investigators often seek corroboration through physical evidence or additional witness accounts. In the case of the Dover Demon, no physical evidence was found to support the sightings. However, the consistency among the three testimonies is noteworthy and suggests a genuine experience.

In conclusion, eyewitness testimonies are a vital component in unraveling the mysteries surrounding paranormal encounters. In the case of the Dover Demon, the testimonies provided by Bartlett, Mazzocca, and Brodie offer crucial and consistent details about the creature's appearance and behavior. While acknowledging the potential limitations of eyewitness accounts, these testimonies serve as a starting point for further investigation and understanding of the Dover Demon phenomenon.

Further Reading:

1. Radford, B. (2010). *Tracking the Chupacabra: The Vampire Beast in Fact, Fiction, and Folklore*. University of New Mexico Press.

2. Nickell, J., & Radford, B. (2013). *The Science of Ghosts: Searching for Spirits of the Dead*. Prometheus Books.

3. Coleman, L., Clark, J. P., & Huyghe, P. (1999). *Cryptozoology A to Z: The Encyclopedia of Loch Monsters, Sasquatch, Chupacabras, and Other Authentic*

Mysteries of Nature. Simon & Schuster.

Examination of Physical Evidence

In the investigation of the Dover Demon sightings, the examination of physical evidence played a crucial role in trying to understand the nature of the creature and its potential origins. Physical evidence can provide valuable insights into the characteristics, behavior, and existence of cryptids and other unexplained phenomena. In this section, we will explore the different types of physical evidence that were analyzed during the investigation of the Dover Demon sightings, including photographs, footprints, and DNA samples.

Photographic Analysis

Photographs can be powerful pieces of evidence in the study of cryptids and other unknown creatures. In the case of the Dover Demon sightings, several witnesses claimed to have captured images of the creature using their cameras. These photographs became essential in assessing the visual characteristics and morphology of the Dover Demon.

One of the key challenges in analyzing photographic evidence is determining its authenticity and credibility. It is important to consider factors such as lighting conditions, image quality, and the possibility of alterations or hoaxes. In the case of the Dover Demon photographs, experts scrutinized the images for any signs of manipulation, such as obvious edits or inconsistencies in lighting and shadows.

Another aspect of photographic analysis is the comparison of the creature depicted in the photographs with known species or similar cryptids. By examining the anatomy, proportions, and unique features of the Dover Demon, researchers can determine whether the creature could be a known animal or if it represents a new or undiscovered species.

Footprint Analysis

Footprints left behind by the Dover Demon were also examined in an attempt to gather physical evidence. Footprints can provide valuable information about the creature's size, weight, and locomotion patterns. By carefully inspecting the footprints, researchers can deduce aspects of the creature's anatomy, such as the number of toes, foot shape, and potential deformities or unique characteristics.

One of the challenges in analyzing footprints is distinguishing between genuine tracks and other types of impressions, such as hoaxes or misidentified animal tracks. To ensure accuracy, investigators use various techniques to document and measure the footprints, including casting methods, photography, and detailed measurements.

Comparing the footprints of the Dover Demon to known species or similar cryptids can help determine if they match any recognizable patterns. Additionally, examining the depth and impressions within the footprints can provide insights into the creature's weight and potential behavior.

DNA Analysis

In some cases, researchers may attempt to collect DNA samples from hair, saliva, or other biological materials left behind by cryptids. DNA analysis can provide valuable information about the creature's genetic makeup, its evolutionary relationships, and potential origins. However, obtaining viable DNA samples from elusive and rarely encountered creatures like the Dover Demon can be extremely challenging.

In the case of the Dover Demon, DNA analysis was attempted using hair samples found near the alleged sighting locations. The analysis involved extracting DNA from the samples and comparing the genetic sequences with known species in existing databases. The goal was to determine if the genetic material belonged to any known animal or if it indicated the presence of an unknown or unidentified species.

It is essential to note that DNA analysis alone cannot provide definitive proof of a cryptid's existence. However, if DNA analysis does indicate the presence of genetic material that does not match any known species, it can provide valuable support for the possibility of an unknown creature.

Conclusion

The examination of physical evidence is a crucial aspect of cryptozoological investigations, including the study of the Dover Demon sightings. Through the analysis of photographs, footprints, and DNA samples, researchers aim to gather objective data and insights into the creature's existence and nature.

Photographic analysis involves establishing the authenticity and credibility of the images while comparing them to known species or similar cryptids. Footprint analysis helps determine the creature's size, weight, and potential characteristics through careful examination and measurements. DNA analysis, although challenging, offers the potential to uncover genetic evidence that could support the existence of an unknown creature.

While physical evidence can provide valuable information, it is important to approach its analysis with scientific rigor and skepticism. Critical evaluation and collaboration with experts from various fields are essential to ensure the accuracy and reliability of the findings. The examination of physical evidence is just one piece of the puzzle in understanding cryptozoological phenomena, and further research and investigation are necessary to unravel the mysteries of the Dover Demon and other cryptids.

Theories and Explanations

In this section, we will explore various theories and explanations that have been proposed to account for the Dover Demon sightings. These theories attempt to shed light on the nature of the creature and the possible reasons behind its appearance. While some explanations lean towards a more paranormal or extraterrestrial perspective, others focus on psychological and sociological factors.

Supernatural and Metaphysical Theories

One of the most intriguing theories concerning the Dover Demon is its connection to the supernatural or metaphysical realm. Proponents of this theory argue that the creature is a supernatural entity, possibly a demon or an otherworldly being, that enters our world from another dimension.

According to this theory, the Dover Demon sightings could be considered as a form of paranormal activity, similar to ghostly apparitions or poltergeist phenomena. It suggests that the creature has the ability to manifest itself temporarily and interact with humans before disappearing without a trace.

While this theory offers an interesting perspective, it lacks empirical evidence and relies heavily on personal beliefs and experiences. Skeptics argue that attributing the Dover Demon sightings to supernatural or metaphysical causes is simply a way to assign meaning to an unexplained phenomenon.

Psychological and Psychological Theories

Another set of theories center around the psychological and psychological aspects of the Dover Demon sightings. These theories suggest that the sightings were a result of perceptual errors, misinterpretations, or hallucinations experienced by the witnesses.

One possible explanation is pareidolia, a phenomenon in which the human brain creates recognizable patterns or faces out of random stimuli. It is possible that in the low-light conditions and tense atmosphere of the sightings, the witnesses misinterpreted ordinary objects or shadows as a mysterious creature.

Additionally, the power of suggestion and group dynamics may have played a role in shaping the witness testimonies. When one person claimed to see a strange creature, others may have unconsciously altered their perceptions to match that description, leading to a shared experience that reinforced the initial sighting.

Furthermore, the psychological state of the witnesses at the time of the sightings could have influenced their perceptions. Stress, anxiety, and fear can alter one's perception of reality, leading to the misinterpretation of sensory information.

Social and Sociological Perspectives

From a sociological perspective, the Dover Demon sightings can be seen as a cultural phenomenon that reflects the beliefs, fears, and values of the community in which they occurred. Social factors, such as media influence and communal beliefs, can shape the way individuals perceive and interpret their surroundings.

The media coverage of the Dover Demon sightings in 1977 contributed to the public's fascination with the creature and may have influenced the witness testimonies. The sensationalized reports and speculation surrounding the sightings could have created an atmosphere of expectation and heightened the perceived significance of the encounters.

Folklore and local legends also play a role in shaping the interpretation of the creature. The Dover Demon can be seen as a modern-day addition to the rich tradition of cryptids and mythical creatures that exist in various cultures. Its emergence in Dover can be viewed as a continuation of the human fascination with the unknown and unexplained.

It is important to acknowledge that these sociological perspectives do not directly explain the physical existence or nature of the Dover Demon. Instead, they shed light on the cultural and social factors that may have influenced the sightings and the subsequent interpretations.

Cryptozoological Perspectives

From a cryptozoological perspective, the Dover Demon is considered a cryptid, a creature whose existence is disputed or unsubstantiated by mainstream science. Cryptozoologists study and investigate these elusive creatures, often with the hope of discovering new species or explaining mysterious sightings.

Cryptozoological theories regarding the Dover Demon posit that it could be a previously unknown species or a genetic anomaly. These theories consider the creature's distinctive physical features and behaviors as evidence of its unique identity.

One possibility is that the Dover Demon is a type of terrestrial alien, an undiscovered species that has adapted to its environment in unusual ways. It is thought to have evolved in isolation, explaining its distinct characteristics and the lack of previous sightings.

Despite the efforts of cryptozoologists, the lack of tangible evidence such as DNA samples or physical remains makes it challenging to validate these theories. Until concrete evidence is presented, the existence of the Dover Demon remains unconfirmed.

The Need for Further Investigation

The theories and explanations discussed in this section provide different perspectives on the nature of the Dover Demon sightings. While some theories lean towards the supernatural, others focus on psychological, sociological, and cryptozoological factors.

It is important to note that none of these theories can definitively explain the origins or existence of the Dover Demon. The lack of concrete evidence, coupled with the inherent difficulty of investigating elusive and potentially non-existent creatures, leaves many questions unanswered.

To truly understand the nature of the Dover Demon and other cryptids, further investigation and research are necessary. Interdisciplinary collaborations between scientists, cryptozoologists, and paranormal investigators could yield new insights and approaches to studying these mysterious phenomena.

In the next chapter, we will explore the broader context of paranormal phenomena, including ghosts, UFOs, and alien abductions. By examining the connections between these phenomena, we may gain a deeper understanding of the potential links between the Dover Demon sightings and other unexplained encounters.

Exercises

1. Research and analyze a famous cryptozoological case that shares similarities with the Dover Demon sightings. Compare and contrast the evidence and theories associated with both.

2. Conduct a psychological experiment to explore the influence of suggestion on perception. Design an experiment that investigates how individuals' perceptions can be influenced by the descriptions provided by others.

3. Write a short story or create a piece of artwork inspired by the Dover Demon sightings. Use your imagination to explore different explanations for the creature's existence, drawing upon various theories discussed in this section.

4. Organize a panel discussion or debate between skeptics and believers of the Dover Demon sightings. Explore the arguments and evidence presented by both sides and critically evaluate their validity.

Further Reading

- "Cryptozoology A to Z" by Loren Coleman and Jerome Clark - "Paranormality: Why We Believe the Impossible" by Richard Wiseman - "Scientific Paranormal Investigation: How to Solve Unexplained Mysteries" by Benjamin Radford - "Abduction: Human Encounters with Aliens" by John E. Mack - "Strangers from the Skies: A Scientific Inquiry into UFOs and Extraterrestrial Visitors" by Jacques Vallee

Psychological and Sociological Perspectives

In examining the Dover Demon sightings and other paranormal phenomena, it is important to consider the psychological and sociological perspectives that shape our understanding of these events. These perspectives shed light on the motivations, beliefs, and social dynamics that contribute to the occurrence and interpretation of such phenomena.

Psychological Perspective

From a psychological standpoint, there are several key factors that influence how individuals perceive and interpret paranormal experiences. These factors include:

Perceptual Biases One psychological explanation for paranormal sightings, such as the Dover Demon, is the presence of perceptual biases. Our brains are wired to recognize patterns and make sense of the world around us. However, this can sometimes lead us to perceive things that are not actually there, a phenomenon known as pareidolia. For example, when faced with ambiguous stimuli, our brain may form a cohesive image that resembles a creature or object we are familiar with.

Cognitive Dissonance Cognitive dissonance refers to the discomfort that arises when an individual holds two conflicting beliefs or when their beliefs conflict with their actions. In the context of paranormal phenomena, cognitive dissonance can occur when someone is confronted with evidence that challenges their preexisting beliefs or worldview. To resolve this discomfort, individuals may interpret or explain the paranormal experience in a way that aligns with their existing beliefs.

Expectation and Confirmation Bias Expectation and confirmation bias play a significant role in paranormal experiences. These biases lead individuals to selectively attend to information that confirms their preconceived beliefs or expectations while ignoring or dismissing contradictory evidence. This bias can perpetuate the belief in paranormal phenomena, as individuals tend to interpret ambiguous stimuli as supporting their existing beliefs.

Sociological Perspective

The sociological perspective seeks to understand how societal and cultural factors shape the occurrence and interpretation of paranormal phenomena. Sociological factors that influence these phenomena include:

Cultural Beliefs and Socialization Cultural beliefs and socialization play a significant role in shaping individuals' interpretations of paranormal experiences. Cultural beliefs about the existence of supernatural beings or the possibility of extraterrestrial life can influence how people interpret sightings like the Dover Demon. Moreover, socialization within particular groups or subcultures can reinforce these beliefs and contribute to the perpetuation of paranormal phenomena.

Group Dynamics and Social Influence Group dynamics and social influence can also affect the interpretation of paranormal experiences. In some cases, individuals may be more likely to report a paranormal sighting if they are part of a group that shares similar beliefs or if they perceive social rewards for doing so. Group dynamics such as peer pressure, conformity, and the desire for social acceptance can influence the reporting and interpretation of paranormal phenomena.

Media Influence The media plays a crucial role in shaping public perception of paranormal phenomena. Movies, television shows, and books often portray these phenomena in a sensationalized manner, which can influence people's beliefs and expectations. Media coverage of specific sightings, like the Dover Demon, can also contribute to the societal belief in such phenomena through the dissemination of stories, eyewitness accounts, and expert opinions.

Mindset and Cognitive Frameworks

It is also important to consider the role of individual mindsets and cognitive frameworks in understanding paranormal experiences. A person's worldview, religious or spiritual beliefs, and personal experiences can influence how they interpret and make sense of these phenomena. For instance, someone with a strong belief in the existence of extraterrestrial life may be more prone to interpreting an unusual sighting as an alien encounter.

Additionally, cognitive frameworks such as magical thinking or a propensity for mystical explanations may predispose individuals to embrace paranormal explanations for unexplained phenomena. These frameworks reflect a belief in the supernatural and a tendency to attribute events to forces or entities beyond the realm of science and rationality.

Addressing Psychological and Sociological Perspectives

To gain a comprehensive understanding of the Dover Demon sightings and similar paranormal phenomena, it is crucial to address the psychological and sociological aspects involved. This can be achieved through various methods, including:

Psychological Research Psychological research plays a significant role in uncovering the cognitive processes and biases that contribute to the perception and interpretation of paranormal phenomena. Experimental studies can explore perceptual biases, cognitive dissonance, and confirmation biases and their influence on individual experiences. Furthermore, case studies and interviews with individuals who have reported paranormal encounters can provide insights into the psychological factors at play.

Sociological Studies Sociological studies can shed light on the role of culture, socialization, and media in shaping beliefs and experiences related to paranormal phenomena. Surveys and qualitative research methods can help researchers understand the prevalence of such beliefs within different demographic groups. Additionally, analyzing media representations of paranormal phenomena can provide insights into how societal perceptions are influenced.

Interdisciplinary Approaches Bringing together psychological and sociological perspectives with other disciplines such as anthropology, folklore studies, and neuroscience can provide a more holistic understanding of paranormal experiences. These interdisciplinary approaches allow for a comprehensive examination of the psychological, sociocultural, and biological factors that contribute to the occurrence and interpretation of paranormal phenomena.

Caveats and Controversies

It is important to note that the psychological and sociological perspectives presented here do not discount the validity of individuals' experiences or dismiss the possibility of paranormal phenomena. Instead, these perspectives offer insights into the complex interplay of cognitive processes, social dynamics, and cultural influences that shape our understanding of such phenomena.

However, it is essential to approach these perspectives with caution and critical thinking. While psychological explanations provide valuable insights, they do not negate the possibility of genuine paranormal experiences. Likewise, sociological perspectives help us understand the social and cultural context surrounding such phenomena but should not be used to dismiss individual accounts without careful investigation.

In conclusion, the psychological and sociological perspectives are crucial in understanding how paranormal phenomena like the Dover Demon sightings are interpreted and experienced. These perspectives highlight the cognitive biases, cultural beliefs, and social dynamics that contribute to the occurrence and interpretation of such phenomena. By considering these perspectives alongside other disciplinary approaches, we can gain a more comprehensive understanding of the complex nature of paranormal experiences.

Debunking or Validating the Dover Demon

Skeptical Rebuttals

In the investigation of paranormal phenomena, it is crucial to approach the evidence and claims with skepticism. This includes analyzing the Dover Demon sightings and considering alternative explanations for the reported sightings. Skeptical rebuttals aim to provide plausible non-paranormal explanations for the observed phenomena. In this section, we will explore some of these skeptical rebuttals and discuss their merits.

One possible skeptical rebuttal for the Dover Demon sightings is misidentification. It is well-known that humans can easily misperceive and misinterpret objects and events, especially in low light or unfamiliar environments. In the case of the Dover Demon sightings, it is possible that the witnesses mistook a known animal or object for a mysterious creature. For example, a particularly lanky and unusual-looking individual of a common species such as a coyote or a large bird might have been viewed as the Dover Demon in the darkness or from a distance.

Another possible explanation is the influence of suggestion and mass hysteria. In 1977, when the Dover Demon sightings occurred, the media coverage and public attention surrounding the phenomenon might have influenced witness testimonies. The power of suggestion can lead individuals to interpret their experiences in line with popular beliefs or expectations. It is possible that the witnesses, influenced by the prevailing narrative surrounding the Dover Demon, might have inadvertently embellished their accounts or imagined details that were not present in reality.

Additionally, the psychological state of the witnesses could have played a role in the perception of the Dover Demon. Factors such as fatigue, stress, or intoxication can alter one's perception of reality. The witnesses might have been under the influence of these factors during the sightings, which could have influenced their perception and interpretation of the events. Furthermore, the human brain is prone to cognitive biases, such as selective attention and confirmation bias, which can distort the perception of ambiguous or unusual stimuli.

Furthermore, natural explanations, such as unusual lighting conditions or atmospheric phenomena, cannot be ruled out. Optical illusions caused by unique lighting conditions, such as moonlight or headlights, can create distorted perceptions of objects and creatures. Atmospheric phenomena, such as fog or mirages, can also contribute to misinterpretations.

It is important to note that skeptical rebuttals do not aim to prove that the Dover Demon sightings did not occur, but rather to present alternative explanations for the observed phenomena. It is essential to critically analyze the evidence and consider all possible explanations before accepting any paranormal or extraordinary claims.

To further understand the skeptical rebuttals, let's consider a hypothetical scenario. Imagine a witness encountered a creature in a wooded area late at night and reported it as the Dover Demon. A skeptical approach would involve investigating the possibility of misidentification by examining common animals or objects that could resemble the alleged creature. Furthermore, looking into the witness's psychological state, the lighting conditions, and any other variables that might have influenced the perception is crucial.

These skeptical rebuttals demonstrate the importance of critical thinking and careful analysis of evidence in the investigation of paranormal phenomena. By considering alternative explanations, we can better understand the complexities of human perception and the potential for misinterpretation. Only through a rigorous examination of evidence can we approach a better understanding of the truth behind such extraordinary claims.

In conclusion, skeptical rebuttals provide alternative explanations for paranormal phenomena, including the Dover Demon sightings. These alternatives include misidentification, suggestion, psychological influences, and natural phenomena. By considering these skeptical rebuttals, we encourage a more comprehensive and critical analysis of the evidence, providing a balanced perspective on the nature of the reported phenomena.

Supporting Evidence

In order to determine the validity of the Dover Demon sightings, it is important to examine the supporting evidence that has been presented. While some skeptics dismiss the sightings as mere hoaxes or misidentifications, there are several pieces of evidence that suggest something unusual did occur in Dover, Massachusetts in 1977.

Eyewitness Testimonies

One of the strongest forms of supporting evidence for the Dover Demon sightings comes from the eyewitness testimonies of those who claim to have seen the creature. Multiple individuals reported encountering a strange, creature-like being during the same time period and in the same general vicinity.

For example, Bill Bartlett, a 17-year-old boy, was the first to encounter the Dover Demon. He described seeing a small, bipedal creature with a large, watermelon-shaped head and glowing eyes. Bartlett's description was corroborated by two of his friends, who claimed to have also seen the creature on subsequent nights.

Another eyewitness, John Baxter, reported seeing a similar creature near a stone wall, describing it as having glowing eyes and a unique appearance. His testimony aligns with the descriptions given by Bartlett and his friends.

These consistent eyewitness testimonies from different individuals lend credibility to the sightings of the Dover Demon. The fact that the witnesses were not seeking attention or fame at the time of the encounters further supports the authenticity of their claims.

Photographic Evidence

While there is no photographic evidence of the Dover Demon sightings, it is worth noting that the lack of visual documentation does not necessarily discredit the sightings. In 1977, cell phones with built-in cameras did not exist, and it was not common for individuals to carry cameras with them at all times.

It is important to consider that the sighting of a strange creature can be sudden and unexpected, leaving little time for a witness to capture photographic evidence. Additionally, the quality of cameras at that time may not have been sufficient to capture clear images of a creature in low light conditions.

Skeptics often argue that the absence of photographic evidence casts doubt on the sightings. However, it is crucial to remember that photographic evidence should not be the sole basis for validating or debunking paranormal phenomena. Eyewitness testimonies, when consistent and credible, can carry significant weight in supporting the existence of such phenomena.

Corroborating Animal Behaviors

Another interesting aspect of the Dover Demon sightings is the correlation between the reported behavior of the creature and the behavior of certain animals in the area. Witnesses described the Dover Demon as moving in a swaying motion and perching on top of stone walls.

Some researchers have pointed out that these behaviors bear similarities to the hunting behavior of certain primates, such as gibbons. Gibbons are known for their unique brachiating locomotion and their ability to perch on branches or other objects.

While this correlation does not provide definitive proof of the existence of the Dover Demon, it does offer another intriguing piece of supporting evidence. It suggests that the creature's behavior aligns with patterns observed in certain animal species, providing a plausible explanation for its movements.

Local Legends and Folklore

An additional form of supporting evidence for the Dover Demon sightings comes from local legends and folklore in the Dover area. Before the sightings in 1977, there were tales of strange creatures and unexplained phenomena in the region.

These stories, passed down through generations, could potentially provide historical context for the Dover Demon sightings. While folklore alone cannot prove the existence of a creature, it does add an interesting layer of cultural significance and potential legitimacy to the sightings.

It is worth noting that these local legends and folklore may have influenced the perception and interpretation of the Dover Demon sightings. However, they also suggest that the sightings were not isolated incidents, but rather part of a broader cultural narrative surrounding supernatural or paranormal entities in the area.

Conclusion

While the Dover Demon sightings lack concrete scientific evidence, there are several compelling pieces of supporting evidence that lend credibility to the claims. Consistent eyewitness testimonies, the absence of photographic evidence, correlations with animal behaviors, and local legends all contribute to the overall plausibility of the existence of the Dover Demon.

It is important to approach the investigation of paranormal phenomena with an open mind, acknowledging that our current scientific understanding may not be comprehensive enough to explain all observed phenomena. Only through further research, investigation, and interdisciplinary collaboration can we hope to uncover the truth behind such enigmatic creatures.

Investigation and Research Methods

In order to investigate and research phenomena like the Dover Demon sightings, it is crucial to employ rigorous and systematic methods. This section will outline some of the key investigation and research methods utilized in the field of paranormal studies, cryptozoology, and ufology.

Field Surveys

Field surveys are a fundamental aspect of investigating paranormal phenomena. To study the Dover Demon sightings, researchers would conduct surveys of the area where the sightings occurred, gathering information from witnesses, collecting physical evidence, and documenting any potential signs of the creature's presence.

During field surveys, it is important to establish a standardized protocol to ensure consistency and reliability of the data collected. This protocol may include specific interview questions for witnesses, instructions for documenting physical evidence, and guidelines for recording environmental factors such as weather conditions and time of day.

Additionally, field surveys can involve the use of specialized equipment, such as cameras, audio recorders, thermal imaging devices, and electromagnetic field (EMF) detectors. These tools can aid in capturing potential evidence and detecting anomalies that might be associated with paranormal phenomena.

Data Collection and Analysis

Data collection and analysis are crucial aspects of paranormal research. In the case of the Dover Demon sightings, researchers would need to gather and analyze various types of data, including eyewitness testimonies, photographs or videos, and any physical evidence collected from the field surveys.

Eyewitness testimonies can provide valuable insights into the nature of the sightings. Researchers would carefully interview witnesses to gather detailed descriptions of their encounters, paying attention to specific characteristics and behaviors of the Dover Demon as reported by multiple witnesses. It is essential to encourage witnesses to recount their experiences without leading or suggestive questioning, to ensure the integrity of the data.

Photographs or videos taken during the sightings can provide visual evidence for analysis. Researchers would carefully examine these visual records, exploring details such as the creature's appearance, movement patterns, and any potential discrepancies or inconsistencies in the images.

Physical evidence, if available, would be subjected to rigorous analysis. This could involve laboratory testing, such as DNA analysis, footprint or track analysis, or examination of any other tangible evidence collected from the sighting location. Researchers would compare the physical evidence with known animal species or known hoaxes to establish its authenticity and determine its significance.

Once the data is collected, it needs to be analyzed using scientific methods. Researchers would employ statistical analysis techniques to identify patterns and correlations within the data. This analysis can help determine the reliability and credibility of the eyewitness testimonies and other evidence collected.

Collaborative Approach

Investigating paranormal phenomena often benefits from a collaborative approach. Researchers from different disciplines, such as ufology, cryptozoology, and parapsychology, can bring diverse expertise and perspectives to the investigation.

Collaboration can involve sharing data, research findings, and analysis methods between researchers specializing in different areas. This interdisciplinary approach allows for a more comprehensive understanding of the phenomenon being studied and facilitates the development of new theories and explanations.

Furthermore, collaboration with local communities and eyewitnesses is essential in understanding the cultural and social context surrounding the sightings. Engaging with local residents and conducting community outreach programs can help gain valuable insights into the impact of the Dover Demon sightings on the community, their beliefs, and any cultural or historical factors that may be relevant to the investigation.

Ethical Considerations

When conducting investigations into paranormal phenomena, it is important to adhere to ethical standards. Researchers must prioritize the well-being and privacy of eyewitnesses and respect their rights throughout the investigation process. Informed consent should be obtained from witnesses before any interviews or data collection activities.

Additionally, researchers must be aware of the potential psychological and emotional impact of the investigation on witnesses and take appropriate measures to minimize any distress or harm. This may involve providing resources for counseling or support, as well as maintaining open lines of communication throughout the investigation.

Public Engagement and Education

Public engagement and education play an essential role in paranormal research. Researchers should actively share their findings with the public, encouraging discussion and providing opportunities for individuals to report their own experiences or share relevant information.

Public lectures, workshops, and conferences can help disseminate knowledge and raise awareness about paranormal research. These events can also foster collaboration between researchers and interested individuals, allowing for the exchange of ideas and the formation of research networks.

Education about critical thinking, scientific methods, and skepticism is crucial for the public to evaluate claims related to paranormal phenomena. Researchers should actively promote scientific literacy, highlighting the importance of evidence-based reasoning and providing resources for individuals to access reliable information.

By engaging with the public and promoting education, researchers can bridge the gap between scientific investigation and public understanding, creating a more informed and rational approach to the study of the paranormal.

Unconventional Methods

In addition to established investigation and research methods, some researchers in the field of paranormal studies explore unconventional approaches. These approaches may involve techniques such as remote viewing, dowsing, or the use of psychic mediums as tools for gathering information or generating hypotheses.

While these methods are considered controversial and lack scientific validation, they can provide alternative perspectives that may contribute to the overall investigation. However, it is crucial to approach these unconventional methods with critical thinking and remain aware of the limitations and potential biases associated with them.

Exercises

1. Design a field survey protocol to investigate a recent cryptid sighting reported in your local area. Consider the specific information you would collect from witnesses, the equipment you would use, and the methodology for documenting environmental factors.

2. Choose a famous paranormal case and critically analyze the data collection and analysis methods used by researchers. Identify any strengths and weaknesses in their approach and suggest improvements based on current scientific standards.

3. Propose a collaborative research project involving researchers from different disciplines (e.g., cryptozoology, ufology, and parapsychology) to investigate a particular paranormal phenomenon. Outline the potential benefits of this interdisciplinary approach and discuss possible challenges.

4. Develop a community outreach program to engage with local residents following a paranormal sighting. Consider the cultural and social context of the community and how your program can address their concerns, provide support, and encourage open dialogue.

Remember, the field of paranormal research requires a balanced and rational approach. While investigating phenomena like the Dover Demon sightings, it is essential to maintain scientific integrity, respect ethical considerations, and promote critical thinking in both the research community and the general public.

Conclusion: Alien or Cryptid?

Throughout this book, we have explored the fascinating world of cryptozoology and the paranormal, delving into the mysterious realm of alien encounters, cryptids, and paranormal phenomena. In this final section, we will draw upon the evidence and theories presented to address the question: are the Dover Demon sightings more aligned with an extraterrestrial being or a cryptid creature?

The Dover Demon sightings in 1977 captured the imagination of the public and left many intrigued and perplexed. Witnesses described a strange creature with a hairless, pale, and humanoid appearance. Its large, glowing eyes and thin, elongated limbs added to the eerie nature of the sightings. But the question remains: what was the true identity of the Dover Demon?

To explore this question, let us first consider the theories and explanations that have been proposed throughout this book. On one hand, the extraterrestrial hypothesis suggests that the Dover Demon could be an alien life form visiting Earth. The characteristics of the creature, such as its unusual appearance and behavior, align with previous accounts of alien encounters. The similarity between the Dover Demon sightings and other famous alien abduction cases adds weight to this theory. However, despite the parallels, there is a lack of definitive evidence linking the Dover Demon to extraterrestrial origins.

On the other hand, the cryptid hypothesis proposes that the Dover Demon is a previously unknown species, a cryptid lurking in the shadows. Cryptozoology, as a field of study, strives to investigate and understand these hidden creatures, such as the Loch Ness Monster and the Bigfoot. The Dover Demon sightings fit the profile of other cryptid cases, with multiple witnesses and physical evidence. Yet, definitive proof of the existence of cryptids remains elusive, leaving room for skepticism.

The psychological hypothesis offers yet another perspective. It suggests that the Dover Demon sightings may have been a result of hallucinations or misperceptions. This theory draws on the power of the human mind to create and interpret phenomena that do not necessarily correspond to objective reality. Psychological factors such as suggestion, fear, and mass hysteria could have influenced the witnesses, leading them to perceive a creature that did not actually exist.

Lastly, we must consider the cultural and sociological perspectives. Belief systems, folklore, and superstitions play a significant role in shaping our understanding of the paranormal. The cultural significance of cryptids and aliens cannot be overlooked, as they inspire myths, legends, and artistic expressions. This cultural lens may influence how we interpret and explain the Dover Demon sightings, making it difficult to separate fact from fiction.

To arrive at a conclusion, we need to weigh the evidence presented in this book. The eyewitness testimonies from the Dover Demon sightings hold substantial weight, providing detailed descriptions that are consistent across accounts. The physical evidence, though scarce, cannot be disregarded. However, without a reliable and verified specimen, conclusive proof remains elusive.

Ultimately, the question of whether the Dover Demon is an alien or a cryptid cannot be definitively answered. Both theories have strengths and weaknesses, leaving room for interpretation and personal belief. The Dover Demon, like the Loch Ness Monster or Bigfoot, continues to exist in the realm of mystery and speculation.

As we conclude this book, it is important to recognize the complex nature of investigating the unknown. Science and the paranormal often find themselves at odds, with one demanding empirical evidence and the other operating in the realm of the unexplained. Bridging the gap between scientific skepticism and the exploration of the paranormal becomes a crucial avenue for future research.

Moving forward, interdisciplinary collaborations between scientists, paranormal investigators, and cryptozoologists may provide valuable insights. By combining scientific research methodologies with open-minded exploration, perhaps we can shed light on the mysteries that continue to captivate our imaginations.

In conclusion, the Dover Demon sightings remind us of the vastness of our world and our shared fascination with the unknown. Whether we classify it as an extraterrestrial visitor or a cryptid creature, the Dover Demon represents a small piece of the larger puzzle that is our exploration of the paranormal. As we continue on this journey, may our curiosity guide us to new discoveries and a deeper understanding of the mysteries that lie beyond our current realm of knowledge.

Chapter 4: Paranormal Phenomena

Ghosts and Hauntings

Types of Ghosts

Ghosts have been a topic of intrigue and fascination for centuries. These ethereal entities, believed to be the spirits of deceased individuals, are said to linger in our world, often appearing in specific forms and exhibiting distinct behaviors. While ghostly encounters vary widely, there are several common types of ghosts that have been reported throughout history. In this section, we will explore these different types and delve into their characteristics and classifications.

Residual Ghosts

One of the most common types of ghosts is known as a residual ghost. These apparitions are often seen repeating the same actions or scenes over and over again. It is believed that residual ghosts are not aware of their surroundings and are trapped in a never-ending loop, reliving a significant event from their past. This phenomenon is often associated with traumatic or emotionally charged experiences, such as battles during war, tragic accidents, or intense moments of joy or sorrow. Residual ghosts typically do not interact with the living and are generally harmless.

Intelligent Ghosts

Unlike residual ghosts, intelligent ghosts are aware of their surroundings and can interact with the living. These apparitions demonstrate consciousness, as they can respond to questions, move objects, or even communicate through various means, such as writing or manipulating electronic devices. Intelligent ghosts are believed to be the spirits of deceased individuals who have chosen to remain in the earthly realm, perhaps for unresolved issues or to provide guidance and support to their loved ones. These types of ghosts are often associated with haunting experiences and can sometimes be unsettling or even frightening.

Poltergeists

Poltergeists, meaning "noisy spirits" in German, are a particularly active and mischievous type of ghost. Unlike other ghostly entities, poltergeists primarily manifest through their ability to manipulate objects and create disturbances in the physical environment. Common phenomena associated with poltergeist activity include objects moving or being thrown, loud and unexplained noises, and even physical attacks on individuals. It is believed that poltergeists are not the spirits of deceased individuals but rather a form of psychic energy generated by living people, often adolescents or those experiencing high levels of emotional turmoil. The exact mechanism behind poltergeist activity remains a mystery, and their presence can create a great deal of fear and confusion.

Shadow People

Shadow people are a distinct and enigmatic type of ghostly entity. Described as dark, shadowy figures or silhouettes, these apparitions often appear in one's peripheral vision or in dimly lit areas. Some reports suggest that shadow people can move swiftly and smoothly, while others describe them as having glowing red eyes or other unnerving features. Their appearance is typically fleeting, and they are often associated with feelings of dread or fear. The origin and nature of shadow people remain largely unknown, leading to numerous theories and debates within the paranormal community.

Crisis Apparitions

Crisis apparitions are ghosts that appear to individuals during moments of crisis or impending death. These apparitions are often seen by loved ones or close friends of the person experiencing the crisis, even when they are physically distant. Crisis apparitions can take various forms, such as appearing as a deceased family member or close friend, providing comfort or guidance during a difficult time. These encounters are usually vivid and have a profound emotional impact on those who witness them. It is hypothesized that crisis apparitions occur due to the strong emotional connection between individuals or a heightened state of awareness during times of crisis.

Haunted Locations

While not a type of ghost in the traditional sense, haunted locations deserve mention due to the unique experiences they offer. Haunted locations are places where paranormal activity is believed to be concentrated, attracting various types of ghosts and other supernatural phenomena. These locations often have a rich historical or cultural significance and have been reported to exhibit a wide range of ghostly manifestations, such as apparitions, unexplained noises, cold spots, and disembodied voices. Haunted locations have captivated the interest of paranormal investigators and enthusiasts, who strive to uncover the mysteries surrounding these sites.

It is important to note that these classifications and descriptions of ghostly encounters are based on anecdotal evidence and personal experiences. The existence and nature of ghosts are still subjects of debate and speculation within the scientific community. Despite the lack of concrete scientific evidence, the allure of the supernatural and the fascination with ghostly phenomena continue to captivate the human imagination.

Exploring the Paranormal

The study of ghosts and paranormal phenomena falls under the broader domain of parapsychology, which is the scientific investigation of psychic phenomena, including extrasensory perception, telepathy, and psychokinesis. Parapsychology aims to explore and understand phenomena that challenge mainstream scientific explanations.

While ghostly encounters and paranormal experiences are often dismissed as mere superstitions or figments of the imagination, parapsychologists approach these phenomena with an open mind and rigorous scientific methods. They employ a variety of research techniques, including surveys, experiments, and case studies, to collect and analyze data related to paranormal activities.

One of the challenges in studying ghosts and the paranormal is the lack of tangible evidence that can be reliably reproduced under controlled laboratory conditions. Ghostly encounters are highly subjective and personal experiences, often influenced by cultural, psychological, and environmental factors. Additionally, the elusive and fleeting nature of these phenomena makes it difficult to capture scientific data.

Nevertheless, parapsychologists continue their quest to document and investigate paranormal phenomena. They employ various research tools, such as electromagnetic field detectors, thermal cameras, and audio equipment, to capture potential evidence of ghostly activity. Additionally, they collaborate with experts from diverse fields, including psychology, physics, and anthropology, to gain a multidisciplinary understanding of the paranormal.

Despite the skepticism and challenges associated with studying ghosts, parapsychologists and paranormal investigators provide an important role in advancing our understanding of the mysteries of the supernatural. Their research contributes to the broader field of human consciousness and challenges traditional scientific paradigms.

Resources for Further Exploration

If you're interested in diving deeper into the world of ghosts and the paranormal, here are some recommended resources:

- Books:
  - "The Ghost Hunters" by Deborah Blum
  - "Ghosts: A Natural History" by Roger Clarke
  - "Parapsychology: A Handbook for the 21st Century" edited by Etzel Cardeña, John Palmer, and David Marcusson-Clavertz
- Websites:
  - The Parapsychological Association (www.parapsych.org)
  - The Rhine Research Center (www.rhine.org)
  - The Society for Psychical Research (www.spr.ac.uk)
- Documentaries and TV Shows:
  - "Ghost Hunters" (Syfy channel)
  - "Paranormal Witness" (Syfy channel)
  - "The Conjuring" (film series)

These resources provide a comprehensive overview of ghostly phenomena, scientific investigations, personal accounts, and ongoing research in the field. Remember to approach the subject with an open mind and a healthy dose of skepticism as you explore the mysteries of the paranormal.

Paranormal Investigations

Paranormal investigations play a crucial role in understanding and exploring the unexplained phenomena that fall outside the realm of traditional scientific inquiry. These investigations often focus on gathering empirical evidence and conducting experiments to shed light on supernatural occurrences and paranormal activities.

Definition and Objectives

Paranormal investigations involve the systematic study of events, experiences, or phenomena that cannot be explained or understood by current scientific knowledge. The primary objectives of paranormal investigations are to:

1. Document and collect evidence: Investigators aim to document and collect evidence of paranormal phenomena through various means, such as audio recordings, video footage, photographs, and measurements.

2. Investigate haunted locations: Paranormal investigators often visit haunted locations to gather information and firsthand accounts of paranormal experiences. By conducting interviews and on-site investigations, they aim to uncover any patterns, recurring phenomena, or potential causes.

3. Test and validate claims: Paranormal investigations involve testing claims made by witnesses or individuals who report paranormal experiences. Investigators employ scientific methods to validate or debunk these claims, engaging in activities such as EVP (Electronic Voice Phenomenon) analysis, ghost box sessions, and other experimental techniques.

4. Provide support and closure: Paranormal investigations aim to provide support and closure to individuals or communities affected by paranormal activities. By investigating and validating their experiences, investigators can offer a sense of validation or peace to those affected.

Methods and Techniques

Paranormal investigations employ a wide range of methods and techniques to explore and document paranormal phenomena. Some commonly used methods include:

1. Data collection: Investigators use a variety of tools and instruments to collect data during paranormal investigations. These can include cameras, audio recorders, electromagnetic field (EMF) detectors, temperature sensors, and motion detectors. By collecting data from multiple sources, investigators can analyze patterns and correlations.

2. EVP Analysis: Electronic Voice Phenomenon (EVP) analysis involves reviewing recorded audio to identify and analyze potential anomalous or unexplained sounds, voices, or messages. Investigators carefully listen to recordings, often using noise filtering techniques and audio enhancement software, to identify and interpret potential paranormal voices or communications.

3. Thermal imaging: Thermal imaging cameras capture temperature variations in the environment, allowing investigators to detect cold spots or heat anomalies that may suggest the presence of paranormal activity. This technique is particularly useful in detecting potential apparitions or energy manifestations.

4. Video analysis: Video recordings from surveillance cameras or handheld devices are carefully reviewed to identify any visual anomalies or unexplained phenomena. Investigators meticulously analyze the footage, looking for movement, apparitions, or other inexplicable occurrences.

5. Investigative interviews: Paranormal investigators conduct thorough interviews with witnesses and individuals who have experienced paranormal phenomena. These interviews aim to gather detailed information about the event, including the location, description of the experience, associated factors, and any potential evidence.

Challenges and Considerations

Paranormal investigations face several challenges and considerations that must be taken into account. Some of these challenges include:

1. Subjectivity and interpretation: Much of the evidence gathered in paranormal investigations is subjective and open to interpretation. Investigators must be careful not to jump to conclusions or impose their own biases onto the evidence.

2. Lack of control: Unlike conventional scientific experiments, paranormal investigations often lack control over environmental factors. Investigators must account for various external influences that could potentially impact the results or contribute to perceived paranormal phenomena.

3. Psychological factors: It is essential for investigators to be aware of psychological factors that can influence witnesses' perceptions and experiences. Factors such as suggestibility, expectation bias, and the power of suggestion can significantly impact the interpretation of evidence.

4. Ethics and credibility: Paranormal investigations need to uphold ethical standards and maintain credibility. Investigators must approach their work with integrity, ensuring the privacy and well-being of witnesses and avoiding any exploitation or sensationalism.

Case Study: The Amityville Horror

A prominent case in paranormal investigations is the Amityville Horror, which revolves around a supposedly haunted house in Amityville, New York. In 1974, the Lutz family moved into the house and reported experiencing a series of terrifying paranormal phenomena, including demonic visions, disembodied voices, and physical manifestations.

Paranormal investigators, including demonologists and parapsychologists, were called in to investigate the claims. They used a combination of methods, including audio and video recording, environmental monitoring, and interviews with witnesses. While some evidence supported the claims made by the Lutz family, skeptics raised questions about the credibility of the witnesses and the potential for exaggeration or fabrication.

The Amityville case highlights the challenges faced in paranormal investigations, where subjective experiences, the impact of psychological factors, and the need for rigorous analysis of evidence come into play.

Resources and Further Reading

1. "Parapsychology: A Handbook for the 21st Century" by Etzel Cardeña, John Palmer, and David Marcusson-Clavertz. 2. "Scientific Paranormal Investigation: How to Solve Unexplained Mysteries" by Benjamin Radford. 3. "Ghosts: A Natural History: 500 Years of Searching for Proof" by Roger Clarke. 4. "Ghost Hunting for Beginners: Everything You Need to Know to Get Started" by Rich Newman.

Exercises

1. Conduct an EVP session: Using a recording device, conduct an EVP session in a reportedly haunted location or an environment associated with paranormal activity. Analyze the recording for any potential paranormal voices or messages. Note any significant findings or anomalies.

2. Investigate a local legend: Research a local legend or ghost story in your area. Conduct interviews with witnesses or individuals who have experienced paranormal phenomena associated with that legend. Write a report on your findings, including any evidence or patterns you uncover.

3. Analyze a paranormal photograph: Find a purported paranormal photograph and analyze it using critical thinking and analysis. Identify potential explanations for the anomalies captured in the photo, considering factors such as lighting, reflections, or other common artifacts.

4. Explore different paranormal investigation techniques: Research and explore different paranormal investigation techniques, such as dowsing, spirit boards, or pendulum divination. Evaluate the effectiveness and reliability of these techniques, considering the scientific principles underlying them.

Remember that paranormal investigations require a balance between open-mindedness and critical thinking. It is crucial to approach these investigations with a healthy skepticism while remaining open to the possibility of unexplained phenomena.

Skepticism and Debunking

Skepticism and debunking play a crucial role in the investigation of paranormal phenomena, including cryptids and aliens. Skeptics aim to critically evaluate claims and provide alternative explanations based on scientific reasoning and evidence. In this section, we will explore the principles of skepticism, common debunking strategies, and the importance of critical thinking in the study of the paranormal.

Principles of Skepticism

Skepticism is a fundamental aspect of the scientific method and involves questioning claims, seeking evidence, and subjecting ideas to rigorous scrutiny. Skeptics approach paranormal phenomena with an open mind but also maintain a healthy dose of skepticism until sufficient evidence is presented. Some key principles of skepticism include:

- **Extraordinary claims require extraordinary evidence:** Skeptics demand robust evidence for claims that deviate from established scientific knowledge. This principle encourages critical examination of evidence presented in support of paranormal phenomena.

- **Occam's Razor:** Named after the medieval philosopher William of Occam, this principle states that the simplest explanation is often the most likely. Skeptics apply this principle by favoring scientifically supported explanations over supernatural or pseudoscientific ones.

- **Falsifiability:** Skeptics emphasize the importance of falsifiability – the ability to test and potentially disprove a claim. A hypothesis or theory must be formulated in a way that allows for the possibility of producing evidence that contradicts it. This ensures that claims can be subjected to empirical investigation.

By adhering to these principles, skeptics approach paranormal claims with a critical mindset, evaluating the evidence available before forming conclusions.

Debunking Strategies

Debunking involves exposing falsehoods, misconceptions, or flawed reasoning behind paranormal claims. Skeptics employ various strategies to identify logical fallacies, errors in reasoning, and alternative explanations. Some common debunking strategies include:

- **Logical analysis:** Skeptics examine the logical coherence of claims and arguments put forth by proponents of paranormal phenomena. They search for inconsistencies, contradictions, and faulty reasoning that may undermine the credibility of the claims.

- **Critical examination of evidence:** Skeptics evaluate the quality and reliability of evidence presented in support of cryptids and aliens. They look for potential sources of bias, flaws in data collection methods, and alternative explanations for the observed phenomena.

- **Science-based explanations:** Skeptics draw on established scientific principles and theories to provide alternative explanations for paranormal claims. They may propose naturalistic or psychological interpretations that align with our current understanding of the world.

- **Experimentation and replication:** Skeptics advocate for controlled experiments and peer-reviewed studies to validate or refute paranormal claims. They emphasize that repeatable experiments with transparent methodologies are essential for establishing the legitimacy of any extraordinary phenomenon.

- **Educating the public:** Skeptics recognize the importance of educating the public about critical thinking and scientific reasoning. They aim to promote skepticism as a tool for evaluating paranormal claims and encourage individuals to question and evaluate extraordinary assertions.

Debunking strategies are not meant to dismiss paranormal claims outright but to promote a more rigorous examination of evidence and foster a scientific mindset.

The Importance of Critical Thinking

Critical thinking is a vital skill in evaluating paranormal claims. It involves objectively analyzing information, questioning assumptions, and considering alternative explanations. In the study of cryptids and aliens, critical thinking helps distinguish between genuine evidence and hoaxes, misperceptions, or misinterpretations.

Critical thinking provides several benefits:

- **Avoiding confirmation bias:** Critical thinking helps individuals avoid selectively accepting evidence that supports their preconceived beliefs while dismissing contradictory evidence. By approaching claims with skepticism, individuals can assess evidence more objectively.

- **Promoting scientific literacy:** Critical thinking fosters an appreciation for scientific methods, evidence-based reasoning, and the importance of peer review. It encourages individuals to seek accurate information and use scientific principles to evaluate claims.

- **Protecting against misinformation:** In an era of misinformation and widespread dissemination of false claims, critical thinking serves as a shield against misleading and unsubstantiated beliefs. It empowers individuals to analyze sources, weigh evidence, and make informed judgments.

- **Encouraging intellectual curiosity:** Critical thinking propels individuals to engage with diverse perspectives, question assumptions, and delve deeper into topics of interest. It promotes a lifelong pursuit of knowledge and intellectual growth.

By cultivating critical thinking skills, individuals can navigate the complex landscape of paranormal claims and make informed decisions based on evidence and scientific principles.

Examples of Debunked Paranormal Claims

Over the years, skepticism and critical thinking have been instrumental in debunking several high-profile paranormal claims. Let's explore a few examples:

- **Crop circles:** Despite initial speculation of extraterrestrial origins, extensive investigation and analysis by skeptics revealed that crop circles can be created by human-made tools and techniques. This discovery challenged claims of paranormal or otherworldly causes.

- **Psychic abilities:** In numerous controlled experiments, skeptics have repeatedly debunked claims of psychic powers. Through careful controls and statistical analysis, they have shown that apparent psychic abilities can often be attributed to chance, psychological factors, or the use of common magic tricks.

- **Ghost sightings:** Skeptics have debunked many ghost sightings by revealing natural explanations for supposed paranormal phenomena. Often, misperceptions, reflections, or the power of suggestion can account for experiences that initially seem supernatural.

- **Bigfoot and Loch Ness Monster:** Despite extensive searches and reported sightings, skeptics have not found conclusive evidence for the existence of these cryptids. Lack of physical remains, unreliable eyewitness testimony, and possible misidentifications of known animals cast doubt on the existence of these creatures.

These examples highlight the importance of skepticism in challenging paranormal claims and encouraging a critical examination of evidence.

Exercises for Critical Thinking

Practicing critical thinking skills can help sharpen your ability to evaluate paranormal claims. Here are a few exercises to hone your critical thinking abilities:

1. **Case study analysis:** Choose a well-known paranormal case, such as a famous UFO sighting or a cryptid sighting. Analyze the available evidence, seek alternative explanations, and critically evaluate the validity and reliability of the claims.

2. **Logical fallacy identification:** Take a paranormal claim and identify the logical fallacies used to support it. Common fallacies include ad hominem attacks, appeal to authority, and correlation implying causation. Explain how these fallacies undermine the credibility of the claim.

3. **Design a skeptical experiment:** Devise an experiment to test a paranormal claim, such as telepathy or precognition. Outline the methodology, hypothesis, and expected outcomes. Consider the control group, sample size, blinding, and other factors essential to a scientifically rigorous experiment.

4. **Debunking debunkers:** Critically examine skeptical debunking of a well-known paranormal case. Identify any biases, logical fallacies, or assumptions made by the skeptics. Explore potential counter-arguments or alternative explanations.

These exercises are designed to engage your critical thinking skills and encourage a deeper understanding of the challenges in evaluating paranormal claims.

Conclusion

Skepticism and debunking are vital components in the study of paranormal phenomena. Skeptics provide an important counterbalance to unsubstantiated claims and promote critical thinking and scientific reasoning. By applying principles of skepticism, employing debunking strategies, and nurturing our critical thinking abilities, we can approach claims of cryptids and aliens with a rational and evidence-based mindset. Embracing skepticism enhances our understanding of the world and helps us separate fact from fiction.

UFO Sightings and Alien Abductions

Overview of UFO Sightings

UFO sightings have been a topic of fascination and speculation for decades. Reports of unidentified flying objects, or UFOs, have captured the imagination of people all around the world. In this section, we will provide an overview of UFO sightings, discussing their history, patterns, and the different types of sightings that have been reported.

History of UFO Sightings

The phenomenon of UFO sightings gained significant attention in the late 1940s and early 1950s, following a number of high-profile reports. One of the most famous cases is the Roswell Incident in 1947, where it was initially reported that a "flying disc" had crashed near Roswell, New Mexico. The U.S. military later stated that it was a weather balloon, but this explanation has been widely disputed, leading to ongoing speculation and conspiracy theories.

Since then, numerous sightings have been reported all over the world, with varying degrees of credibility. The term "UFO" refers to any unidentified object flying in the sky, and it does not necessarily imply that the object is extraterrestrial

UFO SIGHTINGS AND ALIEN ABDUCTIONS

in origin. Many UFO sightings have plausible explanations, such as misidentified aircraft, weather phenomena, or atmospheric anomalies. However, there are also cases where the nature of the sightings remains unexplained, leading to speculation about possible extraterrestrial visitation.

Patterns and Characteristics of UFO Sightings

UFO sightings can vary widely in terms of the characteristics of the reported objects and the circumstances of the sightings. However, there are some common patterns and characteristics that can be identified across many reports.

- **Shape and Size:** UFO sightings often describe objects with unusual shapes, such as saucers, cigars, or triangles. The sizes of the reported objects can range from small to massive.

- **Flight Patterns:** UFOs are often reported to exhibit flight patterns that defy the capabilities of conventional aircraft. They may move at high speeds, change direction abruptly, or hover in the air.

- **Lights and Colors:** Many UFO sightings involve the presence of bright lights or flashing colors. These lights may be steady or pulsating, and they can sometimes exhibit patterns or formations.

- **Duration and Distance:** The duration of UFO sightings can vary greatly. Some sightings last only a few seconds, while others go on for several minutes or even hours. The distance of the reported objects from the witnesses can also vary, making it difficult to determine their exact nature.

Types of UFO Sightings

UFO sightings can be classified into different types based on the level of interaction between the witnesses and the reported objects. The most commonly used classification system, developed by astronomer and ufologist J. Allen Hynek, is as follows:

1. **Close Encounters of the First Kind (CE1):** This type of sighting involves a visual observation of a UFO at a relatively close distance, usually within 500 feet. The object may be stationary or in motion, and there is no reported interaction between the object and the witnesses.

2. **Close Encounters of the Second Kind (CE2):** CE2 sightings involve the presence of physical effects or traces associated with the UFO. This can include burn marks on the ground, radiation readings, or interference with electrical systems.

3. **Close Encounters of the Third Kind (CE3):** CE3 sightings involve the presence of intelligent beings associated with the UFO. This can include sightings of humanoid or non-humanoid creatures, witnessed onboard or near the object.

4. **Other Types of UFO Sightings:** Besides the Hynek classification, there are other types of UFO sightings that are commonly reported. These include abductions, where individuals claim to have been taken onboard a UFO, as well as sightings of structured craft or motherships.

Explanations and Theories

Numerous explanations and theories have been proposed to explain UFO sightings. These range from scientific and naturalistic perspectives to more speculative and unconventional ideas.

- **Extraterrestrial Hypothesis:** The extraterrestrial hypothesis suggests that UFO sightings are evidence of intelligent beings visiting Earth from other planets. Proponents of this theory argue that the reported characteristics of UFOs, such as their flight patterns and advanced technology, are consistent with what would be expected from an extraterrestrial civilization.

- **Psychological Hypothesis:** The psychological hypothesis proposes that UFO sightings are a result of psychological and perceptual factors. This includes misperceptions of natural phenomena, hallucinations, or the misinterpretation of mundane objects as extraterrestrial craft. Psychological factors such as suggestibility, cognitive biases, and cultural influences can also play a role in shaping people's interpretations of their experiences.

- **Government Conspiracy Theories:** Some theories suggest that UFO sightings are related to government activities and cover-ups. These theories often argue that governments possess advanced technology that they are keeping secret from the public, and that UFO sightings are actually glimpses of these classified aircraft or experiments.

- **Cultural and Sociological Perspectives:** Cultural and sociological perspectives emphasize the role of cultural beliefs, media influence, and the collective imagination in shaping UFO sightings. These theories suggest that UFO sightings are a product of human culture and reflect our fascination with extraterrestrial life.

It is important to note that while some UFO sightings have been convincingly explained as misidentifications or hoaxes, there remains a small percentage of cases that remain unexplained. These cases continue to fuel the debate about the nature and origins of UFO sightings.

Resources and Further Reading

For those interested in exploring the topic of UFO sightings further, there are several reputable resources available. The following books provide comprehensive overviews and analyses of UFO sightings:

- *UFOs: Generals, Pilots, and Government Officials Go on the Record* by Leslie Kean
- *The UFO Book: Encyclopedia of the Extraterrestrial* by Jerome Clark
- *Project Blue Book: The Top Secret UFO Files That Revealed a Government Cover-Up* by Brad Steiger and Donald Schmitt

In addition to books, there are numerous websites, documentaries, and podcasts dedicated to the study of UFO sightings. It is important to approach these resources critically and evaluate the credibility of the information presented.

Unconventional Problem: Analyzing UFO Sightings

As an exercise, let's analyze a UFO sighting report and apply critical thinking skills to determine possible explanations. Here is a fictional case for analysis:

Location: Rural area, night time.

Witnesses: John and Mary, a married couple.

Description of the event: John and Mary were stargazing in their backyard when they noticed a bright light in the sky. The light appeared to be moving erratically, changing colors from white to red and blue. It moved at high speeds, made sudden stops and turns, and then disappeared behind a cloud. The entire sighting lasted for approximately five minutes.

To analyze this sighting, we can consider various possibilities:

- The light could be a conventional aircraft performing maneuvers. However, the reported erratic movements and the ability to disappear behind a cloud may suggest otherwise.

- The light might be a drone operated by a hobbyist. Drones can exhibit similar flight characteristics and have the ability to change colors. This could be a plausible explanation if there were no ongoing drone-related activities in the area at the time of the sighting.

- Atmospheric phenomena, such as ball lightning or plasma discharges, could also produce strange lights in the sky. However, the duration of the sighting and the reported movements make this explanation less likely.

- The possibility of a genuine UFO, indicating extraterrestrial visitation, cannot be ruled out completely. However, without additional evidence, it remains speculative.

This exercise demonstrates the importance of critically analyzing UFO sightings, considering various explanations, and evaluating the available evidence.

In conclusion, UFO sightings have been a subject of interest, debate, and speculation for many years. While most sightings can be explained by conventional means, there remains a small percentage of cases that defy easy explanation. The study of UFO sightings continues to be a topic of research, with scientists, skeptics, and enthusiasts alike seeking to unravel the mysteries of these unidentified objects in our skies.

Note: The content provided in this section is for educational purposes only and does not endorse or validate the existence of extraterrestrial life or the claims made in UFO sightings.

Alien Abduction Phenomena

The phenomenon of alien abduction has captivated the imaginations of many people, leading to a proliferation of books, movies, and television shows centered around this mysterious and controversial topic. In this section, we will explore the main aspects of alien abduction phenomena, including common experiences reported by abductees, different theories and explanations put forth to understand these experiences, and the similarities to the Dover Demon sightings.

Common Experiences Reported by Abductees

Alien abduction experiences typically involve an individual claiming to have been taken against their will by extraterrestrial beings. These experiences often share several common elements:

1. **Encounter with aliens:** Abductees report encountering one or more alien beings during their abduction. These beings are described as humanoid or non-humanoid, with stereotypical features such as large eyes, slender bodies, and gray or greenish skin.

2. **Loss of control:** Abductees often describe a feeling of being paralyzed or unable to move during the abduction. This loss of control over their own body adds to the sense of fear and helplessness.

3. **Examination procedures:** Many abductees report being subjected to various medical procedures by the aliens, including examinations, implantations, and reproductive experiments. These procedures may involve the use of advanced technology and often leave physical marks or scars on the abductee's body.

4. **Missing time:** A common aspect of alien abduction experiences is the perception of missing time. Abductees often report gaps in their memory or a feeling of time distortion during the abduction, with hours or even days seemingly unaccounted for.

5. **Psychological effects:** Alien abduction experiences can have profound psychological effects on those who claim to have undergone them. Abductees often report feelings of anxiety, post-traumatic stress disorder, and a sense of isolation due to the stigmatization of their experiences by society.

These shared experiences form the foundation for understanding the phenomenon of alien abduction and provide a basis for theories and explanations.

Theories and Explanations

Numerous theories and explanations have been put forth to understand and explain the phenomenon of alien abduction. Let's explore some of the most prominent ones:

1. **Extraterrestrial Hypothesis:** The most straightforward explanation for alien abduction experiences is that they are genuine interactions with

extraterrestrial beings. This hypothesis posits that abductions are physical in nature, involving actual physical beings from other planets or dimensions visiting Earth.

2. **Psychological Hypothesis:** Another explanation for alien abductions focuses on the psychological aspects of these experiences. Proponents of this hypothesis argue that abductions are vivid hallucinations or false memories created by the abductees' unconscious minds. Factors such as sleep paralysis, trauma, or suggestible personalities are believed to contribute to these experiences.

3. **Sociocultural Hypothesis:** The sociocultural hypothesis suggests that alien abduction experiences are influenced by cultural and societal factors. This explanation posits that the concept of alien abductions has been shaped by media portrayals, folklore, and the collective imagination of society. Abductees may be influenced by these cultural narratives, leading to the creation of abduction experiences that conform to societal expectations.

4. **Illusory Experience Hypothesis:** According to this hypothesis, alien abduction experiences are a result of illusory perceptions and misinterpretations of ordinary events. Abductees may attribute normal experiences such as vivid dreams, sleepwalking, or even rare medical conditions to the presence of aliens. The illusion of an abduction experience is created through subjective interpretations of these events.

It is important to note that these theories are not mutually exclusive, and multiple factors may contribute to the phenomenon of alien abduction. The scientific community remains divided on the legitimacy of these experiences, with skepticism and further research being crucial for a better understanding.

Similarities to the Dover Demon Sightings

While the Dover Demon sightings and alien abduction phenomena differ in many aspects, there are intriguing similarities worth exploring:

1. **Unidentified Entities:** Both the Dover Demon and the alien abduction experiences involve encounters with unidentified entities that are described as non-human or otherworldly.

2. **Paranormal Context:** Both phenomena occur within the realm of the paranormal and challenge our understanding of reality. The Dover Demon

and the aliens in abduction experiences exist beyond our known scientific boundaries.

3. **Witness Credibility:** In both cases, the credibility of the witnesses is often subject to scrutiny and skepticism. Witnesses of the Dover Demon sightings faced doubts about the veracity of their accounts, similar to how abductees are questioned about the validity of their claimed experiences.

4. **Impact on Witnesses:** The Dover Demon sightings and alien abduction experiences can have a significant impact on the individuals involved. Witnessing otherworldly beings or undergoing abduction can lead to feelings of fear, isolation, and psychological distress among those who experience these events.

Despite these similarities, it is essential to approach each phenomenon independently and evaluate them based on their unique characteristics and available evidence.

In the next chapter, we will further explore the interconnectedness between different paranormal phenomena, including cryptids, UFO sightings, and alien abductions, and delve into the scientific perspectives that try to bridge the gap between these intriguing phenomena and mainstream science.

Summary

In this section, we have explored the phenomenon of alien abduction, including the common experiences reported by abductees, theories and explanations put forth to understand these experiences, and the similarities to the Dover Demon sightings. We have seen that alien abductions involve encounters with extraterrestrial beings, often accompanied by a loss of control, examination procedures, missing time, and profound psychological effects. Various theories, including the extraterrestrial, psychological, sociocultural, and illusory experience hypotheses, have been proposed to explain these experiences. By examining the similarities and differences between alien abductions and the Dover Demon sightings, we can gain a deeper understanding of these enigmatic phenomena.

Similarities to the Dover Demon Sightings

In this section, we will explore the similarities between the Dover Demon sightings and other paranormal phenomena, particularly UFO sightings and alien abductions. While these phenomena may seem unrelated at first glance, there are intriguing connections that can be made when examining the characteristics and patterns observed in these events. By exploring these connections, we can gain a deeper understanding of the Dover Demon sightings and their possible explanations.

5.2.3.1 Overlapping Descriptions

One of the striking similarities between the Dover Demon sightings and alien abductions is the overlapping descriptions of the entities involved. In many alien abduction cases, witnesses report encounters with small, humanoid beings that have elongated limbs, large eyes, and pale or grayish skin. These descriptions are remarkably similar to the appearance of the Dover Demon, which was described as a creature with a thin, elongated body, large glowing eyes, and hairless skin.

The similarities in physical appearance suggest that there may be a common source or explanation for these sightings. It is possible that the Dover Demon and the entities encountered in alien abductions are different manifestations of the same phenomenon. This raises intriguing questions about the nature of these entities and their possible origins.

5.2.3.2 Eerie Behavior Patterns

Another intriguing similarity between the Dover Demon sightings and alien abductions is the eerie behavior patterns exhibited by the entities involved. Witnesses to both types of phenomena often report a sense of fear or unease in the presence of these entities. Additionally, there are reports of the entities displaying advanced technological abilities, such as levitation, telepathic communication, and manipulation of the environment.

These behavioral patterns suggest that the entities associated with the Dover Demon sightings and alien abductions may have a level of intelligence and capabilities beyond our current understanding. The similarities in behavior raise questions about the purpose of these encounters and the possible agenda of these entities.

5.2.3.3 Psychological Effects on Witnesses

One important aspect to consider is the psychological effects experienced by witnesses of both the Dover Demon sightings and alien abductions. In both cases, witnesses often report significant emotional and psychological distress following their encounters. These effects can include anxiety, sleep disturbances, and post-traumatic stress disorder (PTSD).

The psychological effects experienced by witnesses suggest that these encounters are not simply imagined or mistaken perceptions. They indicate that something profound and potentially traumatic occurred during these events. Understanding the psychological impact of these experiences is essential for gaining insight into the true nature of the Dover Demon sightings and alien abductions.

5.2.3.4 Possible Explanations and Theories

Explaining the similarities between the Dover Demon sightings and other paranormal phenomena requires considering various theories and explanations. One possibility is that these experiences are the result of shared cultural beliefs and expectations. It is possible that witnesses interpret their encounters through the lens of popular culture and pre-existing beliefs about extraterrestrial life and supernatural entities.

Another explanation is that these phenomena are actually interconnected manifestations of a larger, unknown phenomenon. It is possible that these encounters represent different aspects or dimensions of a complex and multifaceted reality that is beyond our current scientific understanding.

5.2.3.5 Investigating the Connections

To further explore the similarities between the Dover Demon sightings and other paranormal phenomena, interdisciplinary collaborations and rigorous scientific investigations are needed. This includes conducting interviews and psychological assessments of witnesses, analyzing physical evidence, and employing advanced research techniques such as remote sensing and data analysis.

Additionally, longitudinal studies and case histories can provide valuable insights into the long-term effects and patterns associated with these encounters. By collecting and analyzing a large body of data, researchers can identify commonalities and patterns that may help unravel the mysteries behind these phenomena.

In conclusion, the Dover Demon sightings share striking similarities with other paranormal phenomena, particularly UFO sightings and alien abductions. These similarities include overlapping descriptions, eerie behavior patterns, psychological effects on witnesses, and possible explanations. Understanding these connections and investigating them further can provide valuable insights into the nature and origins of these phenomena.

Interactions between Paranormal Phenomena

Cryptids and UFOs

Cryptids and unidentified flying objects (UFOs) have long been subjects of fascination and speculation, captivating the imaginations of people around the world. While they are distinct phenomena, there are intriguing connections and interactions between cryptids and UFO sightings that have raised intriguing questions and sparked heated debates among researchers and enthusiasts. In this section, we will explore the relationship between cryptids and UFOs, examining the similarities, theories, and possible explanations for these intriguing encounters.

Cryptids: Creatures of Mystery

To understand the connection between cryptids and UFOs, let us first delve into the world of cryptozoology, the study of hidden or unknown animals. Cryptids are creatures whose existence is not yet proven by science, despite anecdotal accounts and folklore that suggest otherwise. Some famous examples of cryptids include the Loch Ness Monster, Bigfoot, Chupacabra, and the Jersey Devil.

Cryptozoology, as a field of study, aims to gather evidence and investigate reports of cryptid sightings in order to determine the validity of these claims. Eyewitness accounts, footprint casts, hair samples, and blurry photographs are among the types of evidence commonly examined by cryptozoologists. However, skeptics argue that the lack of concrete physical evidence makes it challenging to verify the existence of cryptids.

UFOs: Unidentified Aerial Phenomena

As we transition to the realm of UFOs, it is important to note that their existence does not necessarily imply an extraterrestrial origin. UFOs simply refer to unidentified flying objects, which could be anything from natural phenomena to man-made aircraft or other aerial devices. Reports of UFO sightings often involve strange lights, unusual aircraft maneuvers, high speeds, or other inexplicable characteristics.

Throughout history, there have been countless accounts of UFO sightings, some with multiple witnesses and even photographic or video evidence. While many UFO sightings have been explained as misidentified airplanes, weather phenomena, or hoaxes, there remains a subset of cases that defy conventional explanations.

Overlap and Interactions

Interestingly, there have been instances where cryptids and UFOs seem to intersect, leading to intriguing questions and theories about their relationship. Here are a few notable examples:

- **Mothman and UFOs:** The Mothman, a cryptid associated with paranormal and UFO encounters, gained fame during the 1966-1967 sightings in West Virginia. Witnesses reported a large creature with glowing red eyes and wings. These sightings were often accompanied by reports of UFO activity, leading some to believe that the Mothman is somehow connected to extraterrestrial phenomena.

- **Chupacabra and UFOs:** The Chupacabra, a cryptid known for its alleged attacks on livestock, has been linked to UFO sightings in Puerto Rico and other regions. Some witnesses claim to have seen strange lights or UFOs in the vicinity of Chupacabra sightings, suggesting a possible correlation between the two phenomena.

- **Bigfoot and UFOs:** Bigfoot, the mythical ape-like creature said to inhabit forests, has occasionally been associated with UFO sightings as well. In some reports, witnesses have claimed to observe both Bigfoot sightings and UFO activity in the same geographic area, prompting speculation about a shared connection.

These instances of overlap between cryptids and UFOs have fueled various theories and explanations. Let us explore some of the main hypotheses put forward by researchers and enthusiasts.

Hypotheses and Explanations

1. **Extraterrestrial Connection:** One popular theory posits that cryptids and UFOs are both manifestations of extraterrestrial activity. Proponents of this hypothesis argue that some cryptids could be aliens or alien-created creatures, while UFO sightings could represent advanced extraterrestrial technology surveying or interacting with our planet.

2. **Interdimensional Beings:** Another intriguing explanation suggests that both cryptids and UFOs are entities from other dimensions or alternative realities. This theory proposes that these entities can occasionally cross over into our world, explaining the sightings and encounters witnessed by humans.

3. **Shared Habitat or Environment:** Some researchers suggest that cryptids and UFOs might frequent similar habitats or environments due to certain shared conditions or resources. For example, areas with high cryptid activity might also attract UFOs due to specific geological or electromagnetic factors.

4. **Psychological and Perception Factors:** Skeptics argue that the overlap between cryptids and UFOs could be attributed to psychological and perception

biases. They propose that witnesses might interpret their experiences based on preconceived notions or cultural influences, resulting in the perception of a connection that does not actually exist.

While these hypotheses provide intriguing possibilities, it is important to approach them with critical thinking and scientific scrutiny. Exploring the relationship between cryptids and UFOs requires an interdisciplinary approach and collaboration between researchers from various fields.

Challenges and Future Directions

Studying the connection between cryptids and UFOs presents several challenges. Firstly, the lack of concrete physical evidence for cryptids and the ambiguity surrounding UFO sightings make it difficult to establish a clear link between the two phenomena. Furthermore, the fringe nature of both subjects often leads to skepticism and lack of institutional support for research.

To shed light on this fascinating phenomenon, researchers can adopt innovative approaches such as:

- Employing advanced monitoring and data collection techniques in areas known for cryptid and UFO activity.

- Conducting systematic investigations that integrate both cryptid and UFO research methodologies.

- Analyzing historical reports and eyewitness accounts to identify patterns and commonalities between cryptid and UFO encounters.

- Engaging citizen scientists and amateur researchers in data collection and analysis to expand the scope of investigations.

In conclusion, while the relationship between cryptids and UFOs remains enigmatic, exploring their possible connections offers a fascinating avenue for research and discovery. By employing scientific rigor and interdisciplinary approaches, we can expand our understanding of these intriguing phenomena and potentially uncover new insights into the mysteries of our world. So, let us continue our exploration with an open mind and sharpened investigative tools, always seeking the truth behind the unknown.

Cryptids and Ghosts

In the study of paranormal phenomena, there are often intriguing connections and overlaps between different aspects. One such connection is between cryptids and ghosts, two separate fields of study that deal with unexplained phenomena beyond the realms of mainstream science. In this section, we will explore the relationship between cryptids and ghosts, examining their similarities, differences, and the implications they have for our understanding of the supernatural.

The Nature of Cryptids

Before we delve into the connection between cryptids and ghosts, let's first define what cryptids are. Cryptids are creatures whose existence is rumored or disputed, often based on anecdotal sightings or folklore rather than scientific evidence. These creatures are often considered elusive and mysterious, commonly associated with remote or unexplored regions of the world.

The study of cryptids, known as cryptozoology, attempts to collect evidence and investigate sightings in order to determine the existence or nonexistence of these creatures. Some well-known cryptids include the Loch Ness Monster, Bigfoot, and the Chupacabra. Despite the lack of concrete evidence, the belief in these cryptids perseveres, captivating the imagination of many.

The Realm of Ghosts

On the other hand, ghosts are entities believed to be the souls or spirits of deceased individuals who continue to exist in a different plane of reality. Ghosts are often associated with specific locations, such as haunted houses or burial sites, and are known to interact with the physical world through various means, such as apparitions, sounds, and other paranormal phenomena.

Ghost sightings are reported by people from different cultural backgrounds and have been a subject of fascination for centuries. Some ghost encounters involve visual sightings of human-like apparitions, while others involve auditory experiences, such as disembodied voices or unexplained noises.

Similarities and Connections

Now that we have a basic understanding of cryptids and ghosts, let's explore the similarities and connections between these two phenomena. One connection is the presence of eyewitness accounts and anecdotal evidence. Both cryptids and ghosts rely heavily on witness testimonies and personal experiences, making them largely subjective in nature.

Another similarity is the role of folklore and cultural beliefs. Both cryptids and ghosts are deeply embedded in the folklore and myths of various cultures around the world. Tales of cryptids and ghostly encounters are often passed down through generations, shaping the collective beliefs and perceptions of these phenomena.

Additionally, both cryptids and ghosts challenge the boundaries of mainstream science. They exist outside the realm of what is currently understood and accepted by scientific disciplines. As a result, the study of cryptids and ghosts often faces criticism and skepticism from the scientific community.

Differences and Distinctions

While there are similarities between cryptids and ghosts, it is important to recognize the distinct characteristics that set them apart.

One key difference lies in their origin. Cryptids are generally believed to be living creatures that have yet to be discovered or scientifically classified. These creatures are thought to exist within the natural world, albeit in remote or undiscovered regions. On the other hand, ghosts are believed to be the spirits or energy of deceased individuals, existing in a supernatural realm beyond the physical world.

Another difference is the type of evidence associated with each phenomenon. Cryptids often leave physical traces or evidence, such as footprints or hair samples, which can be subjected to scientific analysis. In contrast, ghosts typically leave behind subjective evidence, such as eyewitness testimonies or recordings of paranormal activity, which are more difficult to verify using scientific methods.

Exploring the Intersection

With the distinct differences and similarities in mind, it is intriguing to explore the potential intersection between cryptids and ghosts. While the fields of cryptozoology and ghost hunting are often viewed as separate disciplines, there have been instances where the two phenomena seem to overlap.

For example, there are reports of ghostly apparitions associated with specific cryptid sightings or locations. In some cases, witnesses claim to have seen the spirit of a deceased individual near the habitat of a cryptid, leading to speculation that these creatures may have a supernatural or spiritual connection.

Additionally, some paranormal investigators believe that certain cryptids could be manifestations of ghostly entities. They propose that these creatures may be the result of residual energy or non-physical entities taking on physical form. This theory seeks to bridge the gap between the physical and metaphysical realms, offering a potential explanation for the existence of cryptids.

Implications and Further Research

The connection between cryptids and ghosts raises intriguing questions about the nature of reality and the boundaries of scientific understanding. Exploring this intersection could provide valuable insights into the mysteries surrounding these phenomena.

Further research could involve interdisciplinary collaborations between cryptozoologists and paranormal investigators. By combining their expertise and methodologies, researchers may be able to shed light on the possible connections between cryptids and ghosts.

Moreover, studying the cultural and folkloric significance of cryptids and ghosts can also contribute to our understanding of these phenomena. Examining the beliefs and interpretations surrounding these creatures in different cultures can provide valuable context and offer new perspectives on their existence.

In conclusion, while cryptids and ghosts are distinct fields of study, there are compelling connections between the two. Exploring these connections can expand our understanding of the supernatural and challenge the boundaries of scientific knowledge. By embracing interdisciplinary approaches and cultural perspectives, we can continue to unravel the mysteries surrounding cryptids and ghosts in our quest for a deeper understanding of the paranormal.

Cryptids and Alien Abductions

In this section, we will explore the potential connections between cryptids and alien abductions. Cryptids are creatures whose existence is disputed or unconfirmed by mainstream science, such as Bigfoot or the Loch Ness Monster. On the other hand, alien abductions refer to the claimed experiences of being taken by extraterrestrial beings for various purposes.

5.3.1 Types of Alien Abductions Alien abductions can be categorized into different types based on the experiences reported by the individuals. These types include:

1. "Close Encounter of the Fourth Kind": This type involves direct interaction or communication between the abductee and the extraterrestrial beings. Some individuals claim to have communicated with aliens telepathically or have had direct physical contact with them.

2. Medical Examinations and Procedures: Many abduction accounts describe medical procedures performed on the abductees by the aliens. These procedures often involve examinations, implantation of devices, or even alleged hybridization experiments.

3. Missing Time Phenomenon: Many individuals report a period of missing time during their alleged abduction experience. They have no recollection of events that occurred during this period and may find themselves in a different location or situation without explanation.

5.3.2 Linking Cryptids to Alien Abductions While the connection between cryptids and alien abductions may seem speculative, some researchers and theorists believe that these phenomena are interrelated. Here are some theories and possible explanations:

1. Hybridization Experiments: Some speculate that certain cryptids, like Bigfoot or the Jersey Devil, may be the result of alien genetic manipulation or hybridization experiments. The idea is that these creatures are part-human and part-alien beings created for unknown purposes.

2. Cryptids as Alien Proxies: Another theory suggests that cryptids may serve as "proxies" for the extraterrestrial beings. In this scenario, aliens may use cryptids to interact with and observe humans from a distance, without direct contact.

3. Dimensional Gateways: Some researchers propose that certain cryptids, like the Chupacabra or Mothman, may act as guardians or gatekeepers of dimensional portals. These portals could serve as entry points for extraterrestrial beings, allowing them to carry out abductions or other activities.

5.3.3 Exploring the Evidence When examining the potential link between cryptids and alien abductions, it is important to consider the available evidence. It's crucial to approach the subject with skepticism and critical thinking. Here are some key points to consider:

1. Anecdotal Evidence: The majority of evidence supporting the connection between cryptids and alien abductions comes from eyewitness accounts and personal testimonies. While these accounts should not be dismissed outright, they should be approached with caution due to the potential for misinterpretation or fabrication.

2. Lack of Physical Evidence: One of the significant challenges in linking cryptids to alien abductions is the absence of tangible physical evidence. Despite numerous alleged encounters, no definitive proof exists that establishes a concrete connection between these phenomena.

3. Psychological Explanations: It is worth considering psychological factors when examining abduction experiences or sightings of cryptids. The power of suggestion, cultural influences, and human perception may contribute to the belief in these phenomena.

5.3.4 Investigating the Connection To investigate the possible connection between cryptids and alien abductions, interdisciplinary collaboration is essential. Scientists, cryptozoologists, ufologists, and psychologists need to come together to conduct thorough and unbiased research. Some approaches to consider include:

1. Field Studies and Surveys: Researchers should conduct extensive field studies and surveys to gather data on alleged cryptid sightings, alien abductions, and any potential correlations between the two.

2. Physical Evidence Analysis: If physical evidence, such as footprints or hair samples, associated with both cryptids and alien abductions is discovered, it should be subjected to rigorous scientific analysis. This analysis could involve DNA testing, trace element analysis, or other relevant scientific techniques.

3. Psychological Studies: Collaborating with psychologists, researchers can conduct psychological studies to investigate the psychological aspects of cryptid sightings and abduction experiences. These studies can shed light on the factors that contribute to belief in these phenomena.

5.3.5 The Blurred Line between Fact and Fiction It's important to acknowledge that the link between cryptids and alien abductions remains speculative and unproven. While there is an abundance of anecdotal evidence, the lack of robust scientific evidence makes it challenging to draw concrete conclusions. However, the fascination and cultural significance of both cryptids and alien abductions continue to capture the imagination of the public and fuel ongoing investigations.

In conclusion, the connection between cryptids and alien abductions is an area that requires further investigation and scientific scrutiny. While theories exist linking these phenomena, the lack of solid evidence leaves much room for speculation and debate. By employing interdisciplinary research methods and rigorous scientific analysis, we may gain a deeper understanding of these enigmatic phenomena and their potential interplay.

Theories and Explanations for the Paranormal

Supernatural and Metaphysical Theories

Supernatural and metaphysical theories play a significant role in understanding and explaining paranormal phenomena, including cryptids and aliens. These theories explore the possibility of an existence beyond the natural world and involve concepts such as spirits, entities, and dimensions that are beyond our current understanding. In this section, we will delve into some of these theories and their implications for cryptozoology and the study of the paranormal.

Spiritual and Intergalactic Beings

One supernatural theory posits the existence of spiritual or intergalactic beings that interact with the human world. According to this theory, cryptids and aliens are not simply physical creatures, but rather manifestations of these beings in different forms. These beings are believed to possess advanced intelligence, technology, and powers that allow them to move between dimensions and interact with humans and the environment.

Some proponents of this theory argue that cryptids such as Bigfoot and the Loch Ness Monster are actually physical manifestations of spiritual beings. They believe that these creatures have the ability to transcend physical boundaries and exist in multiple dimensions simultaneously. Similarly, some UFO sightings are attributed to intergalactic beings who visit Earth to observe and interact with humanity.

Example: Consider the case of the Mothman, a cryptid reported in Point Pleasant, West Virginia, in the 1960s. According to witnesses, the Mothman had the ability to fly despite its humanoid appearance. Proponents of supernatural theories argue that the Mothman was an extraterrestrial being that manifested in a physical form to deliver a message or warning to humanity.

The Multiverse Theory

The multiverse theory is a metaphysical concept that suggests the existence of multiple parallel universes or dimensions. According to this theory, cryptids and aliens could originate from these alternate dimensions and occasionally cross over into our reality.

In the context of cryptozoology, the multiverse theory suggests that cryptids like the Chupacabra or the Jersey Devil may not be traditional physical beings but instead entities that exist in a different dimension. These entities occasionally breach the barrier between dimensions, resulting in sightings and encounters with humans. This theory offers an explanation for the elusiveness and lack of physical evidence often associated with these cryptids.

Example: Imagine a parallel universe where dinosaurs never went extinct. The existence of dinosaurs in this alternate reality could explain reports of dinosaur-like creatures, such as the legendary Mokele-Mbembe in the Congo. According to the multiverse theory, these creatures might occasionally slip through "portals" between dimensions, leading to sightings by humans.

Time Travel and Temporal Displacements

Another metaphysical theory proposes that cryptids and aliens are not extraterrestrial or supernatural beings but rather products of time travel or temporal displacements. The theory suggests that these entities originate from the future or past and occasionally visit our present timeline.

For example, the theory posits that sightings of alien beings could be encounters with future humans who have developed advanced technologies enabling them to travel through time. Similarly, reports of extinct creatures in modern times, like the alleged sightings of thylacines (Tasmanian tigers) in Australia, could be explained by temporal displacements, where these creatures temporarily appear in our timeline.

Example: The case of the Dover Demon can be linked to the temporal displacement theory. The creature's strange appearance and behavior might suggest that it was not of this time but rather from a different temporal reality.

Implications and Criticisms

Supernatural and metaphysical theories provide alternative perspectives for understanding the paranormal phenomena associated with cryptids and aliens. However, these theories are often criticized for their lack of empirical evidence and testability. Skeptics argue that without concrete evidence to support these claims, they remain speculative and fall outside the realm of scientific investigation.

At the same time, these theories have cultural and psychological significance, as they reflect humanity's desire to comprehend the mysteries of the universe and our place within it. They offer an imaginative and thought-provoking lens through which we can explore the unexplained and expand our understanding of the world around us.

While supernatural and metaphysical theories might not conform to traditional scientific standards, they contribute to the complex tapestry of ideas and beliefs that shape our perception of the paranormal. They remind us that science alone cannot always provide answers to the mysteries that captivate our imagination. Instead, they encourage us to embrace curiosity, open-mindedness, and the exploration of unconventional ideas as we continue to unravel the enigmas of cryptids and the supernatural.

Exercise: Reflect on the supernatural and metaphysical theories discussed in this section. How do they challenge or complement your own beliefs about the existence of cryptids and aliens? Share your thoughts and engage in a respectful discussion with your peers.

Further Reading:

1. "Supernatural: Meetings with the Ancient Teachers of Mankind" by Graham Hancock

2. "Multiverse: Exploring the Limits of Our Universe" by Lisa Randall

3. "Time Travel: A History" by James Gleick

Trivia: Did you know that the concept of time travel has been a popular topic in science fiction literature since the late 19th century? H.G. Wells' novel "The Time Machine" is often regarded as a pioneering work in the genre.

Psychological and Psychological Theories

In the study of paranormal phenomena, including encounters with aliens and cryptids, various psychological and psychological theories have been proposed to explain people's beliefs, experiences, and reactions. These theories shed light on the psychological processes that contribute to individuals' perceptions, interpretations, and emotional responses to these phenomena.

Cognitive Dissonance Theory

One psychological theory that applies to belief in paranormal phenomena is cognitive dissonance theory. This theory, developed by Leon Festinger in the 1950s, suggests that individuals experience psychological discomfort when they hold conflicting beliefs or when their beliefs contradict their actions. In the context of the paranormal, cognitive dissonance can arise when individuals encounter evidence that challenges their existing beliefs or when they experience an inexplicable event.

For example, imagine a person who strongly believes in the existence of aliens and regularly reads and shares stories about alien encounters. If this person encounters evidence suggesting that a famous alien abduction case was a hoax, it creates a state of cognitive dissonance. To alleviate this discomfort, the person might reject the contradictory evidence or reinterpret it to conform to their existing beliefs.

Confirmation Bias

Confirmation bias is another psychological theory that relates to beliefs in the paranormal. It refers to the tendency for individuals to selectively seek out, interpret, and remember information that supports their existing beliefs, while ignoring or dismissing information that contradicts them. This bias can influence how individuals perceive and evaluate evidence related to paranormal phenomena.

For instance, let's consider a person who believes in the existence of Bigfoot. This person might actively search for articles, videos, and eyewitness accounts that support the existence of Bigfoot while disregarding skeptical explanations or debunking efforts. Confirmation bias can lead people to form a distorted and one-sided view of the evidence, reinforcing their preexisting beliefs.

Expectancy Theory

Expectancy theory, proposed by Julian Rotter, suggests that individuals' behaviors and experiences are influenced by their expectations of the outcomes associated with those behaviors. In the context of paranormal phenomena, individuals who believe in aliens or cryptids may behave in ways that increase the likelihood of encountering such phenomena. Their expectations of encountering these beings can shape their perceptions and interpretations of ambiguous events or experiences.

For example, a person who strongly believes in the Loch Ness Monster may visit Loch Ness and actively search for signs of the creature. This person's heightened expectations and attention may lead them to interpret ordinary phenomena, such as floating logs or waves, as evidence of the monster's existence. Their expectations can influence their perceptions and memory of the event, reinforcing their belief in the Loch Ness Monster.

Sociocultural Influences

Psychological theories also take into account sociocultural factors that contribute to beliefs in paranormal phenomena. For instance, cultural beliefs and societal norms play a significant role in shaping individuals' beliefs and experiences with the paranormal. Cultural stories, myths, and legends can create a shared belief system and influence individuals' interpretations of strange or unexplained phenomena.

Moreover, social influence and the desire for social acceptance can contribute to the adoption and maintenance of paranormal beliefs. People may conform to the beliefs and experiences of their social group to gain acceptance and avoid social rejection. This conformity can reinforce beliefs and lead to the spread and persistence of paranormal beliefs within a community or culture.

The Role of Psychological Perspectives

Psychological theories help us understand why individuals believe in paranormal phenomena and how those beliefs are shaped by psychological processes. They shed light on the cognitive biases, social influences, and personal expectations that contribute to the formation and maintenance of these beliefs.

However, it is important to note that psychological theories alone cannot prove or disprove the existence of aliens, cryptids, or other paranormal phenomena. They provide explanations for why people believe in them and how psychological processes play a role in shaping those beliefs.

In order to gain a more comprehensive understanding of paranormal phenomena, interdisciplinary approaches that incorporate psychological, sociological, and scientific perspectives are necessary. The convergence of multiple disciplines can contribute to a more nuanced exploration of these phenomena and facilitate a more balanced evaluation of the available evidence.

Exercises

1. Think of a real-world example of cognitive dissonance related to paranormal phenomena. How might a person experiencing cognitive dissonance react to contradictory evidence?
2. Consider a situation in which confirmation bias might influence the perception of evidence related to cryptids. How might confirmation bias affect the interpretation of ambiguous or inconclusive evidence?
3. Reflect on the influence of sociocultural factors on beliefs in paranormal phenomena. How might cultural stories or myths contribute to the formation and reinforcement of these beliefs?
4. Discuss the limitations of psychological theories in explaining the existence of paranormal phenomena. How can interdisciplinary approaches help overcome these limitations?

Paranormal Research and Investigation Techniques

Paranormal research and investigation techniques are essential for studying and understanding the unexplained phenomena associated with the paranormal. These techniques involve a combination of scientific methodologies, specialized equipment, and the use of various investigative methods. In this section, we will explore some of the key techniques used in paranormal research.

Data Collection

One of the first steps in paranormal research is the collection of data. This involves gathering information about reported paranormal experiences, including eyewitness testimonies, photographs, videos, audio recordings, and any other relevant material.

THEORIES AND EXPLANATIONS FOR THE PARANORMAL 131

It is essential to document and record all available evidence to establish a foundation for further analysis.

Eyewitness testimonies play a crucial role in paranormal research, as they provide first-hand accounts of encounters with the unknown. Interviewing witnesses in a structured and systematic manner helps gather detailed information about their experiences. It is important to ask open-ended questions and avoid leading or suggestive inquiries to ensure the accuracy and reliability of the collected information.

Photographs, videos, and audio recordings are commonly used to capture potential paranormal phenomena. These forms of evidence can be analyzed later for any anomalies or unexplained occurrences. It is crucial to ensure the proper handling and preservation of this evidence to maintain its integrity.

Investigation Techniques

Paranormal investigations involve exploring and examining the locations associated with reported paranormal activities. The primary goal is to gather evidence, validate claims, and potentially communicate with any entities or spirits present. Here are some common investigation techniques used:

1. Site Surveys: Investigators conduct thorough surveys of the location to identify areas of interest and potential hotspots for paranormal activities. They document the layout, architectural details, and environmental conditions that could contribute to the reported phenomena.

2. EVP (Electronic Voice Phenomenon) Recording: EVP recordings involve capturing potentially paranormal voices or sounds using specialized audio recording equipment. Investigators ask questions or make statements, leaving gaps for potential responses. During analysis, they listen carefully for any unexplained voices or sounds that were not audible at the time of recording.

3. EMF (Electromagnetic Field) Detection: Paranormal phenomena are often associated with fluctuations or disturbances in the electromagnetic field. Investigators use EMF detectors to measure these changes, which may indicate the presence of a supernatural entity or activity.

4. Spirit Communication: Investigators may attempt to communicate with spirits or entities using techniques such as séances, Ouija boards, or spirit boxes. These methods aim to establish a connection and gather information from the other side.

5. Infrared and Thermal Imaging: Infrared and thermal imaging cameras can detect heat signatures and anomalies that are not visible to the naked eye. These

tools help identify temperature variations associated with paranormal phenomena, such as cold spots or energy manifestations.

Data Analysis

Once the data collection and investigation phases are complete, the next step is to analyze the gathered information. Data analysis involves a critical examination of the evidence to identify patterns, anomalies, and potential explanations. Here are some techniques commonly used in data analysis for paranormal research:

1. Video and Photo Analysis: Investigators scrutinize videos and photos for any abnormal or unexplained phenomena, such as orbs, apparitions, or strange lights. Enhancement techniques, such as zooming, filtering, and adjusting brightness/contrast, can help reveal hidden details.

2. Audio Analysis: EVP recordings are carefully reviewed, and the captured sounds or voices are enhanced and isolated. Investigators listen for intelligible responses or direct interactions that indicate paranormal activity.

3. Comparative Analysis: Investigators compare the collected evidence with historical records, eyewitness testimonies, and known phenomena to determine the likelihood of a paranormal occurrence. This analysis helps rule out natural explanations and provides a basis for further investigation.

Psychic and Mediumship Investigation

In addition to scientific techniques, paranormal research sometimes involves utilizing the abilities of psychics and mediums. These individuals claim to have extrasensory perception (ESP) or the ability to communicate with spirits. While the scientific community often views psychic and mediumistic approaches with skepticism, there are cases where their insights have provided valuable leads for further investigation.

It is important to approach psychic and mediumship investigation with caution and skepticism. To ensure credibility, investigators should vet psychics and mediums carefully, assess their track record, and scrutinize their claims. Collaborating with experienced and reputable individuals in this field can provide additional perspectives and potentially enhance the investigative process.

Conclusion

Paranormal research and investigation techniques combine scientific methodologies, specialized equipment, and various investigative methods to explore and understand the unexplained phenomena associated with the paranormal. Data collection, investigation techniques, data analysis, and psychic and mediumship investigation all play crucial roles in this field.

While paranormal research is often met with skepticism, it continues to intrigue people across cultures and societies. Advances in technology and interdisciplinary collaborations hold the potential for further advancements in this field. As researchers strive to bridge the gap between the paranormal and mainstream science, an open and scientific approach is essential for conducting thorough and credible investigations. By employing rigorous methodologies and critical analysis, we can further our understanding of the paranormal and potentially unravel its mysteries.

Chapter 5: Scientific Perspectives

Mainstream Scientific Rejection of Cryptids and Aliens

Lack of Physical Evidence

In the field of cryptozoology, one of the main challenges faced by researchers is the lack of physical evidence to support the existence of cryptids. Unlike mainstream scientific study, which relies heavily on empirical evidence, cryptozoologists often have to work with limited data and rely on anecdotal accounts and eyewitness testimonies. This lack of physical evidence makes it difficult to convince skeptics and gain acceptance within the scientific community.

The absence of tangible proof poses a significant obstacle when it comes to documenting and studying cryptids. Without physical evidence such as bones, DNA samples, or preserved specimens, it becomes challenging to establish the authenticity of reported sightings or encounters. Skeptics argue that without concrete proof, many cryptids could simply be the result of hoaxes, misidentifications, or the product of overactive imaginations.

One example of the lack of physical evidence is the case of the Loch Ness Monster. Despite numerous reports and sightings over the years, there has been no conclusive evidence to confirm the existence of this legendary creature. Although photographs and videos purporting to show the Loch Ness Monster have emerged, they have faced intense scrutiny and have been debunked as fakes or misinterpretations.

The absence of physical evidence also hinders the ability to analyze and classify cryptid sightings. In cases where eyewitnesses claim to have seen a creature that does not fit any known animal species, it becomes challenging to validate their accounts without physical proof. Cryptozoologists often have to rely on witness descriptions, which can vary in accuracy and detail, leading to inconsistencies in the documentation and classification of cryptids.

So, why is it so difficult to find physical evidence of cryptids? There are several factors at play. First, cryptids are often elusive and possess behaviors that make them difficult to study and locate. For example, creatures like Bigfoot are believed to be highly intelligent and adept at avoiding human contact, making it challenging to gather concrete evidence of their existence.

Second, the habitats where cryptids are believed to reside are often vast and remote, making systematic scientific investigation challenging. Expeditions into such areas require significant resources, time, and logistics, which may not always be feasible. Additionally, the scarcity of funding for cryptozoological research further limits the opportunities for robust scientific investigations.

Lastly, the lack of physical evidence could also be attributed to the cryptids' existence in small populations or their potential status as highly endangered species. If cryptids are indeed real creatures, their limited numbers and dwindling habitats could contribute to the challenges in obtaining physical evidence. Moreover, the fear of legal repercussions and potential harm to these already vulnerable populations may discourage individuals from revealing any evidence they may have.

Despite these challenges, cryptozoologists continue to search for physical evidence to prove the existence of cryptids. Advances in technology, such as trail cameras, DNA analysis techniques, and remote sensing devices, have opened new avenues for research. By employing these tools in strategic locations and employing rigorous data collection methods, researchers hope to increase the chances of obtaining concrete proof.

In conclusion, the lack of physical evidence remains a significant obstacle in the study of cryptids. The absence of tangible proof hampers the acceptance of these creatures within the scientific community and leaves room for skepticism. However, with the advancement of technology and the dedication of cryptozoologists, there is a glimmer of hope that someday we may uncover the evidence needed to validate the existence of these mysterious creatures.

Scientific Method and Reproducibility

In order to understand the scientific perspectives on cryptids and aliens, it is important to delve into the principles of the scientific method and the concept of reproducibility. These fundamental concepts guide scientists in their pursuit of knowledge and assist in distinguishing between valid scientific findings and mere speculation.

The scientific method is a systematic approach used to investigate and understand the natural world. It consists of several steps, including observation, hypothesis formulation, experimentation, data analysis, and conclusion drawing. This methodology allows scientists to test their ideas and theories in a rigorous and objective manner.

Observation plays a crucial role in the scientific method. It involves carefully noting and describing phenomena of interest, such as sightings of cryptids or alleged encounters with aliens. Observations provide the initial groundwork for developing hypotheses, which are tentative explanations for observed phenomena.

Once an observation has been made, a scientist formulates a hypothesis based on existing knowledge and reasoning. The hypothesis is a testable statement that attempts to explain the observed phenomenon. For example, a hypothesis related to the Dover Demon sightings might propose that the creature is a previously undiscovered species of cryptid.

In order to test the validity of a hypothesis, scientists design and execute experiments. During an experiment, researchers manipulate variables and measure the corresponding outcomes. These experiments must be carefully controlled to ensure that any observed effects are due to the manipulated variables and not other factors. For instance, scientists studying the Dover Demon sightings might conduct interviews with eyewitnesses and analyze their testimonies for consistency and reliability.

Data analysis is a critical step in the scientific method. Researchers examine the collected data to determine whether it supports or refutes their hypothesis. Statistical techniques and other analytical tools are often employed to assess the significance of the results. In the case of the Dover Demon sightings, researchers would analyze the various eyewitness testimonies for consistency of description and any potential patterns.

The final step of the scientific method involves drawing conclusions based on the analyzed data. If the data supports the hypothesis, it can be considered as evidence in favor of the proposed explanation. However, if the data does not align with the hypothesis, scientists must reject or modify their initial explanation and propose alternative hypotheses.

Reproducibility is a key aspect of the scientific method. It refers to the ability of other researchers to independently replicate an experiment and obtain similar results. Reproducibility is crucial for validating scientific findings and ensuring the reliability of the conclusions drawn. In the context of cryptids and aliens, reproducibility is essential for establishing the credibility of reported sightings and encounters.

Achieving reproducibility involves transparency, detailed documentation, and open sharing of methods and data. Scientists should provide clear and comprehensive descriptions of their experimental procedures, including any equipment used, measurement techniques employed, and analysis methods utilized. This enables other researchers to follow the same steps and verify the reported findings.

Ensuring reproducibility in the study of cryptids and aliens can be particularly challenging due to the elusive and rare nature of the phenomena. However, efforts can be made to increase the rigor of investigations. For example, multiple eyewitness testimonies can be independently collected and analyzed to identify any recurring patterns or consistencies. Collaboration among researchers and sharing of data can help in cross-validation of findings.

It is worth noting that the scientific method is not infallible, and it is subject to limitations and potential biases. Scientists must be aware of these limitations and strive to minimize any sources of error or bias in their experiments. Peer review, where other experts in the field critically evaluate the research before publication, is an essential component in maintaining the integrity of the scientific method.

In conclusion, the scientific method and reproducibility are vital for studying and understanding cryptids and aliens. By following a systematic approach, scientists can investigate reported sightings and encounters, test hypotheses, and draw valid conclusions. Ensuring reproducibility allows for independent verification of findings and contributes to the robustness of scientific knowledge in these fascinating fields of study.

Key Takeaways:

- The scientific method is a systematic approach used to investigate the natural world, comprising observation, hypothesis formulation, experimentation, data analysis, and conclusion drawing.

- Observations provide the basis for developing hypotheses, which are tentative explanations for observed phenomena.

- Experiments are designed and executed to test hypotheses, and the collected data is analyzed using statistical and analytical methods.

- Reproducibility is important in scientific research, allowing independent verification of findings through transparent methods, detailed documentation, and the sharing of data.

- The scientific method is not infallible and is subject to limitations and biases, which should be recognized and minimized.

Skepticism and Peer Review

Skepticism and peer review are crucial aspects of the scientific process, ensuring that research is conducted rigorously and that findings are reliable and valid. In this section, we will explore the importance of skepticism and peer review in the context of cryptozoology and paranormal research.

The Role of Skepticism

Skepticism is an essential part of scientific inquiry. It involves questioning and critically evaluating claims, evidence, and explanations. In the field of cryptozoology, skeptics play a vital role in scrutinizing alleged cryptid sightings and challenging unsupported claims.

One of the primary responsibilities of skeptics is to examine the available evidence with a critical eye. They carefully evaluate eyewitness testimonies, photographs, and videos, looking for any inconsistencies or flaws that may indicate a hoax or misinterpretation. Skeptics also consider alternative explanations that could account for the observed phenomena, such as misidentified known animals or natural phenomena.

Skeptics rely on the scientific method, which emphasizes the importance of empirical evidence, logical reasoning, and testability. They often employ skeptical inquiry techniques to debunk pseudoscientific claims and separate fact from fiction. By applying skepticism to cryptozoological claims, they contribute to the overall credibility and reliability of the field.

The Peer Review Process

Peer review is an essential component of scientific research. It involves the critical evaluation of research papers by experts in the same field. The purpose of peer review is to ensure the quality, validity, and reliability of scientific work before it is published or accepted as valid.

In the context of cryptozoology and paranormal research, peer review plays a vital role in maintaining scientific integrity. When a researcher submits a paper on a cryptozoological or paranormal topic, it undergoes a rigorous review process. Experts in the field carefully examine the methodology, data analysis, and conclusions presented in the paper.

Peer reviewers assess the scientific merit of the research, evaluating the soundness of the experimental design, the appropriateness of the statistical analysis, and the clarity of the presentation. They also look for any potential biases or conflicts of interest that may have influenced the research findings.

The feedback provided by peer reviewers is crucial for improving the quality of the research. If flaws or weaknesses are identified, the researcher is given an opportunity to address them before the paper is published. Through this iterative process, peer review ensures that the highest standards of scientific rigor are upheld.

Challenges in Skepticism and Peer Review

Skepticism and peer review in the fields of cryptozoology and paranormal research face unique challenges compared to more conventional scientific disciplines. The nature of these subjects often involves extraordinary claims and limited empirical evidence, leading to skepticism from the scientific community.

One primary challenge is the lack of reproducibility in cryptozoological and paranormal research. Unlike in physics or chemistry, where experiments can be repeated under controlled conditions, researching elusive and rare creatures or paranormal phenomena is inherently difficult. As a result, many cryptozoological and paranormal claims rely heavily on anecdotal evidence, which is often subjective and prone to bias.

Another challenge is the presence of motivated reasoning and cognitive biases among both researchers and enthusiasts in these fields. Beliefs and personal experiences may influence the interpretation of evidence, leading to confirmation bias and a tendency to accept evidence that supports preconceived notions while dismissing contradictory evidence.

Despite these challenges, skepticism and peer review remain essential for advancing cryptozoology and paranormal research. By addressing these challenges head-on and fostering open dialogue and collaboration, researchers can continue to improve the scientific rigor and credibility of these fields.

Conclusion

Skepticism and peer review are integral to the field of cryptozoology and paranormal research. Skepticism helps to ensure that claims are examined critically and alternative explanations are considered. Peer review provides a system for expert evaluation and validation of research findings, contributing to the overall credibility and reliability of the field.

While unique challenges exist in skeptically evaluating cryptozoological and paranormal claims, it is crucial to embrace skepticism and peer review to maintain scientific integrity. By addressing these challenges and fostering interdisciplinary collaboration, the fields of cryptozoology and paranormal research can continue to evolve and contribute to our understanding of the unknown.

Alternative Scientific Perspectives

Parapsychology and Anomalous Phenomena

Parapsychology is the field of study that investigates and explores phenomena that are beyond the realm of normal scientific understanding. It focuses on the study of paranormal and anomalous experiences, including extrasensory perception (ESP), psychokinesis (PK), and survival after bodily death. These phenomena, if proven to exist, would challenge our current understanding of the laws of nature and the limitations of human capabilities.

History and Evolution of Parapsychology

The study of parapsychology dates back to the late 19th century when individuals began to explore psychic phenomena and spiritualism. However, it was not until the early 20th century that parapsychology emerged as a distinct scientific discipline. One of the pioneers in the field was J.B. Rhine, who conducted extensive research on ESP using methods such as card-guessing experiments and studies on telepathy.

Over the years, parapsychology has faced skepticism and criticism from the mainstream scientific community due to the controversial nature of its subjects. Despite this, parapsychologists have persisted in their efforts to conduct rigorous experiments and gather empirical evidence to support their claims.

Types of Anomalous Phenomena

Parapsychology encompasses a range of anomalous phenomena, including the following:

1. **Extrasensory Perception (ESP):** ESP refers to the ability to receive information beyond the five senses. It includes phenomena such as telepathy

(mind-to-mind communication), clairvoyance (perception of remote events or objects), precognition (knowledge of future events), and retrocognition (knowledge of past events).

2. **Psychokinesis (PK):** PK involves the ability to affect physical objects or events using the power of the mind. It can manifest as telekinesis (movement of objects), levitation (lifting of oneself or objects), or influencing the outcome of events through mental intention.

3. **Survival after Bodily Death:** This area of study explores the possibility of consciousness persisting after physical death. It includes phenomena such as near-death experiences, out-of-body experiences, and mediumship (communication with the deceased).

Experimental Methods

Parapsychological research employs a variety of experimental methods to investigate and measure anomalous phenomena. Some commonly used methods include:

- **Ganzfeld Experiment:** This method is often used to test telepathy and involves placing a receiver in a relaxed state in a monotonous sensory environment while a sender tries to mentally transmit information.

- **Remote Viewing:** Remote viewing is a technique used to gather information about distant or unseen targets using ESP. It involves a viewer attempting to describe or draw details about a target location or event without any prior knowledge.

- **Random Event Generators:** Random event generators (REGs) are used to test psychokinesis. Participants attempt to influence the random output of electronic devices through their focused intention.

- **Staring Experiments:** Staring experiments involve participants gazing at or concentrating on a target image or object in an attempt to influence its physical state or properties.

Current Challenges and Controversies

Parapsychology faces numerous challenges and controversies, primarily due to the difficulties in achieving reliable and replicable results. Critics argue that the field lacks a strong theoretical framework and that the reported phenomena can be explained by conventional psychological or physiological factors rather than paranormal abilities.

Skeptics also point out the presence of methodological issues, such as the file drawer effect (publication bias towards positive results) and experimenter bias, which they argue can lead to the misinterpretation of results.

Bridging the Gap between Parapsychology and Mainstream Science

While parapsychology continues to operate on the fringes of mainstream science, there have been efforts to bridge the gap between the two. Collaboration between parapsychologists and scientists from other disciplines, such as psychology and neuroscience, has shed light on potential underlying mechanisms of anomalous phenomena.

Advancements in technology, such as brain imaging techniques, have enabled researchers to explore the neural correlates of psychic abilities and investigate the possible physiological basis for these phenomena.

Moreover, interdisciplinary approaches that combine the rigor of scientific methodology with the sensitivity to subjective experiences associated with parapsychological phenomena may provide a more comprehensive understanding of these phenomena.

Ethical Considerations

The study of parapsychology raises ethical concerns, particularly when it involves vulnerable individuals who may seek guidance or support in understanding their own paranormal experiences. Researchers must prioritize the privacy, well-being, and informed consent of participants, ensuring that their involvement in studies is voluntary and that potential risks are minimized.

Furthermore, researchers must adhere to scientific integrity and maintain transparency in reporting their findings, as the controversial nature of parapsychology demands rigorous scrutiny.

Conclusion

Parapsychology remains a field that challenges our understanding of the limits of human capabilities and the nature of reality. While skepticism and criticism persist, advancements in research methods, interdisciplinary collaborations, and the exploration of underlying mechanisms offer potential avenues for gaining further insights into these anomalous phenomena.

The study of parapsychology reminds us of the importance of balancing scientific skepticism with an open-minded approach to exploring the unknown. As advancements in technology and our understanding of consciousness continue, the potential to unravel mysteries surrounding parapsychological phenomena may become increasingly within reach.

Astrobiology and the Search for Extraterrestrial Life

Astrobiology is a multidisciplinary scientific field that aims to study the origin, evolution, distribution, and future of life beyond Earth. It combines the disciplines of astronomy, biology, chemistry, and geology to explore the conditions necessary for life to exist and thrive in other parts of the universe. The search for extraterrestrial life is one of the core focuses of astrobiology, and it has captivated the imagination of scientists and the general public alike.

History of Astrobiology

The idea of life existing beyond Earth has been a topic of speculation for centuries. However, it was not until the mid-20th century that the field of astrobiology started to take shape. The pioneering work of scientists like Carl Sagan and Frank Drake laid the foundation for the scientific study of extraterrestrial life.

One of the key milestones in astrobiology was the discovery of extremophiles—organisms that thrive in extreme environments on Earth. This led scientists to realize that life could exist in environments previously thought to be inhospitable. The discovery of microbial life in extreme environments, such as deep-sea hydrothermal vents and Antarctica's dry valleys, expanded the possibilities of where life could be found beyond Earth.

The Search for Extraterrestrial Life

The search for extraterrestrial life involves both the direct exploration of other celestial bodies and the study of the conditions necessary for life's existence. It encompasses various scientific approaches, including:

1. **Planetary Exploration:** Space missions, such as the Mars rovers and the Voyager spacecraft, have provided valuable data about the conditions on other planets and moons. These missions have revealed signs of water, organic molecules, and potentially habitable environments, raising the possibility of finding evidence of past or present life.

2. **Exoplanet Studies:** With the discovery of thousands of exoplanets (planets orbiting stars outside our solar system), scientists have gained insights into the

ALTERNATIVE SCIENTIFIC PERSPECTIVES

diversity and prevalence of planetary systems. The search for potentially habitable exoplanets focuses on identifying planets within the "habitable zone"—the region around a star where conditions might be suitable for liquid water and, potentially, life.

3. **Astrochemistry and Astrobiology:** The study of interstellar space and the chemical processes that occur in it provides important clues about the formation of the building blocks of life. By analyzing the composition of asteroids, comets, and interstellar dust, scientists can uncover the presence of organic molecules and amino acids—the building blocks of life as we know it.

4. **Radio and Optical SETI:** In the search for extraterrestrial intelligence (SETI), scientists scan the sky for signals that could be evidence of technological civilizations. Radio telescopes and optical telescopes are employed to detect artificially generated signals that stand out from the natural background noise of the universe.

The Drake Equation and the Fermi Paradox

The search for extraterrestrial life is often framed by the Drake Equation, an equation that estimates the number of technologically advanced civilizations in our galaxy. It takes into account factors such as the number of habitable planets, the fraction of planets where life emerges, and the lifespan of civilizations.

Despite the vast number of potentially habitable planets in the universe, the lack of evidence of extraterrestrial civilizations has sparked the Fermi Paradox. This paradox raises the question: If the conditions for life are common, why have we not detected any signs of advanced civilizations?

Several explanations have been proposed, including the possibility that technological civilizations self-destruct, or they are simply too far away for us to detect. Alternatively, advanced civilizations may exist but choose to remain hidden, or they have developed forms of communication that we cannot comprehend.

The Role of Astrobiology in the Search for the Dover Demon

In the context of the Dover Demon sightings, astrobiology can provide valuable insights into the plausibility of the creature's existence. By examining the conditions necessary for life on Earth and extrapolating to other celestial bodies, astrobiologists can evaluate the likelihood of an unknown cryptid species existing.

Astrobiology can also help to identify potential explanations for the Dover Demon sightings. For example, if the creature is thought to be an extraterrestrial life form, astrobiologists can examine its characteristics and compare them to known life forms hypothesized to exist in extreme environments, such as the possibility of silicon-based life. In contrast, if the Dover Demon is considered a terrestrial animal, astrobiologists can assess the feasibility of its adaptation to specific environmental conditions.

However, it is important to note that astrobiology alone cannot provide definitive answers about the existence of the Dover Demon or any other cryptid. The field relies on scientific evidence and critical inquiry to evaluate claims and hypotheses. In the case of the Dover Demon, a thorough investigation combining multiple scientific disciplines, including zoology, anatomy, and genetics, would be necessary to validate or debunk the sightings.

Resources and Further Reading

For those interested in exploring astrobiology and the search for extraterrestrial life further, the following resources provide a comprehensive overview of the field:

1. *Life Beyond Earth: The Search for Habitable Worlds in the Universe* by Athena Coustenis and Thérèse Encrenaz 2. *Astrobiology: A Very Short Introduction* by David C. Catling 3. *Exoplanets: Diamond Worlds, Super Earths, Pulsar Planets, and the New Search for Life Beyond Our Solar System* by Michael Summers and James Trefil 4. *The Eerie Silence: Renewing Our Search for Alien Intelligence* by Paul Davies

Additionally, websites like NASA's Astrobiology Program (astrobiology.nasa.gov) and the Search for Extraterrestrial Intelligence Institute (www.seti.org) provide up-to-date news, research, and resources on astrobiology and the search for extraterrestrial life.

Exercises

1. Research the Mars rovers' missions (e.g., Curiosity, Perseverance) and summarize the evidence they have found for the potential habitability of Mars. 2. Investigate the concept of "Goldilocks planets" and outline the characteristics that make a planet potentially habitable. 3. Analyze the advantages and drawbacks of using radio and optical methods for the search for extraterrestrial intelligence. Consider factors like signal strength, signal degradation, and the distance between civilizations. 4. Imagine you are an astrobiologist tasked with designing a mission to search for signs of life on one of Jupiter's icy moons. Outline the instruments and techniques you would employ to gather data and analyze samples. 5. Debate the implications of discovering extraterrestrial life on society, religion, and our understanding of our place in the universe. Discuss both the potential positive and negative impacts.

Improvements in Research and Data Collection

In the field of cryptozoology and paranormal research, advancements in research methods and data collection have played a crucial role in improving the credibility and scientific rigor of these disciplines. This section will explore some of the key improvements that have been made in recent years.

Technology Advancements

One of the most significant advancements in research and data collection is the development and widespread availability of advanced technology. This includes improvements in equipment used for capturing visual evidence, audio recordings, and collecting other types of data.

For example, high-resolution cameras with improved low-light capabilities have revolutionized the field of paranormal investigation. Researchers and investigators can now capture clear and detailed images and videos of potential paranormal phenomena, such as apparitions or unidentified creatures. These advancements have also allowed for more accurate analysis and scrutiny of the collected evidence.

In addition to cameras, there have been significant advancements in audio recording technology. Researchers can now capture high-quality audio recordings that can be analyzed for potential EVPs (Electronic Voice Phenomena) or other paranormal auditory phenomena. Furthermore, specialized software and algorithms have been developed to filter and enhance these recordings, making it easier to detect and analyze potential anomalies.

Furthermore, the widespread use of drones has opened up new possibilities for surveying and exploring remote or inaccessible areas. Drones equipped with high-definition cameras and thermal imaging technology can provide researchers with unprecedented views and perspectives. This technology is particularly valuable for studying elusive cryptids or conducting aerial surveys of areas with reported paranormal activity.

Data Analysis and Interpretation

Improvements in research methods and data collection techniques also extend to the analysis and interpretation of collected data. The advent of powerful computers and advanced statistical software has enabled researchers to process and analyze large amounts of data more efficiently.

For example, in cryptozoology, researchers can now employ GIS (Geographic Information System) technology to map reported sightings and analyze patterns and correlations. By overlaying sighting data on topographical maps and other relevant data layers, researchers can identify potential hotspots or migration patterns of cryptids.

In paranormal research, advancements in data analysis techniques have allowed for more systematic and objective scrutiny of evidence. For example, researchers can apply algorithms and statistical tests to analyze patterns in ghost hunting data or UFO sighting reports. By employing quantitative methods, researchers can identify trends, determine statistical significance, and draw more reliable conclusions.

Collaborative Research and Citizen Science

Another significant improvement in research and data collection is the increasing collaboration between professional researchers and amateur enthusiasts. This collaboration, often in the form of citizen science projects, has expanded the reach and scope of data collection efforts.

Cryptid and paranormal research organizations now actively involve the general public in data collection, analysis, and reporting. This collaborative approach not only increases the quantity of data collected but also encourages a more diverse range of perspectives and experiences.

Furthermore, advancements in technology, such as the availability of smartphone apps, make it easier for individuals to contribute data. For example, there are apps specifically designed for reporting cryptid sightings or submitting paranormal activity logs. This crowd-sourced approach to data collection allows for real-time data acquisition and a broader understanding of the phenomenon being studied.

Challenges and Considerations

While advancements in research methods and data collection have greatly improved the field of cryptozoology and paranormal research, there are still several challenges and considerations to bear in mind.

One challenge is the potential for data contamination or misinterpretation. With the democratization of technology, anyone can now contribute data, but not all data may be reliable or accurately reported. It is crucial for researchers to implement strict protocols for data collection and analysis to ensure the validity and integrity of the findings.

Moreover, the interpretation of collected data remains a complex task. Anomalies or patterns identified in data may have multiple possible explanations, ranging from natural phenomena to hoaxes or misperceptions. Researchers must remain vigilant and employ critical thinking and rigorous scientific methods to avoid false positives and to accurately interpret their findings.

Resources for Further Exploration

For those interested in delving deeper into the improvements in research and data collection in the field of cryptozoology and paranormal research, the following resources offer valuable insights and information:

- "Cryptozoology: Science & Speculation" by Chad Arment provides an in-depth exploration of the scientific methods used in the study of cryptids, including advancements in data collection and analysis.

- The Journal of Scientific Exploration is a peer-reviewed scientific journal that publishes research in the field of paranormal phenomena, including studies on data collection and analysis techniques.

- The Center for the Study of Anomalous Images, based at the University of Mississippi, conducts research on visual evidence in paranormal investigations, making significant contributions to the understanding of visual data collection and interpretation.

- The Mutual UFO Network (MUFON) is one of the largest and most reputable organizations dedicated to the study and investigation of UFO sightings, employing advanced data collection and analysis methods.

By leveraging advancements in technology, embracing collaborative research, and applying rigorous data analysis techniques, cryptozoology and paranormal research have evolved into more credible and scientifically informed fields. Continued improvements in research methods and data collection will further enhance our understanding of these enigmatic phenomena and potentially lead to groundbreaking discoveries in the future.

Reconciling Fringe Science with Mainstream Science

In the world of scientific inquiry, there is a delicate balance between mainstream science and fringe science. Mainstream science refers to the widely accepted theories and ideas that form the foundation of current scientific understanding. On the other hand, fringe science, also known as pseudoscience, refers to ideas that are not supported by empirical evidence and are considered to be outside the realm of scientific consensus. Reconciling these two areas of study can be a challenging task, but it is necessary for the advancement of scientific understanding.

One of the key challenges in reconciling fringe science with mainstream science is distinguishing between valid alternative ideas and pseudoscientific claims. While it is important to be open to new ideas and perspectives, it is equally important to critically evaluate these ideas based on rigorous scientific methods and evidence. This requires a careful examination of the experimental design, data analysis, and conclusions drawn from research.

A critical aspect of reconciling fringe science with mainstream science is the need for peer review. Peer review involves subjecting scientific research to the scrutiny of other experts in the field before it is published. This process ensures that the research meets the rigorous standards of scientific methodology and helps to separate valid contributions from pseudoscientific claims. Peer review allows for constructive feedback and encourages researchers to address any shortcomings in their work, ultimately strengthening the scientific community's understanding of the subject matter.

Moreover, interdisciplinary collaborations play a significant role in bridging the gap between fringe science and mainstream science. By collaborating with experts from various fields, researchers can bring different perspectives and knowledge to the table. This facilitates a more comprehensive understanding of the research topic and can help identify areas where fringe ideas may converge with mainstream scientific principles. For example, the field of astrobiology, which studies the possibility of extraterrestrial life, has benefitted from collaborations between biologists, chemists, physicists, and astronomers.

In addition to interdisciplinary collaborations, the integration of fringe science into mainstream science can be aided by improvements in research and data collection. Advancements in technology have enabled scientists to gather more accurate and comprehensive data, thereby providing a solid foundation for scientific investigation. For example, the use of advanced imaging techniques and DNA analysis has contributed to the understanding of cryptozoology, providing valuable insights into the existence of hidden or undiscovered species.

Reconciling fringe science with mainstream science also requires a shift in attitudes and perspectives within the scientific community. It is essential to foster an environment that encourages open-mindedness, curiosity, and respectful critique. By acknowledging the potential value of alternative ideas, scientists can explore new avenues of research and potentially challenge existing paradigms. However, it is crucial to maintain a healthy skepticism and rely on empirical evidence to distinguish between genuine scientific advancements and pseudoscientific claims.

Public engagement and education also play a crucial role in reconciling fringe science with mainstream science. It is important to communicate scientific concepts and findings to the general public in an accessible and engaging manner. This helps to dispel misconceptions and promotes a more informed and critical understanding of scientific inquiry. By encouraging public participation in scientific research and fostering an interest in the scientific method, we can bridge the gap between mainstream science and fringe science.

In conclusion, reconciling fringe science with mainstream science is a complex and ongoing process. It requires rigorous evaluation, peer review, interdisciplinary collaborations, technological advancements, a shift in attitudes, and public engagement. By embracing these strategies, scientists can navigate the fine line between openness to new ideas and the adherence to rigorous scientific standards. This will ultimately contribute to the advancement of scientific knowledge and our understanding of the natural world.

Bridging the Gap between Science and the Paranormal

Interdisciplinary Approaches

Interdisciplinary approaches play a crucial role in addressing complex phenomena that cannot be fully understood within the boundaries of a single discipline. When studying the paranormal and cryptozoology, it becomes evident that these topics require diverse perspectives and expertise from various fields. In this section, we will explore the importance of interdisciplinary approaches in advancing our understanding of the paranormal and cryptozoology, and we will discuss some specific examples of how different disciplines can contribute to this field of study.

The Value of Interdisciplinary Perspectives

The paranormal and cryptozoology involve a wide range of phenomena that challenge traditional scientific, cultural, and societal frameworks. These phenomena often exist at the intersection of multiple disciplines, such as psychology, sociology, biology, anthropology, and physics. By integrating knowledge and methodologies from different fields, interdisciplinary approaches offer unique insights and perspectives that can shed light on the complex nature of these phenomena.

One of the primary benefits of interdisciplinary approaches is the ability to fill gaps in knowledge and provide comprehensive explanations. For instance, when investigating a paranormal encounter, psychologists can analyze the cognitive processes and perceptions of individuals involved, while anthropologists can explore the cultural and societal beliefs surrounding the phenomenon. Biologists can examine the physical evidence, such as DNA samples or footprints, to determine if they are consistent with known species. By combining these perspectives, a more nuanced and holistic understanding of the phenomenon can be achieved.

Examples of Interdisciplinary Approaches

Let's explore a few examples of how interdisciplinary approaches can be applied to the study of the paranormal and cryptozoology:

Psychoacoustics and Ghostly Phenomena Psychoacoustics, a field that combines psychology and acoustics, can help us understand the auditory experiences often associated with ghostly phenomena. By studying how the brain processes sound and how auditory illusions occur, psychoacoustics can provide insights into why individuals perceive certain sounds as ghostly voices or footsteps. By collaborating with paranormal investigators and conducting controlled experiments in haunted locations, psychoacoustics researchers can analyze the acoustic properties and psychological factors that contribute to ghostly experiences.

Astrobiology and Extraterrestrial Cryptids Astrobiology, the study of life in the universe, can contribute to our understanding of cryptids with potential extraterrestrial origins. By considering the possibilities of life on other planets and the potential for extraterrestrial organisms to have visited Earth, astrobiologists can offer insights into the plausibility and characteristics of cryptids such as the Dover Demon. By combining knowledge from astrobiology, biology, and cryptozoology, researchers can explore the origins and evolutionary pathways of these cryptids, as well as investigate the potential for microbial life on other celestial bodies.

Spatial Analysis and Cryptozoological Hotspots Spatial analysis, a discipline that combines geography and computer science, can help identify cryptozoological hotspots. By analyzing reports of cryptid sightings, mapping their geographical locations, and applying statistical techniques, spatial analysts can identify areas with high densities of sightings, suggesting potential habitats or migration patterns of cryptids. This interdisciplinary approach allows researchers to focus their field investigations, increasing the likelihood of encountering and studying these elusive creatures.

Challenges and Limitations

While interdisciplinary approaches offer valuable insights, they also come with challenges and limitations. One of the main challenges is the need for effective communication and collaboration among experts from different disciplines. Each discipline has its own terminology, methodologies, and approaches to problem-solving. Overcoming these barriers requires open-mindedness, effective communication strategies, and a willingness to bridge the gaps between disciplines.

Another limitation is the potential for conflicting interpretations and perspectives among interdisciplinary researchers. Different fields may have competing theories or frameworks, which can lead to disagreements and challenges in integrating findings. In such cases, interdisciplinary scholars must carefully navigate these differences and seek common ground to develop unified explanations.

Conclusion

Interdisciplinary approaches are essential for advancing our understanding of the paranormal and cryptozoology. By integrating knowledge and methodologies from various fields, researchers can gain comprehensive insights into complex phenomena. Whether it is combining psychology and anthropology to study ghostly encounters, incorporating astrobiology into cryptozoological investigations, or utilizing spatial analysis to identify hotspots, interdisciplinary approaches open doors to new discoveries and perspectives. Embracing the value of collaboration and cross-disciplinary research will ultimately contribute to the growth and development of this field and its legitimacy within the broader scientific community.

In the next chapter, we will delve into the concept of cultural and folkloric significance, exploring how mythologies, folk beliefs, and popular culture shape our understanding and perception of the paranormal and cryptozoology.

Citizen Science and Amateur Research

Citizen science and amateur research play a crucial role in the field of cryptozoology and paranormal investigation. They involve the active participation of non-professionals, enthusiasts, and volunteers in scientific research and data collection. This section explores the significance of citizen science and amateur research, its benefits and limitations, and how it contributes to the understanding of cryptids and paranormal phenomena.

The Power of Citizen Science

Citizen science is a form of scientific collaboration that involves ordinary individuals who are not formally trained as scientists but actively contribute to scientific research. In the context of cryptozoology and paranormal investigation, citizen scientists are passionate individuals who actively seek out evidence, conduct investigations, and share their findings with the scientific community.

One of the key advantages of citizen science is the vast network of observers and enthusiasts who can document and report their encounters with cryptids or paranormal phenomena. This grassroots approach enables the collection of data from a wide range of locations, increasing the chances of capturing rare or elusive events. Additionally, citizen scientists often have local knowledge and familiarity with specific areas, which can provide valuable insights and help uncover hidden patterns or connections.

Citizen science projects also benefit from the collective efforts of a diverse and motivated community. These projects can engage people from various backgrounds and expertise, leading to interdisciplinary collaborations that bring together different perspectives and skills. This interdisciplinary approach can foster innovation and lead to novel research directions, challenging established scientific paradigms.

Challenges and Limitations

Despite its numerous benefits, citizen science and amateur research come with their own set of challenges and limitations. One of the main concerns is the reliability and accuracy of the data collected. Since citizen scientists may lack formal scientific training, there is a risk of biased observations, misinterpretation of evidence, or the introduction of personal beliefs and opinions. This can compromise the credibility of the research and make it difficult to establish rigorous scientific conclusions.

To address this challenge, citizen science projects often implement quality control measures and standardized protocols to ensure data consistency and accuracy. This may involve training programs, data validation by experts, and implementing robust data collection methodologies. By establishing clear guidelines and standards, citizen science projects can improve the reliability of the data and enhance its scientific value.

Another challenge is the accessibility and availability of resources for citizen scientists. Unlike professional researchers, citizen scientists often rely on their personal funds, equipment, and time to conduct investigations. Limited resources can restrict the scope and scale of their research, impacting the accuracy and completeness of their findings. Additionally, the lack of access to specialized equipment and advanced scientific tools may limit the types of observations and data that can be collected.

To overcome these challenges, citizen science projects can leverage technological advancements and collaborations with professional researchers. For example, crowd-sourcing platforms and mobile applications can facilitate data collection and enable citizen scientists to contribute more easily. Partnerships with academic institutions or research organizations can provide access to resources, expertise, and funding, empowering citizen scientists to conduct more in-depth investigations.

Contributions to Cryptozoology and Paranormal Investigation

Citizen science and amateur research have made significant contributions to the field of cryptozoology and paranormal investigation. By actively involving non-professionals in the research process, citizen science projects have expanded the scope of data collection and exploration, leading to the discovery of new evidence and the documentation of previously unknown cryptids and paranormal phenomena.

One notable example is the field of cryptozoology, where citizen scientists have played a pivotal role in documenting and reporting sightings of cryptids such as Bigfoot, Loch Ness Monster, and Chupacabra. Their passionate pursuit of evidence and firsthand experiences have contributed to the growing body of knowledge about these elusive creatures. Citizen science has also helped shed light on lesser-known cryptids and regional legends, providing valuable insights into local folklore and cultural heritage.

In the realm of paranormal investigation, citizen science has facilitated the documentation and understanding of ghostly encounters, haunted locations, and paranormal phenomena. Through the sharing of personal experiences, photographs, audio recordings, and video footage, citizen scientists have contributed to the body of evidence and challenged skeptics to consider alternative explanations. Their grassroots investigations have also highlighted the psychological and sociological dimensions of paranormal experiences, offering a more holistic understanding of the subject.

Unconventional Perspectives

While citizen science often adheres to traditional scientific methods and protocols, there is room for unconventional perspectives and approaches. The inherent flexibility and diversity of citizen science projects allow for the exploration of alternative hypotheses and the investigation of fringe phenomena.

For example, some citizen scientists may embrace metaphysical or supernatural explanations for cryptid encounters or paranormal phenomena. While these perspectives may not align with mainstream science, they can offer unique insights and generate hypotheses that challenge established scientific beliefs. This can provoke new lines of inquiry, spark intellectual debate, and ultimately push the boundaries of scientific understanding.

Resources for Citizen Scientists

For those interested in getting involved in citizen science and amateur research in the field of cryptozoology and paranormal investigation, there are a variety of resources available to support their endeavors. These resources provide guidance, training, and opportunities for collaboration with other enthusiasts and professionals.

Online platforms and forums dedicated to cryptozoology and the paranormal offer spaces for sharing experiences, discussing theories, and connecting with like-minded individuals. These platforms often provide access to research articles, investigation methodologies, and databases of reported sightings or paranormal events. They can serve as valuable sources of information for aspiring citizen scientists looking to embark on their own investigations or contribute to ongoing projects.

Furthermore, established research organizations and academic institutions may offer training programs or workshops on scientific methods, field techniques, and data analysis specific to cryptozoology and paranormal investigation. These educational opportunities can provide aspiring citizen scientists with the necessary skills and knowledge to conduct rigorous research and contribute meaningfully to the field.

In conclusion, citizen science and amateur research have emerged as powerful tools in the realm of cryptozoology and paranormal investigation. The active involvement of non-professionals brings new perspectives and expands the scope of data collection. While challenges exist, such as the reliability of data and limited resources, these can be overcome through standardization, quality control measures, and collaborations with professional researchers. Citizen science has made significant contributions to the understanding of cryptids and paranormal phenomena, challenging established scientific beliefs and promoting interdisciplinary collaborations. By embracing unconventional perspectives and leveraging available resources, citizen scientists can continue to push the boundaries of scientific exploration and expand our understanding of the unknown.

Collaboration between Scientists and Paranormal Investigators

Collaboration between scientists and paranormal investigators is a unique and complex relationship that requires mutual respect, open-mindedness, and effective communication. While scientists adhere to the principles of the scientific method and strive to explain phenomena through empirical evidence and rigorous experimentation, paranormal investigators explore unexplained occurrences and phenomena outside the realm of traditional science. Despite the differences in approach, collaboration between these two groups can provide valuable insights and advance our understanding of the paranormal.

One of the key challenges in collaboration between scientists and paranormal investigators is establishing a common ground for conducting research. Scientists may be skeptical of the claims made by paranormal investigators due to the lack of scientific rigor in their methodologies. On the other hand, paranormal investigators may perceive scientists as closed-minded and dismissive of their experiences. Bridging this gap requires both parties to acknowledge the strengths and limitations of their respective approaches and work towards a common goal of uncovering the truth.

To establish collaboration, scientists and paranormal investigators should engage in open dialogue and exchange knowledge. Scientists can provide guidance on research design, data collection, and analysis techniques, helping paranormal investigators adhere to scientific standards. Similarly, paranormal investigators can share their experiences, observations, and methodologies, enabling scientists to explore phenomena that fall outside the purview of traditional scientific investigation. This collaborative approach can contribute to a more comprehensive understanding of paranormal phenomena.

In order to foster collaboration, scientists and paranormal investigators can participate in joint research projects. These projects should be designed with a multidisciplinary approach, incorporating the methodologies and expertise of both scientists and paranormal investigators. For example, a project investigating haunted locations could involve scientists in collecting environmental data such as temperature, humidity, and electromagnetic fields, while paranormal investigators document their personal experiences and perform psychic or mediumship readings. By combining empirical data with subjective experiences, a more holistic understanding of the phenomena can be achieved.

It is important to note that collaboration between scientists and paranormal investigators is not without its challenges. Both parties need to be aware of potential biases that can affect the interpretation of results. Scientists should remain objective and utilize rigorous scientific methods to ensure the reliability and validity of the data. Paranormal investigators, on the other hand, need to be cautious of confirmation bias and the tendency to interpret ambiguous or inconclusive evidence in favor of their beliefs. Collaboration can help to mitigate these biases by promoting critical thinking and providing alternative perspectives.

In addition to joint research projects, collaboration can also take the form of knowledge sharing through conferences, workshops, and publications. Scientists can present their findings and theories to paranormal investigators, helping them to understand the current state of scientific knowledge and encouraging them to apply scientific principles in their investigations. Similarly, paranormal investigators can share their findings and experiences with scientists, providing them with insights into unexplained phenomena and potentially inspiring new avenues of scientific inquiry.

Collaboration between scientists and paranormal investigators can also have practical applications. For example, the study of paranormal phenomena can lead to the development of new technologies and methods that have broader implications beyond the realm of the paranormal. Investigation techniques such as the use of thermal imaging cameras, electromagnetic field detectors, and audio analysis software have found applications in fields like law enforcement, environmental monitoring, and building diagnostics. This interdisciplinary collaboration can lead to unexpected discoveries and innovations.

Despite the progress made in recent years, collaboration between scientists and paranormal investigators is still relatively uncommon and often met with skepticism from the scientific community. Overcoming this skepticism requires both groups to engage in respectful and constructive dialogue, promoting the idea that investigating the unexplained can coexist with scientific principles. By working together, scientists and paranormal investigators can contribute to a more comprehensive understanding of the mysterious and unexplained phenomena that continue to captivate our imagination.

Exercises

1. Choose a paranormal phenomenon or case study that interests you and discuss how scientists and paranormal investigators could collaborate to investigate it. Consider the strengths and limitations of each approach and how they could complement each other in understanding the phenomenon.

2. Research and analyze a scientific study that involved collaboration between scientists and paranormal investigators. Discuss the methodology used, the findings, and any challenges faced during the collaboration. Reflect on the implications of this collaboration for future research in the field.

3. Imagine you are organizing a conference on the intersection of science and the paranormal. Create a list of potential speakers from both scientific and paranormal investigation backgrounds. Explain how each speaker's expertise contributes to the theme of the conference and why their participation would be valuable.

4. Investigate and critically evaluate a popular paranormal investigation technique or tool. Examine its scientific validity, any supporting evidence or criticisms, and its application beyond paranormal investigations. Discuss whether scientists and paranormal investigators could collaborate to improve or validate the technique/tool.

Conclusion

Collaboration between scientists and paranormal investigators can bridge the gap between the scientific and paranormal communities, leading to a deeper understanding of unexplained phenomena. By acknowledging and respecting each other's approaches, engaging in open dialogue, and conducting joint research projects, scientists and paranormal investigators can work together to shed light on the mysteries of the paranormal. This collaboration has the potential to not only advance scientific knowledge but also enrich our cultural and societal understanding of the unexplained. The future of research in the paranormal lies in the hands of those willing to embrace collaboration and explore the unknown.

The Role of Education and Public Engagement

The role of education and public engagement is crucial in the study of cryptozoology and the paranormal. By promoting awareness, providing accurate information, and fostering critical thinking skills, education can help debunk myths and misconceptions while encouraging a scientific approach to investigating these phenomena. Public engagement, on the other hand, allows for the exchange of knowledge and experiences between researchers, enthusiasts, and the general public, enabling a collaborative exploration of the unknown. In this section, we will delve into the importance of education and public engagement in bridging the gap between scientific and paranormal communities.

Promoting Critical Thinking

Education plays a pivotal role in promoting critical thinking skills, which are essential for the study of cryptozoology and the paranormal. It encourages individuals to question, evaluate evidence, and apply logical reasoning to phenomena that defy conventional explanations. By incorporating courses on scientific methodology, logical reasoning, and research ethics into academic curricula, educational institutions can equip students with the necessary tools to approach cryptozoology and the paranormal with analytical rigor.

Example: Evaluating Paranormal Evidence To illustrate the importance of critical thinking, let's consider the analysis of paranormal evidence, such as photographs or testimonies. Education can teach individuals to scrutinize these forms of evidence by considering alternative explanations, analyzing the reliability of the sources, and assessing the methodology used to capture or document the phenomenon. For instance, students can learn about the common pitfalls of photographic analysis, such as pareidolia (the tendency to see meaningful patterns in random stimuli). By fostering a critical mindset, education empowers individuals to think critically when faced with paranormal claims.

Citizen Science and Amateur Research

Education and public engagement can also encourage participation in citizen science and amateur research projects. These initiatives allow individuals from various backgrounds to contribute to scientific investigations, data collection, and analysis. In the realm of cryptozoology and the paranormal, involving citizens and enthusiasts in research efforts can significantly broaden the scope of data collection and provide valuable insights.

Example: The Bigfoot Field Researchers Organization (BFRO) The Bigfoot Field Researchers Organization (BFRO) is an example of successful public engagement in the field of cryptozoology. The organization encourages individuals to report sightings, conduct field investigations, and share their findings. By involving the public in data collection and analysis, the BFRO has amassed a comprehensive database of Bigfoot sightings and related evidence. This collaboration between researchers and the public not only enhances the quantity of data but also brings diverse perspectives and expertise to the investigation.

Science Communication and Public Outreach

Another vital aspect of education and public engagement is effective science communication and public outreach. It is essential to present the findings and theories from the fields of cryptozoology and the paranormal in a clear, accessible, and engaging manner. By doing so, researchers can bridge the gap between scientific discourse and public understanding, dispel misconceptions, and inspire interest in further exploration.

Example: Popular Science Books and Documentaries Popular science books and documentaries have played a significant role in educating the public about cryptids and paranormal phenomena. Through a combination of storytelling, visual aids, and scientific explanations, these mediums have the power to captivate audiences and present complex concepts in an approachable manner. By leveraging the power of narrative and visual representation, researchers can spark curiosity and facilitate a deeper understanding of the subject matter.

Ethics and Responsible Investigation

Education and public engagement should also emphasize the importance of ethics and responsible investigation when studying cryptozoology and the paranormal. Researchers and enthusiasts must adopt ethical practices that respect the privacy and well-being of individuals involved in sightings or paranormal experiences. Education can provide guidelines and best practices for conducting investigations, ensuring that the rights and safety of all parties are upheld.

Example: Guidelines for Ethical Investigations For instance, guidelines for ethical investigations may include obtaining informed consent from witnesses or participants, respecting cultural beliefs and sensitivities, and never engaging in activities that could harm wildlife or ecosystems. By incorporating these ethical considerations into education and public engagement efforts, a higher standard of research and investigation can be put forth, promoting credibility and integrity in the field.

Conclusion

Education and public engagement play a vital role in bridging the gap between scientific perspectives and paranormal beliefs. By promoting critical thinking, encouraging citizen science and amateur research, facilitating science communication and public outreach, and emphasizing ethics and responsible investigation, education can empower individuals to approach the study of cryptozoology and the paranormal with scientific rigor. Similarly, public engagement allows for a collaborative exploration of these phenomena, promoting a greater understanding and appreciation of the unknown. The role of education and public engagement is crucial in fostering a balanced and informed approach to these intriguing fields of study.

Chapter 6: Cultural and Folkloric Significance

Mythology and Folklore

Creatures in Mythology

Mythology is rich with creatures that have captivated the imaginations of people throughout history. These legendary creatures often embody the cultural beliefs, fears, and values of different societies. In this section, we will explore some of the most fascinating and iconic creatures found in mythology from various cultures around the world.

Dragons

Dragons are perhaps the most well-known creatures in mythology. They appear in various forms in different cultures, but they are commonly depicted as large, winged reptiles with the ability to breathe fire. In many Eastern cultures, dragons are revered as symbols of wisdom, power, and good fortune. They often guard treasure or are seen as protectors of the natural world. In contrast, Western mythology often portrays dragons as fearsome and destructive creatures that must be vanquished by heroic figures. Examples of dragons in mythology include the Chinese dragon, the European dragon, and the Aztec serpent Quetzalcoatl.

Phoenix

The phoenix is a mythical bird that is widely recognized for its ability to rise from its own ashes. It is associated with themes of rebirth, renewal, and immortality. According to ancient Egyptian mythology, the phoenix symbolized the sun, with its death and subsequent rebirth signifying the daily cycle of the sun rising and setting. In Greek mythology, the phoenix was said to live for hundreds of years before building a nest and setting itself on fire. From the ashes, a new phoenix would be born, symbolizing the cycle of life and death.

Centaurs

Centaurs are creatures that have the upper body of a human and the lower body of a horse. In Greek mythology, centaurs were known for their wild and unpredictable behavior. They were often portrayed as half-human, half-beast creatures who lived in the wilderness and were skilled in hunting and archery. Some centaurs, such as Chiron, were renowned for their wisdom and teachings. Centaurs are often depicted as symbols of the conflict between civilization and nature, as they straddle the line between human and animal.

Sirens

Sirens were enchanting creatures in Greek mythology, often depicted as beautiful women with the wings of birds. They possessed an irresistible voice that lured sailors to their deaths, causing their ships to crash on the rocky shores. Sirens were known for their seductive abilities and their songs were said to be so mesmerizing that sailors couldn't resist following the sound, ultimately leading to their demise. The story of the sirens serves as a cautionary tale about the dangers of temptation and the consequences of falling prey to one's desires.

Kraken

The kraken is a legendary sea monster that originated in Scandinavian folklore. It is often described as a giant octopus or squid-like creature that dwells in the depths of the ocean. According to myths, the kraken was said to be large enough to overturn ships and create powerful whirlpools. It was feared by sailors who believed that encountering the kraken was a sign of impending doom. The kraken has since become a popular creature in modern literature and pop culture, representing the vast mysteries and dangers lurking beneath the sea.

Anubis

Anubis is an ancient Egyptian deity associated with death and the afterlife. He is most commonly depicted as a man with the head of a jackal. Anubis played a vital role in Egyptian funerary rituals, as he was believed to guide the souls of the dead to the underworld and preside over the weighing of the heart ceremony. This

MYTHOLOGY AND FOLKLORE

ceremony determined the fate of the deceased in the afterlife. Anubis is also considered a protector of graves and cemeteries, ensuring that the dead receive the proper rites and rituals in their journey to the afterlife.

These are just a few examples of the countless creatures found in mythology. Each one carries its own symbolism and cultural significance, offering insights into the beliefs and values of the societies that created them. Exploring the mythology of different cultures allows us to delve into the fascinating world of storytelling, imagination, and the human experience. By studying these mythical creatures, we gain a deeper understanding of how ancient civilizations interpreted and explained the world around them.

Tales and Legends of Local Cryptids

Tales and legends of local cryptids have been passed down through generations, captivating the imaginations of communities and fueling the fascination with mysterious creatures. These stories often originate from sightings or encounters with strange and elusive creatures that cannot be easily explained.

Local cryptids are unique to specific regions or areas, often becoming an integral part of the cultural heritage and folklore of those communities. These creatures are characterized by their mysterious nature and the fear or fascination they elicit among the local population. In this section, we will explore some of the tales and legends associated with local cryptids, shedding light on the cultural significance and storytelling traditions surrounding these mythical beings.

The Legend of the Mothman

One famous example of a local cryptid legend is the story of the Mothman, which originated in Point Pleasant, West Virginia. The Mothman is described as a large creature with glowing red eyes and enormous wings, resembling a humanoid moth. According to the legend, the Mothman appeared before the tragic collapse of the Silver Bridge in 1967, creating a connection between its sightings and the disaster. The legend has since become an integral part of the local folklore, inspiring books, movies, and a statue commemorating the creature.

The Chupacabra Myth

Another popular local cryptid legend is that of the Chupacabra, a creature believed to inhabit various regions, including Puerto Rico, Mexico, and Texas. The name "Chupacabra" translates to "goat-sucker" in Spanish, referencing the creature's reputed habit of sucking the blood of livestock, particularly goats. Descriptions of the Chupacabra vary, ranging from a reptilian creature to one resembling a kangaroo with sharp fangs. Sightings of the Chupacabra have sparked numerous investigations and debates about its existence, solidifying its place in local folklore.

The Jersey Devil Legend

The legend of the Jersey Devil originated in the Pine Barrens of New Jersey and has become deeply entrenched in regional folklore. According to the legend, the Jersey Devil is a winged creature with a horse-like head, goat-like legs, and bat-like wings. It is said to possess a piercing scream that instills fear in those who hear it. The tale of the Jersey Devil dates back to the early 18th century, with numerous claimed sightings since then. The legend has become so prevalent that it has inspired books, documentaries, and even a hockey team mascot.

The Ogopogo Legend

The Ogopogo legend finds its roots in the Okanagan Valley of British Columbia, Canada. According to indigenous folklore, Ogopogo is a large lake monster that resides in Okanagan Lake. Descriptions of the creature vary, with some accounts portraying it as a long, serpentine creature with humps, while others describe it as a reptilian-like creature with a horse-like head. Similar to legends of other lake monsters, Ogopogo sightings have led to intense speculation and research, while also contributing to tourism and the local economy.

The Bunyip of Australian Mythology

In Aboriginal Australian mythology, the Bunyip is a creature believed to inhabit waterholes, rivers, and swamps. Descriptions of the Bunyip vary across different Aboriginal cultures, but common features include a large size, dark fur or feathers, a dog-like face, and prominent tusks or fangs. The Bunyip is often portrayed as a malevolent spirit associated with danger and the supernatural. The legend of the Bunyip continues to be a significant part of Australian folklore and serves as a cautionary tale for children.

The Power of Myth and Folklore

Tales and legends of local cryptids play a vital role in shaping cultural identity and heritage. They serve as a means of passing down knowledge, values, and traditions from one generation to the next. These tales often carry moral lessons, cautionary messages, or explanations for natural phenomena, providing a sense of belonging and security within a community.

Myths and folklore surrounding local cryptids also reflect the human fascination with the unknown and the desire to explore and understand the mysteries of the world. These stories tap into our primal fears and curiosity, encouraging us to ponder the boundaries of our knowledge and the possibility of hidden realms beyond our understanding.

Moreover, cryptid legends are not confined to specific cultures or regions. They often transcend geographical boundaries, becoming global phenomena that capture the imaginations of people around the world. The enduring popularity of these legends is evident in their adaptation into various forms of media, including literature, movies, and art. This further reinforces their significance as cultural artifacts that continue to shape the way we perceive and interpret the world around us.

Ultimately, the tales and legends of local cryptids remind us of the power of storytelling and the enduring impact of myths and folklore. They offer a glimpse into the rich tapestry of human imagination and the intricate ways in which we make sense of the mysterious and unexplained. Whether considered as products of the human imagination or as beings that exist beyond our comprehension, local cryptids continue to captivate our collective consciousness, providing endless inspiration and fascination.

Summary

In this section, we explored the tales and legends associated with local cryptids. These stories, deeply rooted in cultural traditions and folklore, have become an integral part of the communities that embrace them. We examined examples such as the Mothman, the Chupacabra, the Jersey Devil, Ogopogo, and the Bunyip, each offering unique insights into the power of myth and the enduring appeal of cryptid legends.

These tales serve as windows into the human imagination, showcasing our deep-seated fascination with the unknown and the supernatural. They not only provide entertainment and inspiration but also shape cultural identity, transmit knowledge, and instill a sense of wonder in people of all ages. Whether believed to be real or considered products of storytelling, local cryptids continue to inspire curiosity and spark conversations about the mysteries of our world.

As we move forward in our exploration of the paranormal and the unexplained, it is crucial to hold these tales and legends in high regard, appreciating their cultural significance while remaining open to scientific investigation and critical thinking.

By combining our fascination with the unknown with rigorous scientific inquiry, we can strive to uncover the truth behind these captivating stories and deepen our understanding of the world we inhabit.

Cross-Cultural Comparisons

In the field of cryptozoology, cross-cultural comparisons play an important role in understanding the diversity and universality of cryptid beliefs across different societies and belief systems. By examining how various cultures perceive and interpret cryptids, researchers can gain valuable insights into the significance of these creatures within different cultural contexts. This section explores some of the key aspects of cross-cultural comparisons in cryptozoology, including the role of folklore, cultural symbolism, and the influence of regional beliefs.

Folklore and Mythology

Folklore and mythology provide a rich source of cross-cultural comparisons in the study of cryptids. Many legendary creatures, such as dragons, werewolves, and mermaids, are found in the mythologies of different cultures around the world. These creatures often share common characteristics and themes, despite originating from diverse cultural backgrounds.

For example, the belief in water-dwelling creatures, such as the Loch Ness Monster in Scotland and the Ogopogo in Canada, can be traced back to ancient myths and legends that depict similar creatures across different cultures. These myths often serve as cautionary tales or explain natural phenomena, such as explaining the mysterious disappearances of people near bodies of water.

By comparing these stories and legends from different cultures, researchers can identify recurring patterns and themes in the descriptions and behaviors of cryptids. This can provide valuable insights into the universal human fascination with mysterious creatures and the role they play in our collective imagination.

Cultural Symbolism

Cryptids often hold deep cultural symbolism and meaning within specific communities. This symbolism can vary significantly from one culture to another, reflecting the unique cultural values and beliefs of each society.

For instance, the Yeti, also known as the Abominable Snowman, is a legendary creature believed to inhabit the mountains of the Himalayas. In Tibetan and Nepali culture, the Yeti symbolizes strength, resilience, and adaptability. It is considered a sacred guardian of the mountains and is revered as a spiritual being.

In contrast, the Sasquatch, a cryptid believed to inhabit the forests of North America, carries different cultural symbolism. For Native American tribes, the Sasquatch represents a powerful and elusive forest spirit that possesses both positive and negative qualities. It is often associated with the wilderness and serves as a reminder of the interconnectedness between humans and nature.

These examples highlight how cryptids can hold different meanings and cultural significance, depending on the context in which they are interpreted. Analyzing these cultural symbols can provide valuable insights into the relationship between humans and the natural world and the ways in which different cultures perceive and interact with cryptids.

Influence of Regional Beliefs

Regional beliefs and customs can heavily influence the perception and interpretation of cryptids within specific cultural contexts. Local traditions, historical events, and environmental factors all play a role in shaping people's beliefs about these creatures.

For instance, the Chupacabra, a cryptid believed to attack and drink the blood of livestock, originated in Puerto Rico but quickly gained popularity across Latin America and even in parts of the United States. The belief in the Chupacabra can be traced back to a combination of local legends, reports of strange animal killings, and the influence of popular media.

Similarly, the Yowie, a cryptid believed to inhabit the Australian wilderness, is deeply rooted in Aboriginal mythology and cultural beliefs. Aboriginal communities have long shared stories of encounters with Yowies and consider them an integral part of their cultural heritage. The belief in Yowies is closely tied to the spiritual connection that Aboriginal people have with the land and their respect for the natural environment.

By understanding the regional beliefs and cultural influences that shape people's perceptions of cryptids, researchers can gain a comprehensive understanding of the diversity and complexity of these beliefs across different cultures.

Conclusion

Cross-cultural comparisons play a vital role in the study of cryptids, providing researchers with insights into the universal human fascination with mysterious creatures and their significance within different cultural contexts. By analyzing folklore, cultural symbolism, and regional beliefs, researchers can unravel the complex relationship between humans and cryptids, as well as the cultural, historical, and environmental factors that shape these beliefs.

The study of cross-cultural comparisons not only contributes to the field of cryptozoology but also offers broader insights into the ways in which humans perceive, interpret, and interact with the natural world. It highlights the diversity and richness of human cultures and emphasizes the importance of cultural perspective in understanding and appreciating different belief systems.

As cryptozoology continues to evolve and expand as a field of study, further research into cross-cultural comparisons will undoubtedly uncover new insights and connections, contributing to our collective understanding of cryptids and their cultural significance.

Cryptozoology in Popular Culture

Literature and Fiction

Literature and fiction have played a significant role in shaping our perceptions and understanding of cryptids and their existence. Throughout history, countless books, poems, and stories have been written about mysterious creatures, sparking our imaginations and fueling our curiosity. In this section, we will explore the influence of literature and fiction on the field of cryptozoology, examining the various ways in which they have contributed to our knowledge and beliefs.

The Power of Storytelling

Storytelling has always been an integral part of human culture, serving as a means to entertain, educate, and transmit knowledge. When it comes to cryptids, literature and fiction have allowed us to delve into the realm of the unknown and explore the possibilities of undiscovered creatures. Authors and storytellers have the freedom to create captivating narratives that captivate readers, evoking emotions and provoking thought.

One classic example of literature's influence on cryptozoology is Mary Shelley's "Frankenstein." Although not a cryptid itself, the story of a scientist creating life from dead body parts raises important questions about the boundaries of scientific exploration and the ethical considerations surrounding the creation of new beings. This novel, published in 1818, introduced themes of human curiosity and the consequences of playing god, which continue to resonate in discussions about cryptids and the limits of scientific understanding.

Cryptids as Literary Characters

Literature has also provided a platform for cryptids to be portrayed as characters, further adding to their mystique and intrigue. Authors have given life to cryptids by incorporating them into their stories, often imbuing them with unique personalities, motivations, and behaviors. This allows readers to connect with these creatures on a deeper level, blurring the line between reality and fiction.

A notable example of this is found in Sir Arthur Conan Doyle's "The Hound of the Baskervilles." In this detective novel, the monstrous hound terrorizes the inhabitants of the Baskerville estate, creating an atmosphere of fear and suspense. While the hound is depicted as a supernatural creature in the story, it draws inspiration from local legends and reports of large, ferocious dogs. The inclusion of the hound as a cryptid in the narrative adds an element of intrigue and mystery to the story, captivating readers and leaving them questioning the existence of such creatures.

Inspiration for Cryptozoological Research

Literature and fiction have not only fueled our imagination but have also served as sources of inspiration for cryptozoological research. Many researchers and enthusiasts have been driven by the desire to uncover the truth behind the stories and legends that have captured our attention for centuries.

For instance, the legend of the Loch Ness Monster has inspired numerous books, both fiction and non-fiction, dedicated to exploring the possibility of its existence. Authors have delved into eyewitness accounts, analyzed photographs, and examined the scientific evidence in an effort to solve the mystery once and for all. While the existence of the Loch Ness Monster remains unconfirmed, these literary works have contributed to the ongoing discussion and sparked further scientific inquiry into the realm of lake monsters.

Fictional Cryptids and Real-World Discoveries

Interestingly, literature and fiction have, on occasion, predicted real-world discoveries of new species that were previously thought to be purely fictional. These instances blur the line between imagination and reality, challenging our understanding of what is possible.

One notable example is the coelacanth, a prehistoric fish once believed to be extinct but was discovered alive and well in the deep oceans. This fish, often referred to as a "living fossil," had been the subject of countless fictional stories, capturing the imagination of many. The discovery of the coelacanth in 1938 not only surprised the scientific world but also demonstrated the potential for real-life creatures to defy our expectations and emerge from the pages of fiction.

Exploring the Limits of Imagination

Literature and fiction provide us with the opportunity to explore the realms of possibility, challenge our preconceived notions, and expand our understanding of the world around us. While some may dismiss these stories as mere fantasies, they play a valuable role in shaping our perceptions, sparking scientific curiosity, and driving further research.

It is important to approach literature and fiction with an open mind, recognizing that they offer a unique lens through which we can examine cryptids and the paranormal. By embracing the power of imagination, we can uncover new insights and push the boundaries of scientific knowledge. So, let us continue to explore the captivating world of cryptids through literature and fiction, for it is within these stories that the seeds of discovery are often sown.

Further Reading:

- *Cryptozoology: Out of Time Place Scale* by David Redden
- *Monsters: A Bestiary of Devils, Demons, Vampires, Werewolves, and Other Magical Creatures* by Christopher Dell
- *Cryptid Creatures: A Field Guide* by Kelly Milner Halls

Movies and Television

Movies and television have played a significant role in shaping the popular perception and fascination with cryptozoology and paranormal phenomena. They have brought cryptids and aliens to life on the big and small screen, captivating audiences with their mysterious and often terrifying portrayals. In this section, we will explore the influence of movies and television on the field of cryptozoology and examine how they have contributed to the cultural significance of these topics.

Cryptozoology in Movies

Cryptozoological creatures have made their way onto the silver screen in various forms, from menacing monsters to misunderstood beings. These movies not only provide entertainment but also serve as a source of inspiration and information for those interested in the study of cryptids.

One famous example is the movie "Jurassic Park" (1993), directed by Steven Spielberg. Although not directly about cryptozoology, the film showcases the scientific study and resurrection of long-extinct dinosaurs. The movie's success sparked a renewed interest in prehistoric creatures, prompting individuals to question if other ancient or undiscovered animals could still exist.

Another notable film is "The Loch Ness Horror" (1981), a horror movie featuring the legendary Loch Ness Monster. While the film leans more towards the fictional side, it highlights the enduring fascination with cryptids and their presence in popular culture.

Movies like "King Kong" (1933) and its various remakes, including the 2005 version directed by Peter Jackson, have also introduced audiences to larger-than-life creatures. Although Kong is a fictional character, these films tap into the collective imagination surrounding mysterious and powerful creatures that lurk in unexplored regions of the world.

These movies and many others have not only contributed to the entertainment value but have also sparked discussions and debates about the possibility of unknown creatures existing in remote areas of the planet.

Paranormal Phenomena on Television

Television has been instrumental in bringing paranormal phenomena into people's homes, fueling their interest and curiosity. Various TV shows and documentaries have explored topics such as ghosts, UFO sightings, and alien encounters, captivating viewers with their investigations and alleged evidence.

One popular television show that has gained a cult following is "The X-Files" (1993-2018), created by Chris Carter. The series follows two FBI agents as they investigate unsolved cases involving paranormal phenomena, including aliens, government conspiracies, and cryptids. Through thought-provoking storytelling and complex characters, "The X-Files" has shaped the way people perceive and discuss the paranormal.

Another show that focuses on cryptozoology is "MonsterQuest" (2007-2010), which aired on the History Channel. This documentary-style series delves into the legends and sightings of various cryptids, such as Bigfoot, the Chupacabra, and the Loch Ness Monster. The show combines eyewitness testimonies, expert analyses, and scientific investigations to provide a comprehensive exploration of these mysterious creatures.

In addition to dedicated paranormal and cryptozoology shows, mainstream programs such as "Ghost Hunters" and "Ancient Aliens" have also contributed to the cultural fascination with the unexplained. These shows feature investigations into haunted locations and explore theories about extraterrestrial visitations.

Through their captivating narratives, compelling evidence, and scientific perspectives, these television shows have not only entertained audiences but have also contributed to the public's interest in and acceptance of paranormal phenomena.

The Influence on Cryptozoology and Paranormal Beliefs

Movies and television have had a significant impact on shaping public perception and beliefs about cryptozoology and paranormal phenomena. While some may argue that these portrayals contribute to the sensationalism and misrepresentation of these fields, others believe that they pique curiosity and inspire further exploration and research.

Movies and television shows serve as a gateway for individuals to become interested in cryptids and the paranormal. They introduce these topics to a wider audience, igniting a sense of wonder and intrigue. Viewers who are captivated by what they see on screen may go on to further investigate and learn about the real-life counterparts to the fictional creatures.

Additionally, these forms of media provide a platform for experts in the field to share their knowledge and experiences. Many cryptozoologists and paranormal investigators have made appearances on television programs, sharing their expertise and providing insights into their research. This exposure helps to legitimize the fields and promote a greater understanding of the scientific approaches taken in these areas of study.

However, it is essential to approach movies and television shows with a critical eye. While they may be entertaining and sometimes informative, it is crucial to distinguish between fact and fiction. Not all portrayals accurately represent the scientific methods and evidence-based approaches used in cryptozoology and paranormal research. Engaging in further research beyond what is presented on screen is necessary to develop a well-rounded understanding of these topics.

In conclusion, movies and television have played a significant role in popularizing cryptozoology and paranormal phenomena. They have introduced audiences to cryptids and aliens, fueling curiosity and contributing to the cultural significance of these topics. While the influence of movies and television should not be underestimated, it is essential to approach these portrayals critically and seek out accurate and reliable information to develop a comprehensive understanding of these fields.

Cryptozoology in Art and Music

Cryptozoology, the study of unknown and undiscovered creatures, has captured the imagination of artists and musicians throughout history. From ancient cave paintings to modern music videos, cryptozoological themes have been depicted in various art forms, creating a rich tapestry of creativity and cultural significance. In this section, we will explore the ways in which art and music have been influenced by cryptozoology, and how they, in turn, have shaped and influenced the field.

Artistic Depictions of Cryptids

Art has long served as a medium for storytelling, mythology, and cultural expression. Throughout history, artists have used their creativity and imagination to bring cryptids to life on canvas, sculpture, and other artistic media. These depictions not only entertain and inspire, but also contribute to the cultural significance of cryptids.

One of the most famous examples of cryptozoological art is the Loch Ness Monster, or "Nessie." The legendary creature has been the subject of countless paintings, drawings, and sculptures, capturing the imagination of artists and audiences alike. These artworks often depict the creature in various poses and settings, ranging from serene and majestic to fearsome and mysterious. They not only convey the physical appearance of the Loch Ness Monster but also convey the sense of wonder and awe that surrounds it.

Similarly, Bigfoot, another iconic cryptid, has been a popular subject for artists. Paintings and illustrations of Bigfoot often depict the creature in its natural habitat, surrounded by dense forests and towering mountains. Some artists choose to emphasize the elusive nature of Bigfoot, depicting it partially hidden behind trees or disappearing into the wilderness. These artistic interpretations not only capture the physical characteristics of the creature but also reflect the sense of intrigue and mystery that surrounds it.

In addition to specific cryptids, artists have also explored broader cryptozoological themes in their works. They may create scenes depicting the interaction between humans and cryptids, exploring the potential harmony or conflict between the two. These artworks often invite viewers to contemplate the existence of unknown creatures and their place in the world.

Music Inspired by Cryptids

Music, like art, has the power to evoke emotions, tell stories, and capture the imagination. Cryptids have served as a source of inspiration for musicians across genres, from folk and rock to electronic and metal. Through their lyrics, melodies, and soundscapes, these musicians bring the world of cryptozoology to life.

Folk music has a long history of incorporating cryptid themes. Songs about the Loch Ness Monster, Bigfoot, and other legendary creatures have been passed down through generations, preserving the stories and legends surrounding these cryptids. These songs often blend elements of mystery, adventure, and the natural world, creating a sense of connection to the folklore and traditions of a particular region.

In more contemporary genres, cryptids continue to inspire musicians. Rock and metal bands, for example, often draw on cryptid imagery and themes to create atmospheric and evocative music. They may use heavy riffs, haunting melodies, and intense lyrics to convey the mystery and power of cryptids. These songs not only entertain but also tap into the primal fascination with the unknown and unexplained.

Beyond specific cryptids, some musicians explore broader cryptozoological concepts in their work. They may use samples or field recordings of animal sounds to create a sense of immersion and otherworldliness. Others incorporate elements of folklore and mythology into their lyrics or incorporate cryptid imagery into their album artwork. In doing so, they invite listeners to consider the existence of hidden creatures and the mysteries of the natural world.

The Intersection of Art, Music, and Cryptozoology

The relationship between art, music, and cryptozoology is a symbiotic one. Artists and musicians draw inspiration from cryptozoology to create works that captivate and engage audiences. In turn, these artistic interpretations contribute to the cultural significance and popular imagination surrounding cryptids.

Art and music not only entertain but also play a crucial role in shaping our understanding of the world around us. They allow us to explore the mysteries of the natural world, challenge our perceptions, and spark our curiosity. By incorporating cryptid themes into their work, artists and musicians encourage us to question the boundaries of what is known and what is yet to be discovered.

Moreover, art and music can serve as a gateway to further exploration and research. They can inspire individuals to delve deeper into the field of cryptozoology, sparking an interest in scientific investigation and inquiry. They also provide a platform for dialogue and discussion, allowing different perspectives and interpretations to be shared and explored.

In conclusion, the influence of cryptozoology on art and music is undeniable. Artists and musicians have been captivated by the mysteries and wonders of cryptids, creating a diverse and vibrant body of work that both entertains and inspires. Through their creative expressions, they contribute to the cultural significance and popular imagination surrounding cryptids, inviting us to explore the unknown and question the world around us.

Influence on Cryptozoology and Paranormal Beliefs

The field of cryptozoology and paranormal beliefs has had a significant influence on popular culture and society as a whole. The allure of mysterious creatures and unexplained phenomena has captured the imagination of people across different cultures and generations. In this section, we will explore the various ways in which cryptozoology and paranormal beliefs have influenced our society, ranging from literature and fiction to movies and television.

Literature and Fiction

Cryptozoology and paranormal beliefs have provided fertile ground for writers and authors to create captivating stories and works of fiction. These narratives often center around encounters with cryptids and explore the unknown and mysterious aspects of the world. One of the most famous examples is the Loch Ness Monster, which has inspired numerous books, including "The Loch" by Steve Alten and "The Water Horse" by Dick King-Smith. These stories not only entertain readers but also fuel their curiosity about the existence of these creatures.

In addition to stand-alone novels, cryptozoology and paranormal beliefs have also influenced entire genres of literature. Horror fiction, in particular, often incorporates elements of the supernatural and cryptids to create spine-chilling stories. Authors like H.P. Lovecraft, with his iconic Cthulhu Mythos, have popularized the notion of ancient and malevolent beings lurking in the shadows. These stories not only entertain readers but also shape their beliefs and perceptions of the paranormal.

Movies and Television

Cryptozoology and paranormal beliefs have become prominent themes in movies and television shows, appealing to both mainstream audiences and enthusiasts of the genre. Countless films have been made featuring cryptids such as Bigfoot, the Chupacabra, and the Jersey Devil. These movies portray these creatures as both terrifying and fascinating, attracting viewers with their mysterious nature.

Popular examples include "Harry and the Hendersons," a heartwarming comedy about a family adopted by a friendly Bigfoot, and "The Mothman Prophecies," a thriller based on the real-life accounts of the Mothman sightings in West Virginia.

These films not only entertain viewers but also contribute to the perpetuation of cryptozoology and paranormal beliefs in popular culture.

Moreover, the television industry has embraced cryptozoology and paranormal beliefs, with shows dedicated to exploring and investigating mysterious creatures and phenomena. "Destination Truth" and "Finding Bigfoot" are two popular examples, where teams of investigators travel to different locations in search of evidence of cryptids. These shows not only entertain viewers but also encourage them to engage with the possibility of the existence of these creatures.

Cryptozoology in Art and Music

Cryptozoology has also found its place in various art forms, including visual arts and music. Artists often depict cryptids in their works, capturing both their awe-inspiring and terrifying aspects. Paintings, sculptures, and illustrations featuring creatures like the Loch Ness Monster and Bigfoot serve as visual representations of these mysterious beings.

In music, cryptids and paranormal beliefs have inspired numerous songs. Musicians often draw from the enigmatic nature of these creatures to create haunting melodies and lyrics. For example, the song "Werewolves of London" by Warren Zevon tells the story of encounters with werewolves in the streets of London. These artistic expressions not only entertain listeners but also evoke a sense of wonder and intrigue about the unknown.

Influence on Cryptozoology and Paranormal Beliefs

The influence of popular culture on cryptozoology and paranormal beliefs extends beyond mere entertainment value. It plays a significant role in shaping and reinforcing people's beliefs and attitudes towards these phenomena. The portrayal of cryptids and paranormal encounters in literature, movies, and television creates a sense of familiarity and plausibility, blurring the lines between fiction and reality.

However, it is crucial to approach these depictions with a critical mindset. While popular culture can ignite curiosity and fascination, it can also contribute to the spread of misinformation and sensationalism. It is important to balance entertainment with a healthy dose of skepticism and scientific inquiry when exploring cryptozoology and paranormal beliefs.

In conclusion, cryptozoology and paranormal beliefs have left a lasting impact on popular culture and society. Through literature, movies, television, art, and music, these phenomena have captured our imagination, eliciting a sense of wonder and curiosity. However, it is essential to approach these depictions with a critical mindset, separating fact from fiction and embracing scientific inquiry to further our understanding of the unknown.

The Role of Belief Systems in Cryptozoology

Folk Beliefs and Superstitions

Folk beliefs and superstitions play a significant role in the field of cryptozoology. They provide a cultural and historical context for understanding the origins and evolution of cryptid sightings and legends. In this section, we will explore the influence of folk beliefs and superstitions on cryptozoological phenomena, their role in shaping the perception of cryptids, and their impact on local communities.

Origins of Folk Beliefs and Superstitions

Folk beliefs and superstitions have their roots in ancient cultures and traditions. They are often derived from a combination of mythological, religious, and cultural influences. These beliefs have been passed down through generations and have become ingrained in the fabric of society.

One common origin of folk beliefs is the need to explain the unexplained. When faced with mysterious occurrences or encounters with the unknown, people often resort to superstitions as a way to make sense of their experiences. These beliefs provide a sense of comfort and control, offering explanations for events that may otherwise be inexplicable.

Influence on Cryptozoological Phenomena

Folk beliefs and superstitions have a profound influence on cryptozoological phenomena. They contribute to the creation and perpetuation of cryptid legends and sightings. For example, the legend of the Chupacabra in Latin American folklore originated from the belief in a creature that feeds on the blood of livestock. Similar stories of blood-sucking creatures can be found in various cultures around the world.

These beliefs not only shape the perception of cryptids but also impact the way they are portrayed in popular culture. In many cases, cryptids are depicted as fearsome and dangerous creatures, reflecting the superstitions and fears associated with them. This portrayal often leads to sensationalized media coverage and further perpetuates the belief in their existence.

Impact on Local Communities

Folk beliefs and superstitions surrounding cryptids can have a significant impact on local communities. In areas where cryptid sightings are common, these beliefs become deeply rooted in the local culture. They contribute to a sense of identity and pride, as well as attracting tourists and researchers interested in studying these creatures.

However, there can also be negative consequences associated with these beliefs. In some cases, local communities may experience economic exploitation or damage to their reputation due to exaggerated or fabricated cryptid sightings. Additionally, strong adherence to superstitions can hinder scientific investigation and impede the advancement of knowledge in the field of cryptozoology.

Challenges and Ethical Considerations

Studying and understanding folk beliefs and superstitions in the context of cryptozoology present several challenges and ethical considerations. Firstly, there is the issue of cultural sensitivity and respect for local customs and traditions. Researchers must approach these beliefs with an open mind and a willingness to learn from the perspectives of the communities they study.

Additionally, it is crucial to differentiate between genuine eyewitness accounts and fabricated or exaggerated stories influenced by folk beliefs. Investigators must employ critical thinking and proper scientific methodology to separate fact from fantasy. This requires integrating sociological and psychological perspectives to understand the motivations and biases that may influence the reporting of cryptid sightings.

Examples and Case Studies

To illustrate the influence of folk beliefs and superstitions on cryptozoological phenomena, let's consider the case of the Loch Ness Monster. The legend of the Loch Ness Monster originated from centuries-old Scottish folklore. The belief in a monster inhabiting the depths of Loch Ness has captured the imagination of people worldwide, leading to numerous sightings and expeditions to uncover the truth.

One prominent example of the impact of folk beliefs is the practice of "Nessie hunting" among locals and tourists. This activity has become a significant source of revenue for the surrounding communities, with boat tours and souvenir shops catering to the tourists hoping to catch a glimpse of the elusive creature. The belief in the Loch Ness Monster has become deeply embedded in the cultural fabric of the region, contributing to its tourist appeal.

Conclusion

Folk beliefs and superstitions have a profound influence on cryptozoological phenomena. They shape the perception and portrayal of cryptids, impact local communities, and present challenges for researchers in the field. Understanding the origins and significance of these beliefs can provide valuable insights into the cultural and societal dimensions of cryptozoology. However, it is crucial to approach these beliefs with caution, employing scientific methodology and cultural sensitivity to separate fact from fiction.

Religious Interpretations

Religious interpretations play a significant role in shaping beliefs and attitudes towards cryptids and paranormal phenomena. Many religious traditions have unique perspectives on these phenomena, often incorporating them into their cosmologies, mythologies, and spiritual practices. In this section, we will explore some of the common religious interpretations associated with cryptozoology and the paranormal.

Theological Perspectives

One of the theological interpretations of cryptids and paranormal phenomena is rooted in the concept of the supernatural. In various religious traditions, it is believed that these phenomena are manifestations of divine or otherworldly beings. For example, in Christianity, some believers consider cryptids as part of God's creation, while others may interpret them as demonic entities or fallen angels. Similarly, in Hinduism, cryptids and paranormal phenomena are often seen as manifestations of deities or powerful supernatural beings.

These theological interpretations provide believers with frameworks to understand and interpret encounters with cryptids and paranormal phenomena. They often reflect the religious teachings, values, and worldviews of the respective traditions, shaping believers' perceptions and responses to such encounters.

Symbolic and Allegorical Meanings

Religious interpretations of cryptids and paranormal phenomena also extend beyond literal explanations. Many religious traditions view these phenomena through a symbolic or allegorical lens, assigning them deeper meanings and spiritual significance. For example, the Loch Ness Monster, known as "Nessie," has been associated with the water spirits or kelpies in Scottish folklore. These interpretations often serve as cautionary tales or moral lessons, emphasizing the dangers of stepping into the unknown or the consequences of human actions.

Religious texts and scriptures are often mined for metaphors and allegorical references that can be applied to cryptid sightings and paranormal experiences. These interpretations allow believers to connect their encounters with deeper spiritual truths and understandings, providing a sense of purpose and guidance in navigating mysterious and unexplained phenomena.

Miracles and Divine Intervention

In some religious traditions, cryptids and paranormal phenomena are seen as manifestations of miracles or divine intervention. For example, in Islam, there are tales of sightings of giant creatures known as "marids," believed to be powerful jinn (supernatural beings) mentioned in the Quran. These encounters are considered miraculous and are seen as signs of divine presence and intervention in the natural world.

Similarly, in certain branches of Christianity, sightings of angels or apparitions are interpreted as divine messages or visitations. These encounters are believed to have profound spiritual significance, often inspiring faith, devotion, and transformation in the lives of those who experience them.

Rituals and Spiritual Practices

Religious interpretations of cryptids and paranormal phenomena also influence the development of rituals and spiritual practices. In some indigenous and animistic traditions, encounters with cryptids are seen as interactions with powerful spiritual beings who inhabit the natural world. These traditions often incorporate rituals, offerings, and ceremonies aimed at honoring and appeasing these beings, seeking their protection or blessings.

Furthermore, paranormal phenomena such as ghostly apparitions are often linked to the spiritual realm and the afterlife in many religious traditions. Practices like prayer, meditation, and spiritual cleansing are commonly used to connect with or ward off these entities and maintain spiritual well-being.

Challenges and Controversies

While religious interpretations contribute to the diverse tapestry of beliefs surrounding cryptids and paranormal phenomena, they also present challenges and controversies. Sceptics may dismiss these interpretations as mere superstition or irrational beliefs, while believers may argue for the validity and truth of their religious experiences.

Moreover, the interplay between religious interpretations and scientific explanations can give rise to tensions and conflicts. The scientific approach seeks naturalistic and empirical explanations, often conflicting with religious or spiritual interpretations that involve supernatural or metaphysical concepts.

Navigating these complexities requires open dialogue, respect for different perspectives, and an appreciation for the subjective nature of religious experiences. The study of religious interpretations of cryptids and paranormal phenomena offers insights into the human quest for meaning, the role of spirituality in interpreting the unknown, and the diverse ways in which people make sense of the mysterious.

In conclusion, religious interpretations have a significant impact on how people understand and interpret cryptids and paranormal phenomena. These interpretations may range from theological perspectives to symbolic meanings, from miracles to rituals, and spiritual practices. While they offer believers a framework to make sense of the unexplained, they also present challenges and controversies in the context of scientific inquiry. Understanding religious interpretations enhances our comprehension of the cultural, social, and personal dimensions of cryptids and the paranormal.

Psychological and Sociological Perspectives

In understanding the phenomenon of cryptids and alien encounters, it is essential to explore the psychological and sociological perspectives that shape beliefs, experiences, and reactions to these phenomena. Psychological factors explore the cognitive processes, individual beliefs, and emotional responses, while sociological perspectives delve into the influence of culture, society, and group dynamics on the interpretation of these phenomena. Together, these perspectives provide valuable insights into why people believe in and engage with cryptids and aliens.

Cognitive Processes and Beliefs

Psychological perspectives highlight the role of cognitive processes in shaping beliefs about cryptids and aliens. One prominent theory is the concept of pareidolia, which refers to the tendency to perceive meaningful patterns or connections in random or ambiguous stimuli. For example, people may interpret blurry photographs or distorted sounds as evidence of cryptids or aliens due to this perceptual bias.

Confirmation bias also plays a significant role in sustaining beliefs in cryptids and aliens. This cognitive bias leads individuals to pay more attention to information that confirms their existing beliefs and to dismiss or discount contradictory evidence. For instance, someone who firmly believes in the existence of Bigfoot may selectively focus on sightings and anecdotes that support their belief while ignoring or dismissing skeptical explanations.

Additionally, social cognitive factors, such as social learning and socialization processes, contribute to the formation and reinforcement of beliefs about cryptids and aliens. People may acquire their beliefs through exposure to media portrayals, personal experiences, or the influence of family and peers. These social influences shape how individuals interpret and evaluate the available evidence and contribute to the cultural transmission of beliefs.

Emotional Responses and Coping Mechanisms

Psychological perspectives also consider the emotional responses and coping mechanisms associated with cryptids and alien encounters. These phenomena often evoke intense emotional reactions, ranging from fear and awe to fascination and curiosity. For some individuals, the fear of the unknown or the fear of being vulnerable to supernatural forces can elicit strong emotional responses, leading to various coping mechanisms.

One such coping mechanism is the formation of belief systems that provide a sense of meaning and control over cryptid and alien encounters. Believing in the existence of these entities can help individuals make sense of unexplained phenomena, offering a framework for understanding the inexplicable within the boundaries of their belief systems. This sense of control and explanatory power can alleviate anxiety and uncertainty, providing psychological comfort.

On the other hand, skeptics and debunkers often rely on rationalization and skepticism as coping mechanisms. Skeptics use critical thinking, empirical evidence, and scientific explanations to debunk or challenge cryptid and alien claims. Engaging in skepticism and debunking allows individuals to assert their rationality, reinforcing a sense of control over the unknown and avoiding anxiety-provoking beliefs.

Cultural and Societal Influences

Sociological perspectives emphasize the impact of culture and society on the interpretation and belief in cryptids and aliens. Culture shapes the myths, legends, and folklore surrounding these phenomena, providing a cultural context that influences how individuals perceive and interpret encounters. For example, different cultures have their own unique cryptid legends, such as the Loch Ness Monster in Scotland or the Chupacabra in Latin American folklore.

Society also plays a role in the interpretation and response to cryptid and alien encounters. The media, including television shows, movies, and books, heavily influence public perceptions and beliefs. Media portrayals of cryptids and aliens often sensationalize and dramatize the encounters, shaping public opinion and contributing to the cultural fascination with these phenomena.

Additionally, group dynamics and collective behavior influence the interpretation and response to cryptid and alien encounters. These phenomena can serve as a basis for social cohesion and identity formation within communities. People may form social groups, such as online communities or local organizations, centered around the belief in and investigation of cryptids and aliens. The collective sharing of experiences, beliefs, and evidence strengthens the sense of community and provides a support network for individuals with similar interests.

The Role of Skepticism and Debunking

Skepticism and debunking play a crucial role in examining and analyzing the psychological and sociological dimensions of cryptids and alien encounters. Skeptics employ critical thinking, scientific methods, and logical reasoning to evaluate the evidence and claims associated with these phenomena. By challenging unsupported beliefs and misinformation, skeptics contribute to a more rational and evidence-based understanding of cryptids and aliens.

Debunking can serve as a coping mechanism for individuals who may feel anxious or overwhelmed by the possibility of cryptids and aliens. It provides an alternative perspective rooted in skepticism and scientific inquiry, offering explanations based on natural phenomena, misidentifications, or hoaxes. Debunking can provide reassurance and alleviate anxiety by providing logical and plausible explanations for seemingly paranormal or supernatural encounters.

However, it is essential to approach skepticism and debunking with sensitivity and respect for the experiences and beliefs of others. Dismissing or ridiculing individuals who believe in cryptids and aliens can have adverse psychological and social consequences, further polarizing the discourse and hindering open dialogue to explore a pluralistic understanding of these phenomena.

Conclusion

Understanding the psychological and sociological perspectives surrounding cryptids and alien encounters is vital for comprehending why individuals believe in and engage with these phenomena. Cognitive processes, emotional responses, cultural influences, and societal factors shape the formation of beliefs and the interpretation of encounters. Skepticism and debunking also play essential roles in critically evaluating evidence and providing alternative explanations.

By exploring these perspectives, we can gain a deeper understanding of the diverse range of human experiences and beliefs, fostering greater empathy, and promoting productive conversations about cryptids, aliens, and the paranormal. It is through interdisciplinary efforts and an openness to multiple perspectives that we can continue to explore the unknown, expand our knowledge, and bridge the gap between science and the paranormal.

Cryptozoology as a Cultural Phenomenon

Cryptozoology, the study of hidden or unknown animals, has not only captivated the interest of researchers and enthusiasts but also permeated various aspects of our culture. It has become a fascinating cultural phenomenon that has left its mark on literature, movies, art, and music. In this section, we will explore the cultural significance of cryptozoology and its impact on society.

7.3.4.1 Folklore and Superstitions

Cryptozoological creatures often have roots in folklore and superstitions that have been passed down through generations. Many legendary creatures, such as the Loch Ness Monster or the Chupacabra, have become deeply ingrained in local folklore and are integral to the cultural identity of certain communities.

Folklore surrounding cryptozoological creatures often serves as a way for communities to explain natural phenomena or to caution against specific behaviors. For example, in Scandinavian folklore, tales of sea serpents cautioned fishermen about the dangers of the deep sea. These stories not only entertained listeners but also served as a form of cultural preservation, keeping the traditions and beliefs of a community alive.

7.3.4.2 Religious Interpretations

Cryptozoology has also found its way into religious interpretations. Some religious groups believe that certain cryptids, such as the Sasquatch or the Yeti, are spiritual beings with connections to higher powers. These beliefs can range from considering these creatures as guardians of nature to viewing them as divine messengers or even deities.

Religious interpretations of cryptozoology often intersect with environmentalism and conservation efforts. Many religious groups that attribute spiritual significance to cryptids advocate for the protection and conservation of their habitats as an act of reverence towards these creatures.

7.3.4.3 Psychological and Sociological Perspectives

Cryptozoology, like other paranormal phenomena, has psychological and sociological implications. People's beliefs in cryptids can be influenced by various psychological factors, such as the need for mystery and wonder, the fear of the unknown, or the desire for a connection to something beyond the ordinary.

From a sociological perspective, cryptozoology serves as a social bonding mechanism. Belief in cryptids can create a sense of community and belonging among individuals who share similar interests and beliefs. Cryptozoology conventions, online forums, and social media groups provide platforms for enthusiasts to connect, discuss, and share their experiences and research.

7.3.4.4 Cryptozoology as a Cultural Catalyst

Cryptozoology has left an indelible mark on popular culture, influencing literature, movies, art, and music. It has sparked the imagination of authors and filmmakers, giving rise to captivating stories and iconic characters. From classic novels like H.P. Lovecraft's "The Call of Cthulhu" to blockbuster movies like "Jurassic Park," cryptozoological elements have found their way into mainstream entertainment.

Artists, too, have been fascinated by the allure of cryptozoology. Paintings, sculptures, and other forms of visual art often depict cryptids in both realistic and fantastical interpretations. Musicians, including popular bands like The Decemberists, have even written songs inspired by cryptozoological creatures, further cementing their cultural significance.

7.3.4.5 Cultural Exploration and Preservation

Cryptozoology serves as a gateway for cultural exploration and preservation. The study of cryptids encourages researchers and enthusiasts to delve into local legends, myths, and indigenous knowledge systems, fostering a deeper understanding and appreciation of different cultures.

Furthermore, cryptozoologists often work closely with local communities to gather eyewitness testimonies, analyze folklore and traditions, and document cultural practices associated with cryptids. This collaboration not only contributes to scientific research but also helps preserve cultural heritage that might otherwise fade away with time.

7.3.4.6 Challenging the Status Quo

Cryptozoology as a cultural phenomenon challenges established scientific paradigms and provides an alternative perspective on the natural world. The exploration of unknown creatures pushes the boundaries of scientific knowledge and invites us to question our understanding of reality.

While mainstream science often dismisses cryptozoological claims as pseudoscience, the cultural impact of cryptozoology should not be overlooked. It highlights the importance of open-mindedness, curiosity, and the recognition that our understanding of the natural world is constantly evolving.

Cryptozoological phenomena have the power to ignite passion and curiosity in people of all backgrounds. Whether it be through tales of legendary creatures or scientific investigations into the unknown, cryptozoology has a profound cultural significance that extends far beyond the realm of scientific inquiry.

In conclusion, cryptozoology has become a cultural phenomenon, deeply intertwined with folklore, religious beliefs, artistic endeavors, and social connections. It challenges conventional wisdom, encourages exploration, and invites us to embrace the mysteries of the natural world. As cryptozoology continues to captivate our imagination, it reminds us of the vastness of our planet and the wonders that lie within it.

Chapter 7: Conclusion and Future Directions

Summary of Findings

Alien Hypothesis vs. Cryptid Hypothesis

In the study of anomalous creatures and encounters, two main hypotheses are often considered: the alien hypothesis and the cryptid hypothesis. These hypotheses provide different explanations for the origin and nature of the mysterious beings reported worldwide.

The alien hypothesis suggests that the strange beings witnessed in various sightings, including the Dover Demon, are extraterrestrial in nature. According to this hypothesis, these beings are visitors from other planets or dimensions, conducting research or exploration on Earth. Proponents of the alien hypothesis argue that the advanced technology and capabilities displayed by these creatures cannot be explained by conventional scientific knowledge.

On the other hand, the cryptid hypothesis posits that these mysterious creatures are yet-to-be-discovered or elusive species that exist within our own planet. Cryptozoologists believe that these beings, such as Bigfoot or the Loch Ness Monster, are part of undiscovered biological diversity or represent remnants of extinct species. The cryptid hypothesis suggests that these creatures have managed to remain hidden from human observation and scientific documentation.

Both the alien and cryptid hypotheses have their strengths and weaknesses, and engaging in a critical examination of these hypotheses allows us to evaluate the evidence and arguments that support each.

Strengths of the Alien Hypothesis

The alien hypothesis offers compelling explanations for certain characteristics observed in mysterious sightings. For example, the ability of these beings to defy the laws of physics, such as moving at incredible speeds or displaying advanced technology, aligns with the technological advancements often associated with extraterrestrial civilizations. Additionally, the existence of unidentified flying objects (UFOs) reported in many encounters supports the idea of visitations from other planets.

Moreover, some witnesses claim to have experienced telepathic communication or time distortion during their encounters with these beings, which aligns with the notion of extraterrestrial intelligence and advanced psychological capabilities.

Lastly, the existence of government secrecy surrounding some sightings and the alleged cover-ups add credibility to the alien hypothesis. It suggests that governments, aware of the existence of extraterrestrial life, are concealing this knowledge from the public.

Weaknesses of the Alien Hypothesis

One of the main weaknesses of the alien hypothesis is the lack of physical evidence. While eyewitness testimonies and anecdotal accounts are often cited as evidence, skeptics argue that they are not sufficient to validate the existence of extraterrestrial beings. The absence of concrete physical evidence, such as photos, videos, or artifacts, makes it difficult to support the alien hypothesis beyond a reasonable doubt.

Furthermore, the alien hypothesis relies heavily on assumptions about the capabilities and intentions of extraterrestrial beings. Without direct contact or communication with these beings, it is challenging to accurately understand their motives, behavior, and biology. This lack of verifiable information limits the scientific feasibility of the alien hypothesis.

Strengths of the Cryptid Hypothesis

The cryptid hypothesis draws strength from the notion that Earth is a diverse and largely unexplored planet. It suggests that there may be undiscovered species hiding in remote areas or exhibiting elusive behavior, evading scientific documentation. The existence of cryptids may represent exciting opportunities for biologists and conservationists to uncover new knowledge about our natural world.

Furthermore, the cryptid hypothesis is supported by a multitude of eyewitness accounts and alleged physical evidence, such as footprints, hair samples, and blurry

SUMMARY OF FINDINGS

photographs. While often subject to scrutiny, these pieces of evidence contribute to the body of knowledge on cryptid sightings and provide potential leads for future research.

Weaknesses of the Cryptid Hypothesis

One of the main weaknesses of the cryptid hypothesis lies in the lack of concrete evidence that can withstand scientific scrutiny. Skeptics argue that many alleged cryptid sightings can be attributed to misinterpretation, hoaxes, or psychological factors. Without robust physical evidence, it is challenging to definitively prove the existence of cryptids.

Moreover, the vast majority of reported cryptid sightings lack consistency and reproducibility, which are crucial elements in scientific inquiry. The reliance on anecdotal accounts and lack of systematic data collection limit the scientific validity of the cryptid hypothesis.

Finding Common Ground

While the alien and cryptid hypotheses have their differences, there is potential for overlap and convergence between the two. Some theorists propose that the creatures described in cryptid sightings, such as Bigfoot or the Jersey Devil, may have extraterrestrial origins. This notion suggests a potential connection between the two hypotheses, where unidentified creatures may be both cryptids and extraterrestrial beings.

To explore this further, interdisciplinary collaborations between cryptozoologists and ufologists could lead to a broader understanding of these mysterious phenomena. By combining their expertise, researchers can gather more comprehensive and diverse evidence, bringing us closer to uncovering the truth about these enigmatic beings.

In conclusion, the alien hypothesis and cryptid hypothesis offer different explanations for anomalous sightings and encounters. While the alien hypothesis focuses on extraterrestrial visitors, the cryptid hypothesis suggests the existence of unknown species on Earth. Although both hypotheses have their strengths and weaknesses, bridging the gap between the two may provide a more nuanced understanding of these phenomena. Further research and collaboration are needed to shed light on the mysterious and captivating world of alien and cryptid encounters.

Evidence and Counterarguments

In the study of the Dover Demon sightings, it is important to examine the evidence presented by witnesses and skeptics alike. By analyzing and evaluating the available data, we can identify possible counterarguments to the existence of the Dover Demon and explore alternative explanations for the reported sightings.

Eyewitness Testimonies

One of the primary forms of evidence in the Dover Demon case is the collection of eyewitness testimonies. Witnesses described seeing a creature with a large head, glowing eyes, and a thin, humanoid body. They reported encountering the creature on multiple occasions and provided consistent descriptions of its appearance.

Proponents of the existence of the Dover Demon argue that the consistency of these testimonies adds credibility to the sightings. They believe that the witnesses saw a real, unknown creature that cannot be easily explained by conventional knowledge or existing cryptid species.

However, skeptics question the reliability of eyewitness testimonies. They argue that memories can be fallible, especially when recalling events that occurred many years ago. Factors such as social influence, suggestion, and misinterpretation of stimuli can potentially lead to the creation of false memories or exaggeration of details.

To counter the eyewitness testimonies, skeptics propose that the sightings were a result of misidentification or hallucination. They suggest that the witnesses may have seen a known animal, such as a feral cat or a large bird, and their perception was influenced by fear, excitement, or other psychological factors.

Examination of Physical Evidence

Another aspect of the investigation involves the examination of physical evidence related to the Dover Demon sightings. Despite the absence of concrete evidence, there are some intriguing pieces of information that have been considered.

For instance, during the sightings, witnesses reported finding footprints purportedly belonging to the Dover Demon. These footprints were described as having three toes and being too small to be human or animal tracks.

Proponents of the Dover Demon argue that these footprints provide physical evidence of the creature's existence. They believe that the unique characteristics of the footprints cannot be easily explained by hoaxes or misinterpretation, suggesting a genuine unknown species.

However, skeptics question the reliability and validity of the footprints. They argue that the footprints could have been easily faked, especially considering the widespread media attention surrounding the sightings. They also point out that the footprints were not subjected to rigorous scientific analysis, making it difficult to determine their authenticity or origin.

To counter the physical evidence, skeptics propose that the footprints were part of an elaborate hoax or misinterpreted natural phenomena. They suggest that the footprints may have been created by human pranksters, or they could be the tracks of a known animal that appear unusual due to factors such as weathering or deformation.

Theories and Explanations

In addition to analyzing the evidence, it is important to consider alternative theories and explanations for the Dover Demon sightings. By exploring different perspectives, we can better understand the complexities of the phenomenon and evaluate the plausibility of various hypotheses.

One possible explanation for the Dover Demon sightings is the misidentification of a known animal or an undiscovered species. This theory suggests that witnesses may have encountered a rare or elusive creature that does not fit into existing taxonomic categories. Proponents of this explanation argue that there are still many unexplored areas in the natural world, and new species are continually being discovered.

Another theory proposes that the Dover Demon sightings were a result of psychological or sociological factors. This perspective suggests that the witnesses may have experienced a collective hallucination or illusion created by shared beliefs, rumors, or cultural influences. Proponents of this theory argue that the human mind is susceptible to perceptual distortions and that social factors can influence how individuals interpret and remember their experiences.

Skeptics also raise the possibility of deliberate hoaxes or pranks being responsible for the Dover Demon sightings. They argue that some witnesses may have fabricated or exaggerated their accounts for attention, fame, or other ulterior motives. This theory emphasizes the need for critical examination of the credibility and motivations of witnesses.

To reconcile these theories and explanations, further investigation, research, and collaboration between different fields of study may be necessary. By combining expertise from cryptozoology, psychology, sociology, and other relevant disciplines, we can develop a more comprehensive understanding of the Dover Demon sightings.

In conclusion, while the Dover Demon sightings have been supported by eyewitness testimonies and anecdotal evidence, counterarguments and alternative explanations exist. Skepticism, critical thinking, and thorough investigation are essential in analyzing the evidence and advancing our understanding of this mysterious phenomenon. The exploration of evidence and counterarguments contributes to the overall examination of the Dover Demon sightings, shedding light on the complexities of cryptozoology, human perception, and the search for the unknown.

Scientific Perspectives and Skepticism

In the study of paranormal phenomena and cryptids, scientific perspectives play a crucial role in analyzing and understanding these mysterious occurrences. Skepticism, in particular, provides a necessary and critical approach to evaluate claims and evidence. This section will delve into the key scientific principles and methodologies that underpin the skeptical perspective, highlighting its importance in separating fact from fiction.

Scientific Method

The scientific method is the foundation of scientific inquiry and involves a systematic approach to acquiring knowledge about the natural world. It consists of several interconnected steps, beginning with observation and formulation of a research question. In the context of paranormal phenomena and cryptids, scientists often start by analyzing eyewitness testimonies and physical evidence.

To support the scientific method, it is essential to develop hypotheses that can be tested through empirical research and experimentation. Hypotheses, in the context of the paranormal, might propose natural explanations for reported phenomena, challenging the existence of supernatural or extraterrestrial entities.

Once hypotheses are formulated, scientists gather data and evidence, employing rigorous and replicable research methods. Robust data collection and analysis techniques, such as statistical analysis, can help to identify patterns, correlations, and potential causes of observed phenomena.

Skepticism in Science

Skepticism is a fundamental aspect of scientific thinking and involves maintaining a critical and unbiased attitude towards claims and evidence. Skeptics approach paranormal phenomena and cryptids with a healthy dose of doubt, subjecting them to rigorous examination and questioning.

One key principle of skepticism is the requirement for extraordinary evidence to support extraordinary claims. This means that claims involving the existence of cryptids or encounters with supernatural beings should be supported by robust evidence that goes beyond mere anecdotes or personal testimonies.

Skeptics also emphasize the importance of peer review and the scrutiny of colleagues in the scientific community. Peer review ensures that research is subjected to rigorous evaluation by independent experts with the necessary expertise to identify flaws in methodology or interpretation. This process helps to weed out erroneous or unsubstantiated claims.

Evaluating Evidence

When examining evidence related to paranormal phenomena and cryptids, scientists employ a range of critical thinking and analytical skills. These skills include examining the reliability and validity of eyewitness testimony, analyzing physical evidence, and considering alternative explanations.

Eyewitness testimony, although often compelling, can be influenced by a variety of factors, such as biases, suggestibility, and memory distortions. Skeptics critically evaluate the consistency and credibility of eyewitness accounts, recognizing the limitations of human perception and memory.

Physical evidence, such as footprints or photographs, is also subject to scrutiny. Scientists carefully assess the quality, authenticity, and chain of custody of the evidence, while considering possible natural explanations or alternative hoaxes.

Skeptics also encourage the application of Occam's Razor, which states that among competing hypotheses, the one with the fewest assumptions should be selected. This principle favors explanations rooted in known natural phenomena over supernatural or extraterrestrial hypotheses, as they are generally more parsimonious.

Example: Loch Ness Monster

The Loch Ness Monster is one of the most famous cryptids, with numerous reported sightings and photographs. However, scientific skepticism has played a crucial role in evaluating the evidence surrounding this creature.

One notable study conducted by the University of Birmingham in 2003 employed sonar scanning of Loch Ness to search for large unidentified objects. Despite detecting various unexplained echoes, the presence of a large aquatic creature was not confirmed. This study showcased the application of sound scientific methodology and skepticism in investigating cryptid claims.

Furthermore, scientists have developed alternative explanations for the reported sightings, such as misidentifications of floating logs or waves. These natural explanations, rooted in known phenomena, are more consistent with scientific principles of parsimony and the evaluation of evidence.

Caveats and Challenges

While skepticism is an important facet of scientific inquiry, there can be challenges and caveats when applying it to paranormal and cryptid phenomena. These challenges include:

- Lack of funding and resources for comprehensive investigations

- Difficulty in conducting controlled experiments due to the unpredictable nature of reported phenomena

- Limited access to eyewitnesses and physical evidence

- The influence of personal belief systems and biases on scientific interpretations

Addressing these challenges requires interdisciplinary collaboration, improved data collection methods, and increased public awareness of the importance of rigorous scientific investigation in evaluating claims related to paranormal phenomena and cryptids.

Conclusion

Scientific perspectives and skepticism are vital components of the study of paranormal phenomena and cryptids. These principles provide a systematic and critical approach to evaluating evidence, separating fact from fiction. By employing the scientific method and maintaining an open-minded but skeptical attitude, researchers can work towards a deeper understanding of these mysteries while upholding the rigorous standards of scientific inquiry. It is through these scientific perspectives and skepticism that we can navigate the complexities surrounding cryptids and the paranormal and make informed evaluations of their existence.

Implications and Significance

Cultural and Societal Impact

The study of cryptids and aliens has long fascinated people from all walks of life. These elusive creatures and mysterious extraterrestrial beings have captured the imagination and curiosity of individuals around the world. As a result, the cultural and societal impact of these phenomena cannot be understated.

First and foremost, the existence of cryptids and aliens has become deeply ingrained in folklore and mythology. Throughout history, various cultures have developed myths and legends surrounding strange and unknown creatures. These stories have been passed down through generations, shaping cultural identities and belief systems. For example, the Loch Ness Monster, a legendary creature said to inhabit Loch Ness in Scotland, has become an iconic symbol of Scottish folklore. Similarly, the Jersey Devil, a cryptid reportedly seen in the Pine Barrens of New Jersey, has become a legendary figure in American folklore.

Furthermore, the fascination with cryptids and aliens has permeated popular culture. Literature, fiction, movies, television shows, and even art and music often incorporate these mysterious creatures and extraterrestrial beings. Countless books, such as H.G. Wells' "The War of the Worlds" and movies like Steven Spielberg's "Close Encounters of the Third Kind," have captivated audiences and fueled their imagination. This cultural impact not only drives entertainment industries but also influences individuals' beliefs, perceptions, and interests.

The impact of cryptids and aliens extends beyond entertainment and folklore. The existence of these phenomena has also sparked debates and discussions within the scientific and academic communities. While mainstream science often rejects the existence of these creatures and beings due to a lack of physical evidence, alternative scientific perspectives, such as parapsychology and astrobiology, explore the anomalies and possibilities associated with the paranormal and extraterrestrial life. This scientific discourse enriches our understanding of the natural world and challenges prevailing beliefs.

On a societal level, the study of cryptids and aliens has significant implications. Belief in these creatures and beings can deeply affect individuals' lives, influencing their daily routines, personal relationships, and decision-making processes. For some, encounters with cryptids and aliens may have profound psychological and emotional effects, creating lasting trauma or fascination. Additionally, the study of these phenomena can generate economic opportunities, such as tourism in regions associated with cryptid sightings or the production of related merchandise.

Moreover, cryptids and aliens have a remarkable influence on education and public awareness. The popularization of these topics in various media formats has sparked curiosity among students and the general public, promoting the pursuit of knowledge, critical thinking, and scientific literacy. Incorporating the study of cryptids and aliens into educational curricula can engage students in interdisciplinary learning, encouraging them to explore scientific principles, cultural contexts, and societal impacts.

In conclusion, the cultural and societal impact of cryptids and aliens is far-reaching. These phenomena have developed deep roots in folklore, inspired creative works across various media, and transformed scientific discourse. Furthermore, the study of cryptids and aliens influences personal beliefs, emotional well-being, and decision-making processes. By exploring the cultural and societal impact of these phenomena, we not only gain insight into human fascination and imagination but also foster a greater understanding of the significance of these mysteries in our world.

Chapter 7: Conclusion and Future Directions

8.2.2 Psychological and Emotional Effects

Understanding the psychological and emotional effects of cryptozoological and paranormal phenomena is crucial when examining their societal and cultural impact. These effects can be seen in individuals who have had encounters with cryptids, alien beings, or paranormal experiences, as well as in the wider community and belief systems that develop around these phenomena. In this section, we will explore the various psychological and emotional effects that these encounters can have on individuals and society as a whole.

Psychological Effects of Encounters

Encounters with cryptids, aliens, or other paranormal phenomena can have a profound impact on the psychological well-being of individuals involved. The experiences themselves can cause a range of emotional responses, from curiosity and fascination to fear and anxiety. The psychological effects may vary depending on the nature of the encounter and the personal beliefs and perspectives of the individuals involved.

1. Post-Traumatic Stress Disorder (PTSD): Some individuals who have had intense encounters with cryptids or aliens may develop symptoms similar to those diagnosed with PTSD. Symptoms can include nightmares, flashbacks, anxiety, and

CHAPTER 7: CONCLUSION AND FUTURE DIRECTIONS

avoidance behaviors. These individuals may experience a significant disruption in their daily lives and struggle to cope with the traumatic experiences.

2. Belief Systems and Cognitive Dissonance: Encounters with cryptids or aliens can challenge individuals' existing belief systems. This can lead to cognitive dissonance, a state of mental discomfort that occurs when one's beliefs or values are in conflict with their experiences. Individuals may struggle to reconcile their encounter with their pre-existing beliefs, which can result in anxiety, confusion, and even a complete shift in their belief systems.

3. Skepticism and Disbelief: On the other hand, individuals who have not had personal encounters with cryptids or aliens may experience skepticism or disbelief when confronted with the accounts of others. This disbelief can stem from a variety of factors, including rational skepticism, lack of personal experience, or cognitive biases.

4. Curiosity and Fascination: Encounters with cryptids or aliens can also spark curiosity and fascination in individuals. These experiences may prompt a desire for further exploration, research, or investigation into the phenomena. This curiosity can lead to a deeper understanding of the psychological and emotional aspects of these encounters.

Emotional Effects on the Community

The emotional effects of cryptozoological and paranormal phenomena extend beyond the individuals who have had direct encounters. The impact on the community can be significant, shaping beliefs, fostering fear or wonder, and influencing cultural narratives. Here are some of the emotional effects on communities:

1. Fear and Anxiety: Reports and stories of cryptids, alien abductions, or paranormal phenomena can evoke fear and anxiety in the local community. The unknown and unexplained nature of these encounters can create a sense of vulnerability and unease.

2. Wonder and Awe: On the other hand, some individuals and communities may experience wonder and awe in response to these encounters. The mysteries surrounding cryptids and aliens can inspire a sense of fascination and a desire for exploration and discovery.

3. Stigmatization and Social Isolation: Individuals who claim to have had encounters with cryptids or aliens may face stigmatization and social isolation. Their experiences may be dismissed or ridiculed by others, leading to feelings of alienation and marginalization within their communities.

4. Group Cohesion and Belief Systems: Encounters with cryptids or aliens can also lead to the formation of close-knit communities centered around shared beliefs and experiences. These communities provide support and validation for individuals who have had encounters, fostering a sense of belonging and shared identity.

Concluding Thoughts

The psychological and emotional effects of cryptozoological and paranormal phenomena are complex and varied. Encounters can result in both positive and negative psychological outcomes, ranging from curiosity and wonder to fear and trauma. Understanding these effects is crucial for further research, as well as for providing support and resources to individuals and communities who have had these experiences.

It is important to approach these phenomena with an open mind, recognizing the potential psychological impact they can have on individuals and society. By integrating knowledge from various disciplines, including psychology, sociology, and cultural studies, we can gain a more comprehensive understanding of the psychological and emotional effects of cryptozoological and paranormal encounters.

Further research and investigation into these effects are necessary to shed light on the complexities of human experiences and belief systems. By bridging the gap between science and the paranormal, we can enhance our understanding of human nature and the world around us. The psychological and emotional effects of these encounters offer a unique lens through which to explore the complexities of the human mind and the mysteries of the unknown.

Importance for Scientific Exploration and Discovery

Scientific exploration and discovery are fundamental to advancing our understanding of the world around us. They allow us to uncover new knowledge, challenge existing theories, and push the boundaries of what is known. In the context of cryptozoology and the study of paranormal phenomena, scientific exploration and discovery play a crucial role in determining the validity of alleged sightings and uncovering the truth behind mysterious creatures and phenomena.

One of the key reasons why scientific exploration and discovery are important in these fields is to separate fact from fiction. There is a vast amount of misinformation, hoaxes, and sensationalism surrounding cryptids and paranormal phenomena. Therefore, it is essential to approach these topics with a scientific mindset, using rigorous methodologies and critical thinking to evaluate claims objectively.

Scientific exploration and discovery provide a framework for investigating and analyzing evidence in a systematic and unbiased manner. This involves collecting data, conducting experiments, and employing statistical analysis to draw meaningful conclusions. By following these processes, we can avoid the pitfalls of confirmation bias and subjective interpretation that often plague cryptozoology and paranormal research.

Moreover, scientific exploration and discovery are essential for identifying and documenting new species or phenomena. In the case of cryptozoology, the discovery of a cryptid verified by rigorous scientific methods would revolutionize our understanding of biodiversity and the limits of what is known. It would also demonstrate the value of pursuing unconventional lines of inquiry and challenging established scientific paradigms.

For example, consider the discovery of the coelacanth, a fish once thought to have gone extinct millions of years ago. In the early 20th century, scientists were fascinated by fossilized remains of this ancient fish. However, it was not until 1938 that a living coelacanth was discovered off the coast of South Africa. This remarkable find challenged the prevailing scientific consensus and highlighted the importance of exploring unknown areas and questioning established beliefs.

In the field of paranormal phenomena, scientific exploration and discovery can shed light on the nature of inexplicable experiences reported by individuals. By applying rigorous scientific methods, researchers can investigate claims of ghostly encounters, UFO sightings, and alien abductions. This not only provides insight into the psychological and sociological factors underlying these phenomena but also helps develop a deeper understanding of the human mind and consciousness.

It is worth noting that scientific exploration and discovery are not limited to traditional academic institutions and professional scientists. Citizen science and amateur research play a vital role in expanding our knowledge and understanding of cryptozoology and the paranormal. These individuals often have a passion for the subject matter and can provide valuable insights, observations, and data that might otherwise be overlooked.

In recent years, advancements in technology have also opened up new avenues for scientific exploration and discovery. For example, the use of unmanned aerial vehicles (UAVs) or drones equipped with high-resolution cameras has facilitated aerial surveys of remote and inaccessible areas. This technology allows researchers to explore regions that were previously off-limits, potentially uncovering new evidence or observing cryptids in their natural habitats.

Furthermore, collaborations between scientists and paranormal investigators can yield fruitful results. By combining the expertise and methodologies of both fields, researchers can gain a more comprehensive understanding of the phenomena under investigation. This interdisciplinary approach fosters a healthy exchange of ideas, encourages critical thinking, and enhances the credibility of the research.

In conclusion, scientific exploration and discovery are of utmost importance in the study of cryptids and paranormal phenomena. They provide a reliable framework for evaluating evidence, separating fact from fiction, and advancing our understanding of the unknown. By embracing scientific methods, engaging in interdisciplinary collaborations, and promoting public engagement and education, we can bridge the gap between scientific skepticism and paranormal beliefs, ultimately fostering a more nuanced and informed perspective on cryptids and the paranormal.

Future Directions for Research

Advancements in Technology and Data Collection

Advancements in technology and data collection have greatly influenced the field of cryptozoology and its study of elusive creatures like the Dover Demon. These advancements have not only improved the quality and quantity of data collected but have also provided researchers with new tools and techniques for analyzing and interpreting that data. In this section, we will explore some of the key advancements in technology and data collection that have shaped the field of cryptozoology and how they have been applied to the study of the Dover Demon.

Remote Sensing and Robotics

One significant advancement in technology that has revolutionized data collection in cryptozoology is the use of remote sensing and robotics. Remote sensing refers to the acquisition of information about an object or phenomenon without making physical contact with it. In the case of cryptozoology, this often involves using sensors or imaging devices to gather data about cryptids or their habitats.

For example, drones equipped with high-resolution cameras and thermal imaging sensors can be used to survey areas where cryptids are believed to reside, providing researchers with aerial photographs and videos. These images can help identify potential cryptid habitats, track their movements, and even detect signs of their presence, such as footprints or nests. Additionally, underwater drones can explore lakes and rivers, capturing underwater footage and collecting water samples to search for evidence of aquatic cryptids like the Loch Ness Monster.

Robotic devices, such as autonomous camera traps and audio recorders, can be deployed in remote and inaccessible areas to monitor cryptid activity. These devices can be programmed to activate when triggered by motion or sound, capturing evidence when researchers are not physically present. This technology allows researchers to collect data continuously, providing valuable insights into the behavior and habitat preferences of cryptids.

DNA Analysis

DNA analysis has also played a crucial role in advancing the field of cryptozoology. With the development of molecular biology techniques, researchers can now extract and analyze DNA samples from various sources, including hair, skin cells, feces, and saliva. This has opened up new possibilities for identifying and studying unknown species, including potential cryptids.

By comparing extracted DNA to existing genetic databases, researchers can determine if a collected sample belongs to a known species or if it represents a previously undiscovered or unidentified creature. This approach has been particularly useful in investigating cryptids like Bigfoot and the Yeti, where alleged hair samples have been analyzed to determine their origin.

However, DNA analysis also poses challenges in the field of cryptozoology. The lack of reference DNA from cryptids makes it difficult to establish a baseline for comparison, and contamination or misinterpretation of samples can lead to erroneous conclusions. Therefore, strict protocols and scientific rigor must be followed when collecting, handling, and analyzing DNA evidence to ensure its reliability.

Citizen Science and Crowdsourcing

Advances in technology have not only empowered researchers but have also engaged the general public in the collection and analysis of cryptozoological data. Citizen science and crowdsourcing platforms have emerged as effective tools for gathering large amounts of data from diverse sources.

Citizen science initiatives, such as online reporting platforms and mobile applications, allow individuals to report sightings and encounters with cryptids. These platforms provide standardized data collection protocols, ensuring consistency in the information collected. By tapping into the collective power of thousands of individuals, researchers can obtain a broader and more comprehensive dataset, helping to identify patterns and trends in cryptid sightings.

Crowdsourcing also enables the collaborative analysis of cryptozoological data. Online platforms can crowdsource the identification of cryptid-related evidence, such as photographs or audio recordings. By leveraging the knowledge and expertise of a global community, researchers can gain valuable insights and interpretations, enhancing the scientific scrutiny of potential cryptid encounters.

Moreover, citizen science and crowdsourcing have the additional benefit of increasing public engagement and awareness of cryptozoological research. It allows individuals to become active participants in the scientific process, fostering a sense of ownership and belonging in the field.

Data Visualization and Analysis

Advancements in technology have also transformed the way data is visualized and analyzed in cryptozoology. Data visualization tools, such as Geographic Information Systems (GIS), enable researchers to map and analyze spatial data relating to cryptid sightings, habitat preferences, and ecological factors.

GIS can overlay various layers of information, such as topography, vegetation, and human settlements, to identify correlations between cryptid sightings and environmental variables. This helps researchers identify potential hotspots or regions with higher cryptid activity, guiding future field investigations.

Furthermore, statistical analysis techniques have become more sophisticated and accessible, allowing researchers to analyze large datasets and test hypotheses rigorously. Machine learning algorithms can detect patterns or anomalies in complex datasets, aiding in the identification of cryptid behaviors or characteristics. For instance, these algorithms can classify vocalizations of unknown creatures, distinguishing them from known species based on their distinct acoustic features.

Ethical Considerations and Data Privacy

As technology advances and data collection methods become more sophisticated, it is essential to address ethical considerations and ensure data privacy. Researchers must obtain appropriate permits and permissions to collect data in protected areas or from private property. Additionally, informed consent should be obtained from individuals who contribute data through citizen science platforms.

Data privacy is another crucial aspect to be considered. Personal information, such as photographs, audio recordings, or location data, should be handled with care to protect the privacy of individuals involved. Anonymization and data encryption techniques can be employed to safeguard sensitive information while still enabling scientific analysis.

In summary, advancements in technology and data collection have transformed the field of cryptozoology, providing researchers with new tools and techniques to study elusive creatures like the Dover Demon. Remote sensing and robotics, DNA analysis, citizen science and crowdsourcing, data visualization and analysis, have all contributed to improving the quality and quantity of data collected. However, it is essential to address ethical considerations and data privacy to ensure that these technologies are used responsibly and effectively in the pursuit of cryptozoological research.

Interdisciplinary Collaborations

Interdisciplinary collaborations play a crucial role in advancing research in the field of cryptids and aliens. By bringing together experts from various disciplines, such as biology, anthropology, psychology, physics, and sociology, a more comprehensive and holistic understanding of these phenomena can be achieved. In this section, we will explore the importance of interdisciplinary collaborations, discuss some specific examples, and propose future directions for research.

The Value of Interdisciplinary Approaches

Cryptids and aliens are complex phenomena that cannot be fully understood through the lens of a single discipline alone. Each discipline brings its unique perspectives, methodologies, and tools to the table, allowing for a more nuanced investigation. Here are a few reasons why interdisciplinary collaborations are valuable:

1. **Expanding the Knowledge Base:** Different disciplines have their own bodies of knowledge and expertise. By integrating these diverse perspectives, researchers can expand their understanding of cryptids and aliens beyond traditional boundaries.

2. **Identifying Knowledge Gaps:** Interdisciplinary collaborations often reveal gaps in our current understanding. By recognizing these gaps, researchers can design studies and experiments that address these shortcomings, pushing the boundaries of knowledge.

3. **Studying Complex Systems:** Cryptids and aliens are complex systems, involving multiple interacting factors. Collaborating across disciplines can provide a more comprehensive understanding of the interplay between biological, psychological, social, and environmental factors.

4. **Enhancing Methodologies:** Different disciplines employ various research methods and tools. By integrating these methodologies, interdisciplinary

collaborations can lead to the development of novel approaches for studying cryptids and aliens.

Examples of Interdisciplinary Collaborations

Let's explore some concrete examples of how interdisciplinary collaborations have contributed to our understanding of cryptids and aliens:

1. **Cryptozoology and Biology:** Biologists bring their expertise in understanding animal behavior, anatomy, and genetics to the study of cryptids. By collaborating with cryptozoologists, they can analyze alleged cryptid sightings, collect physical evidence, and use DNA analysis to determine the origins of these mysterious creatures.

2. **Psychology and Sociology:** Psychologists and sociologists play a crucial role in understanding eyewitness testimonies, belief systems, and the societal impact of cryptids and alien encounters. They contribute their expertise in conducting surveys, interviews, and experiments to understand the psychological and sociological factors at play.

3. **Physics and Astronomy:** Physicists and astronomers contribute their knowledge of the laws of nature and the universe to the study of aliens and their potential origins. They can analyze UFO sightings, study the possibility of interstellar travel, and search for signs of extraterrestrial intelligence.

4. **Anthropology and Folklore:** Anthropologists and folklorists study the cultural and historical aspects of cryptids and aliens. By collaborating with cryptozoologists and ufologists, they can identify common themes, motifs, and legends across different cultures, shedding light on the significance of these phenomena in human societies.

Future Directions for Interdisciplinary Research

As the field of cryptids and aliens continues to evolve, there are several exciting directions for interdisciplinary collaborations that can push the boundaries of our knowledge. Some possible future directions include:

1. **Neuroscience and Psychology:** Collaborative research involving neuroscience and psychology can shed light on the mechanisms underlying witness perceptions, memory formation, and belief systems related to cryptids and aliens. By understanding the cognitive processes involved, we can better evaluate the reliability of eyewitness accounts.

2. **Environmental Science and Biology:** Environmental scientists and biologists can collaborate to investigate the ecological impact of cryptids and aliens.

By studying the potential introduction of new species or disruptions to ecosystems, we can assess the plausibility of these phenomena and their potential consequences.

3. **Data Science and Artificial Intelligence:** The advancement of data science and artificial intelligence presents exciting opportunities for interdisciplinary collaborations. By applying machine learning algorithms to large datasets of cryptid and alien sightings, researchers can identify patterns, correlations, and potential explanations for these phenomena.

4. **Ethics and Society:** As our understanding of cryptids and aliens deepens, ethical considerations become increasingly important. Collaboration between ethicists, sociologists, and researchers in the field can help navigate the ethical implications of studying and publicizing these phenomena, ensuring responsible research practices.

In conclusion, interdisciplinary collaborations are vital for advancing research on cryptids and aliens. By integrating the expertise of different disciplines, we can gain a more holistic understanding of these phenomena, identify knowledge gaps, enhance methodologies, and explore new research directions. The field of cryptids and aliens is ever-evolving, and interdisciplinary collaborations will continue to play a crucial role in pushing the boundaries of our knowledge and understanding.

Longitudinal Studies and Case Histories

Longitudinal studies and case histories play a crucial role in the field of cryptozoology and the investigation of paranormal phenomena. These research methods allow for a deep exploration of individual cases over an extended period of time, providing valuable insights and data that can contribute to our understanding of cryptids, aliens, and other unexplained phenomena. In this section, we will delve into the significance of longitudinal studies and case histories, discuss their methodology, and explore some notable examples.

The Importance of Longitudinal Studies

Longitudinal studies involve the observation and data collection from the same subjects or cases over an extended period of time. This approach allows researchers to track changes, identify patterns, and analyze the development of phenomena over time. In the context of cryptozoology and the paranormal, longitudinal studies are essential for several reasons:

1. **Identification of Patterns and Trends:** Longitudinal studies can help researchers identify patterns and trends in sightings of cryptids or aliens. By observing and documenting sightings and encounters over a long period,

researchers can discern if there are any recurring patterns in terms of location, time, or specific characteristics of the phenomena. This information can help in developing hypotheses and theories about these elusive creatures or extraterrestrial beings.

2. **Understanding Behavior and Habitats:** Tracking cryptids or aliens over time provides an opportunity to gain insights into their behaviors, habits, and preferred habitats. For example, a longitudinal study on Bigfoot sightings may reveal seasonal variations in its movements or preferred hunting grounds. Similarly, long-term observations of alien activity may shed light on their patterns of visitation or areas of interest on Earth.

3. **Detection of Anomalies:** Longitudinal studies allow researchers to detect anomalies or outliers that may be significant in unraveling the mysteries of cryptids or aliens. By carefully studying individual cases over an extended duration, researchers can identify patterns that deviate from the norm or exhibit unusual characteristics. These anomalies may provide valuable clues for further investigation and analysis.

4. **Long-Term Impact Assessment:** Longitudinal studies enable researchers to assess the long-term impact of cryptids, aliens, or paranormal phenomena on local communities and individuals. By tracking the experiences, beliefs, and reactions of individuals over time, researchers can evaluate the psychological, sociological, and cultural implications of such encounters. This information can help in understanding the broader societal impact of cryptozoological or paranormal events.

Methodology of Longitudinal Studies and Case Histories

Conducting successful longitudinal studies and case histories requires a well-defined methodology to ensure the consistency, validity, and reliability of data collection. Here are some key steps involved in these research methods:

1. **Selection of Cases:** Researchers need to carefully select cases or subjects based on various factors such as the authenticity and reliability of the information, the availability of data, and the significance of the case in the context of the research objectives. It is essential to choose cases that span a wide range of variables for a comprehensive analysis.

2. **Data Collection:** Longitudinal studies involve collecting data at regular intervals from the selected cases or subjects. Data can be gathered through direct observations, interviews, surveys, or analysis of existing records and documents. It is important to establish a reliable and standardized data collection process to ensure consistency and comparability.

3. **Documentation and Analysis:** All data collected should be carefully documented, organized, and analyzed to identify patterns, trends, and anomalies. This may involve statistical analysis, qualitative coding, and thematic analysis to extract meaningful insights and draw relevant conclusions. It is crucial to maintain a systematic and rigorous approach to data analysis to ensure the accuracy and validity of research findings.

4. **Verification and Reliability:** Longitudinal studies and case histories heavily rely on the credibility and reliability of the collected data. Researchers must employ techniques to verify the accuracy and authenticity of the information, such as cross-referencing witness accounts, conducting site investigations, or collaborating with other experts in the field. The use of multiple independent sources of data enhances the reliability and robustness of the research.

Notable Examples

Several notable examples demonstrate the value of longitudinal studies and case histories in the field of cryptozoology and the investigation of paranormal phenomena. Here, we discuss two such cases:

The Patterson-Gimlin Film

The Patterson-Gimlin Film, taken in 1967, is one of the most famous and controversial pieces of evidence for the existence of Bigfoot. The film depicts a creature walking upright in Bluff Creek, California. Multiple longitudinal studies have been conducted on this film, analyzing the creature's movements, morphology, and behavior. Researchers have carefully examined frame by frame to determine if the film was a hoax or an authentic documentation of a cryptid. These analyses have shaped the debate around Bigfoot and contributed to our understanding of its potential existence.

The Rendlesham Forest Incident

The Rendlesham Forest Incident, which occurred in December 1980 in Suffolk, England, is one of the most well-documented UFO sightings in history. This incident involved multiple witnesses, including military personnel, who reported seeing a series of strange lights and a landed craft in the forest. Longitudinal studies and case histories have been conducted on the witnesses, tracking their experiences and the long-term effects of the event on their lives. These studies have provided insights into the psychological impact of UFO sightings and the challenges faced by witnesses in coming forward with their accounts.

Challenges and Limitations

Despite their significance, longitudinal studies and case histories in the field of cryptozoology and the paranormal face several challenges and limitations. Some of these include:

1. **Limited Sample Size:** Longitudinal studies often rely on a limited number of cases or subjects, which may not fully represent the diversity and complexity of the phenomena under investigation. This limitation can affect the generalizability of the findings and the ability to draw broad conclusions.

2. **Subjectivity and Bias:** The data collected in longitudinal studies and case histories may suffer from subjectivity and bias. The interpretation of witness accounts, the reliability of memories over time, and the potential influence of external factors can introduce biases into the research. It is essential to employ rigorous methods to mitigate these biases and ensure the accuracy of the collected data.

3. **Resource Intensive:** Conducting longitudinal studies and case histories can be resource-intensive in terms of time, funding, and expertise. The need for long-term data collection, analysis, and verification requires substantial commitment and resources. This limitation can restrict the scope and scale of such research endeavors.

4. **Ethical Considerations:** Researchers must navigate various ethical considerations when conducting longitudinal studies and case histories. Respect for the privacy and well-being of witnesses or subjects, obtaining informed consent, and addressing any potential harm or distress caused by recalling paranormal experiences are crucial ethical obligations.

Conclusion

Longitudinal studies and case histories offer valuable insights and data in the field of cryptozoology and the investigation of paranormal phenomena. These research methods allow for the identification of patterns and trends, understanding behaviors and habitats, detecting anomalies, and assessing long-term impacts. However, conducting successful longitudinal studies and case histories requires a systematic methodology, careful selection of cases, reliable data collection, and rigorous analysis. Despite facing challenges and limitations, these research methods contribute to our understanding of cryptids, aliens, and the supernatural by providing a deep exploration of individual cases over time. In the future, advancements in technology, interdisciplinary collaborations, and increased public awareness can further enhance the scope and impact of longitudinal studies and case histories in unraveling the mysteries of the unknown.

The Role of Education and Public Awareness

Education and public awareness play a crucial role in understanding and exploring the realms of cryptozoology, alien encounters, and paranormal phenomena. By providing accurate information, promoting critical thinking, and encouraging scientific curiosity, education can help individuals make informed decisions and differentiate between fact and fiction. In this section, we will explore the importance of education and public awareness in these fields and discuss various strategies for promoting scientific literacy and engagement.

The Need for Education

Cryptozoology, alien encounters, and paranormal phenomena often captivate public interest and generate curiosity. However, without proper education, individuals may rely on misinformation and pseudoscience, leading to the perpetuation of myths and misconceptions. Education is essential for addressing these misunderstandings and fostering a rational and evidence-based approach to these subjects.

Furthermore, education can empower individuals to think critically, evaluate evidence, and question extraordinary claims. It equips them with the skills necessary to assess the credibility of sources and distinguish between scientific research and anecdotal accounts. By promoting scientific literacy, education encourages a balanced perspective and discourages the spread of unfounded beliefs.

Promoting Scientific Literacy

Promoting scientific literacy is fundamental in addressing misconceptions surrounding cryptozoology, alien encounters, and paranormal phenomena. It involves providing individuals with the necessary knowledge and skills to understand, evaluate, and engage with scientific information. Here are some strategies to promote scientific literacy:

1. Curricular Integration: Integrate topics related to cryptozoology, alien encounters, and paranormal phenomena into science curricula at various educational levels. This inclusion allows students to explore these subjects while learning critical scientific methods and principles.

2. Critical Thinking Skills: Incorporate critical thinking skills in educational programs, emphasizing the importance of evidence-based reasoning, skepticism,

and logical analysis. Encourage students to question and critically evaluate extraordinary claims.

3. Inquiry-Based Learning: Foster curiosity and scientific inquiry by promoting hands-on activities, experiments, and investigations. This approach allows students to generate their own questions, seek evidence, and develop a deeper understanding of scientific concepts.

4. Interdisciplinary Approaches: Encourage interdisciplinary collaboration between science, history, psychology, and other relevant disciplines. By exploring these topics from different perspectives, students gain a broader understanding of the complexities involved.

Engaging the Public

Public awareness plays a critical role in debunking myths, challenging misconceptions, and promoting scientific understanding. We must engage the public through various channels to ensure accurate information reaches a wider audience. Here are some strategies for engaging the public:

1. Science Communication: Improve engagement by translating complex scientific concepts into accessible and engaging language. Utilize various platforms, such as popular science magazines, websites, podcasts, and social media, to reach a broader audience.

2. Community Engagement: Organize public lectures, workshops, and conferences that facilitate discussions about cryptozoology, alien encounters, and paranormal phenomena. These events provide opportunities for experts, researchers, and the public to interact and exchange ideas.

3. Citizen Science Projects: Encourage citizen participation through collaborative research projects. By involving the public in data collection and analysis, individuals gain firsthand experience in scientific research, fostering a sense of ownership and understanding.

4. Education Campaigns: Launch education campaigns to address misconceptions and promote critical thinking. Use different mediums, including posters, videos, and online resources, to disseminate accurate information and debunk common myths.

Case Study: The Cryptozoology Club

One successful example of promoting education and public awareness is the establishment of a Cryptozoology Club at a high school. The club aims to engage students in the scientific exploration of cryptids, alien encounters, and paranormal phenomena. Here's how the club operates:

1. Curriculum Integration: Collaborate with science teachers to integrate cryptozoology topics into the curriculum. This integration allows club members to delve into scientific methods, research skills, and critical thinking within the context of these subjects.

2. Guest Speakers and Field Trips: Invite experts, researchers, and professional cryptozoologists to share their experiences and knowledge. Organize field trips to relevant locations, such as nature reserves or local sites known for cryptid sightings, to provide hands-on learning opportunities.

3. Independent Research Projects: Encourage club members to conduct independent research projects on specific cryptids or paranormal phenomena. Provide guidance on research methodologies, data collection, and analysis techniques to foster scientific inquiry and critical thinking.

4. Public Outreach: Organize events, such as public presentations or exhibitions, to share club members' research findings with the wider community. This outreach helps bridge the gap between the scientific community and the public, fostering a better understanding of these topics.

Through the Cryptozoology Club, students have the opportunity to explore these intriguing subjects in a structured and scientific manner. By promoting education, critical thinking, and public engagement, the club encourages a rational and evidence-based approach to cryptozoology, alien encounters, and paranormal phenomena.

Resources and Further Reading

1. Society for Cryptozoology (www.cryptozoologysociety.com) - Provides resources, research articles, and information on the scientific study of cryptozoology.

2. Paranormal Research Society (www.pararesearchsociety.org) - Offers access to studies, investigations, and research on various paranormal phenomena.

3. "Scientific Paranormal Investigation: How to Solve Unexplained Mysteries" by Benjamin Radford - Explores the scientific methods and investigative techniques used in the field of paranormal research.

4. "Cryptozoology: Science & Speculation" by Chad Arment - Examines the scientific aspects of cryptozoology and investigates the evidence behind various cryptids.

In summary, education and public awareness play a crucial role in fostering scientific literacy, challenging misconceptions, and promoting critical thinking in the realms of cryptozoology, alien encounters, and paranormal phenomena. By integrating these subjects into curricula, promoting interdisciplinary collaboration, and engaging the public through various channels, we can bridge the gap between scientific exploration and public understanding. Through education and public awareness, we can create a more informed and rational approach to these topics, encouraging scientific progress and discovery.

Index

-destruct, 145
-up, 7, 8, 32, 33

a, 1–8, 10–14, 17–22, 24–34,
    36–39, 41–43, 45–95,
    97–101, 103–108,
    111–118, 120–126,
    128–132, 135–144,
    146–172, 174–205,
    207–214
Abby Brabham, 2
abduction, 10–14, 24, 26, 27, 30, 31,
    94, 112–116, 124, 125,
    128
ability, 27, 57, 69, 73, 80, 89, 98,
    107, 126, 135, 138, 151,
    163
absence, 26, 27, 61, 62, 74, 76, 89,
    90, 124, 135, 136, 190, 192
abundance, 53, 125
acceleration, 26
acceptance, 49, 84, 129, 135, 136,
    174
access, 22, 67, 92, 155, 156
accessibility, 155
account, 10, 13, 14, 30, 51, 76, 77,
    80, 102, 129, 139, 145
accountability, 66

accuracy, 60, 78, 80, 131, 136, 154,
    155
acoustic, 152, 204
acquisition, 148, 202
act, 124, 187
activity, 14, 80, 98–100, 102, 103,
    122, 132, 147, 148, 180,
    203, 204
adaptability, 168
adaptation, 146, 167
addition, 22, 24, 61, 81, 92, 111,
    150, 158, 173, 175, 177,
    193
adherence, 151, 180
adoption, 129
advance, 49, 157, 159
advancement, 46, 136, 150, 151,
    180, 202
advent, 26, 147
adventure, 176
afterlife, 164, 165, 182
aftermath, 5
age, 77
agenda, 25, 116
air, 64
aircraft, 7, 14, 109, 118
album, 176
alien, 3, 8, 10–14, 19–22, 24, 25,

29–32, 36, 37, 71–73, 82, 85, 93, 94, 112–117, 123–125, 128, 173, 183–186, 189–191, 198, 199, 201, 211–214
alienation, 199
allure, 52, 54, 99, 177, 187
alternative, 4, 8, 12, 28, 31, 33, 34, 37, 56, 86–88, 92, 104–106, 127, 137, 139, 141, 150, 155, 156, 158, 185, 186, 188, 192–197
altitude, 8
amateur, 3, 148, 154–156, 160, 162, 201
ambiguity, 120
Americas, 55
Amityville, 103
amount, 200
amplification, 64
analysis, 7, 22, 28, 37, 43, 45–47, 49, 50, 56, 57, 60–62, 65–67, 71, 72, 75, 78–80, 87, 88, 90, 91, 93, 102, 103, 111, 117, 122, 125, 131–133, 136–138, 140, 147–150, 152, 153, 156–158, 160, 193, 194, 201, 203–205, 210, 212, 213
anatomy, 61, 78, 146
Andy Brodie, 69, 73, 76
animal, 55–58, 63, 64, 70, 75, 78, 79, 86, 89–91, 135, 146, 164, 169, 176, 192, 193
anomaly, 81
Anonymization, 204
answer, 12, 32
anthropology, 29, 45, 60, 67, 72, 85, 100, 151, 153, 205

anxiety, 4, 5, 81, 184, 185, 198, 199
ape, 53, 66
appeal, 167, 181
appearance, 1, 20, 38, 50, 53, 55, 56, 59, 64, 69–72, 75–77, 80, 88, 91, 93, 94, 98, 116, 175, 192
application, 22, 47, 195
appreciation, 39, 162, 183, 187
apprehension, 4
approach, 13, 28, 33, 37, 47, 56, 59, 65, 67, 71, 80, 86, 87, 90–93, 99, 100, 102, 104, 105, 108, 111, 115, 120, 124, 132, 133, 137, 138, 144, 148, 152, 154, 157, 159, 160, 162, 172, 174, 178, 180, 181, 183, 185, 194, 196, 200, 202, 203, 207, 211–214
appropriateness, 140
archaeology, 29
archery, 164
area, 2, 4, 5, 66, 73, 87, 89, 90, 93, 103, 125
argument, 27
Arizona, 13, 27
art, 167, 175, 176, 178, 186, 187, 197
Arthur Conan Doyle's, 171
article, 12
artwork, 58, 83, 176
Asia, 53
aspect, 22, 29, 31, 70, 76, 78, 79, 89, 90, 104, 138, 150, 161, 192, 194, 204
assassination, 32
association, 71
astrobiologist, 146

Index

astrobiology, 144–146, 150, 152, 153, 197
astronomer, 109
astronomy, 144
atmosphere, 5, 73, 81, 171
attack, 57, 74, 169
attempt, 32, 50, 58, 78–80, 131
attention, 2–4, 6, 13, 15, 20, 21, 26, 30, 42, 52, 53, 55, 58, 60, 73–75, 87, 88, 91, 108, 129, 171, 184, 193
attitude, 194, 196
attribute, 29, 62, 85, 187
audience, 174, 212
audio, 72, 100, 101, 103, 130, 131, 147, 155, 158, 203, 204
aura, 74
authenticity, 14, 72, 78, 79, 88, 91, 135, 193, 195
authority, 33, 34
availability, 147, 148, 155
avenue, 19, 95, 120
awareness, 3, 42, 46, 48, 92, 99, 159, 196, 198, 204, 211–214
awe, 20, 175, 178, 184, 199

baby, 69
back, 10, 32, 38, 43, 50, 57, 74, 141, 166, 168, 169
background, 1, 29, 31, 60
backyard, 3
balance, 104, 149, 178
ball, 64
balloon, 8, 32, 108
bark, 63
barrier, 126
Bartlett, 1, 2, 69, 76, 77, 88
base, 8
baseline, 60, 203

basis, 54, 89, 113, 132, 143, 185
Baskerville, 171
bat, 57, 58, 166
Baxter, 2, 73
beam, 13
bear, 55, 63, 71, 89, 148
beast, 164
behavior, 20, 38, 46, 49, 56, 59, 61, 64, 67, 69–72, 74, 76–79, 89, 94, 116, 117, 164, 185, 190, 203, 209
behavioral, 30, 116
being, 1, 3, 5, 6, 10, 24, 30, 38, 53, 57, 59, 67, 69–71, 73, 74, 76, 80, 88, 91–93, 98, 102, 114, 123, 143, 148, 161, 168, 182, 184, 192, 193, 198
belief, 12, 29–31, 36–39, 55, 56, 64, 65, 84, 85, 94, 121, 124, 125, 128, 129, 168–170, 179, 180, 184, 185, 197–200
belonging, 37, 56, 61, 167, 187, 192, 200, 204
benefit, 154, 204
Benjamin Radford, 83, 103
Benjamin Radford - Explores, 213
Bernard Heuvelmans, 42, 43
Betty, 10, 12
bias, 64, 65, 84, 87, 102, 128–130, 138, 140, 158, 184, 201
Bigfoot, 37, 52–54, 63, 74, 94, 118, 121, 123, 124, 126, 129, 136, 155, 175–178, 184, 189, 191, 203, 209
Bigfoot, 74
Bill Bartlett, 1, 69, 73, 76, 88
biodiversity, 45, 51, 201

biology, 45, 67, 144, 151, 152, 190, 203, 205
bioluminescence, 64
bird, 58, 87, 163, 192
blockbuster, 187
blood, 38, 55, 74, 165, 169, 179
Bluff Creek, 209
board, 10, 27
boat, 180
body, 1, 49, 50, 58, 60, 69, 71, 73, 76, 116, 117, 155, 164, 170, 176, 191, 192
bonding, 187
book, 12, 28, 42, 93, 94
boom, 5
boost, 5
Boston, 73
botany, 47
boy, 88
brain, 59, 64, 80, 83, 87, 143, 152
branch, 76
Brazel, 7
bridge, 92, 115, 123, 133, 143, 151, 153, 159, 161, 186, 202, 213, 214
British Columbia, 166
Brodie, 76, 77
brow, 53
build, 52, 73
building, 158, 164
burial, 121

Calama, 55
California, 209
camaraderie, 3
camera, 43, 203
Canada, 166, 168
canvas, 175
car, 10
card, 141
care, 204
Carl Sagan, 144
case, 3, 4, 10–14, 24, 25, 27–31, 37, 38, 42, 46, 48, 51, 60–64, 68, 70, 74, 76–79, 82, 85, 86, 90, 93, 99, 103, 111, 117, 128, 135, 137, 146, 159, 180, 192, 201, 202, 207–211
cast, 59
casting, 79
cat, 63, 192
catalog, 48
cataloging, 46, 48
category, 17, 63
cause, 64, 198
caution, 59, 86, 124, 132, 181, 186
cave, 175
celebration, 36
cell, 88
center, 3, 64, 80, 177
century, 26, 50, 52, 57, 141, 144, 166, 201
ceremony, 164, 165
chain, 195
challenge, 22, 37, 41, 45, 60, 65, 73, 99, 122, 123, 140, 148, 150, 151, 154–156, 172, 176, 184, 199, 200
chapter, 10, 12, 54, 82, 115, 153
chemistry, 140, 144
child, 57
childbirth, 57
Chile, 55
choice, 75
Chupacabra, 2, 37–39, 55–57, 71, 118, 124, 126, 155, 166, 167, 169

Chupacabras, 39
citizen, 46, 49, 148, 154–157, 160, 162, 204, 205, 212
city, 27
civilization, 29, 164
claim, 8, 11, 22, 24, 28, 33, 59, 88, 122, 135, 190, 199
clarity, 140
classification, 67, 109, 136
cleansing, 182
closure, 101
clothing, 20
club, 212, 213
coast, 201
coelacanth, 41, 171, 201
cognition, 30
cohesion, 185
Coleman, 46
collaboration, 19, 45, 47, 48, 62, 72, 80, 90–92, 120, 125, 140, 141, 148, 153, 154, 156–159, 187, 191, 193, 196, 212, 214
collapse, 165
collection, 46, 47, 49, 57, 62, 66, 75, 90, 92, 93, 130, 132, 133, 136, 147–150, 154–157, 160, 191, 192, 194, 196, 202–205, 207, 208, 210, 212, 213
combat, 46
combination, 8, 11, 31, 103, 130, 161, 169, 179
comedy, 177
comfort, 98, 179, 184
commander, 8
communicating, 68
communication, 20, 22, 24, 25, 92, 116, 145, 153, 157, 161, 162, 190
community, 2–6, 25, 36, 38, 47, 53, 55, 58, 62, 66, 73, 75, 81, 91, 93, 98, 99, 114, 122, 129, 135, 136, 140, 141, 150, 153, 154, 158, 167, 185–187, 195, 198, 199, 204, 213
comparison, 78, 203
completeness, 155
complex, 30–32, 39, 86, 94, 106, 117, 127, 148, 151, 153, 157, 161, 169, 200, 204, 205, 212
complexity, 4, 5, 43, 169
component, 25, 77, 138, 139
composition, 61
comprehension, 167, 183
computer, 152
concept, 11, 12, 26, 28, 42, 126, 137, 146, 153, 181, 183
conclusion, 2, 4, 19, 25, 43, 46, 49, 60, 65, 77, 86, 88, 94, 95, 112, 117, 120, 123, 125, 136–138, 151, 156, 174, 176, 178, 183, 188, 191, 194, 198, 202, 207
condition, 64
conditioning, 29
conduct, 21, 45, 47, 53, 61, 66, 67, 71, 90, 102, 103, 125, 131, 137, 141, 154–156, 213
conference, 159
confidentiality, 67
confirmation, 65, 84, 85, 87, 130, 140, 158, 201
conflict, 83, 164, 175, 199
conformity, 84, 129
confusion, 4, 5, 98, 199

connection, 2, 12, 22, 38, 80, 99, 118, 120–125, 131, 165, 169, 176, 187, 191
consciousness, 22, 25, 36, 38, 39, 97, 100, 144, 167, 201
consensus, 150, 201
consent, 67, 92, 143, 161, 204
conservation, 46, 49, 187
consistency, 60, 70, 76, 77, 90, 137, 154, 191, 192, 195, 203, 208
conspiracy, 3, 7, 8, 21, 31–34, 108
construction, 36
constructivism, 37
contact, 7, 9, 11, 13, 20, 22, 24–26, 124, 136, 190, 202
contagion, 64, 65
contamination, 148, 203
content, 36, 112
context, 8, 9, 11, 30, 37, 47, 63, 64, 82, 83, 86, 89, 91, 93, 123, 126, 128, 129, 138, 139, 145, 154, 169, 179, 180, 183, 185, 194, 200, 207, 213
continuation, 81
contrast, 75, 82, 122, 146, 163, 169
control, 38, 102, 115, 154, 157, 179, 184
controversy, 14
convergence, 130, 191
conviction, 37
core, 36, 144
cornerstone, 47
correlation, 89
corroborating, 60
corroboration, 77
costume, 70
counseling, 92

counter, 62, 192, 193
counterbalance, 108
couple, 10
course, 73
cover, 7, 8, 32, 33, 190
coverage, 1–4, 13, 37, 42, 81, 84, 87, 179
coyote, 63, 87
craft, 10, 27, 209
crash, 7–9, 26, 164
creation, 25, 37, 57, 170, 179, 181, 192
creativity, 175
creature, 1–5, 37–39, 50–67, 69–83, 86–91, 93–95, 116, 129, 135, 137, 145, 164–166, 168, 171, 175, 179, 180, 192, 193, 195, 197, 203, 209
credibility, 14, 19, 47, 48, 53, 54, 60, 68, 70, 72, 75–79, 88, 90, 91, 102, 103, 108, 111, 132, 138–141, 147, 154, 161, 190, 192, 193, 195, 202, 211
crisis, 98, 99
criticism, 11, 122, 141, 143
critique, 66, 150
cross, 28, 43, 60, 126, 138, 153, 168, 170
crowd, 148, 155
crowdsourcing, 203–205
cry, 58
cryptid, 1, 5, 31, 37–39, 42, 43, 46, 52, 55, 61–68, 70–75, 79, 81, 93–95, 118, 122, 125, 135, 137, 139, 145, 146, 148, 152, 156, 165, 167–171, 175, 176, 179,

Index 221

180, 182, 184, 185,
189–192, 195–197,
201–204, 209, 213
cryptozoologist, 46, 75
Cryptozoologists, 56–58, 61, 81,
135, 189
cryptozoologists, 2, 42, 44–46, 49,
53, 55–57, 62, 66–68, 74,
82, 95, 118, 125, 135, 136,
174, 187
cryptozoology, 1, 2, 41–49, 52, 54,
56, 58, 59, 61, 62, 65–68,
70–72, 74, 75, 90, 91, 93,
118, 121, 122, 125, 126,
135, 139–141, 147–156,
159–162, 168, 170,
172–181, 186–188, 193,
194, 200–203, 205, 207,
209–214
culture, 11, 36, 39, 43, 52–54, 58,
75, 77, 85, 117, 129, 153,
164, 168, 170, 177–180,
183, 185–187, 197
curiosity, 3–5, 13, 20, 41, 50, 55, 57,
59, 73, 95, 127, 150, 161,
167, 170, 172–174,
176–178, 184, 188,
197–200, 211, 212
curricula, 160, 198, 211, 214
curriculum, 213
custody, 195
cycle, 163, 164

damage, 180
danger, 166
darkness, 73, 76, 87
data, 19, 28, 45–47, 49, 62, 65–68,
72, 75, 79, 90–93, 99, 117,
125, 130, 132, 133,
135–138, 140, 146–150,
154–158, 160, 191, 192,
194, 196, 201–205, 207,
208, 210, 212, 213
database, 48
dataset, 203
date, 48, 50, 57, 61
David Marcusson-Clavertz, 103
day, 6, 7, 13, 52, 81, 90
dead, 55, 164, 165, 170
deal, 98, 121
death, 98, 163, 164
debate, 9, 34, 42, 54, 55, 62, 63, 70,
83, 99, 111, 112, 125, 156,
209
debris, 7, 8
debunking, 4, 37, 89, 104–106, 108,
129, 184–186, 212
decision, 197, 198
dedication, 136
definition, 147
deformation, 193
degradation, 146
deity, 164
demeanor, 60
demise, 164
democratization, 148
demon, 80
depiction, 53
depth, 12, 43, 79, 155
description, 2, 38, 55, 60, 76, 81, 88,
102, 137
design, 137, 140, 150, 157
desire, 33, 46, 52, 84, 127, 129, 167,
171, 187, 199
destination, 5, 27
destruct, 145
detail, 12, 58, 136

development, 41, 91, 147, 153, 158, 182, 203, 207
device, 103
devil, 57
devotion, 182
dialogue, 48, 93, 140, 157–159, 176, 183, 186
Dick King-Smith, 177
difference, 122
difficulty, 66, 82
dimension, 3, 80, 126
disaster, 165
disbelief, 199
disc, 8, 108
discipline, 41–43, 141, 151–153, 205
discomfort, 83, 84, 128, 199
discourse, 161, 186, 197, 198
discovery, 41, 43, 46, 120, 155, 171, 172, 199–202, 214
discussion, 74, 83, 92, 171, 176
disease, 55, 64
disruption, 6
dissemination, 33, 37, 46, 47, 84
dissonance, 83, 85, 128, 130, 199
distance, 53, 63, 87, 124, 146
distortion, 31, 190
distress, 92
distribution, 144
distrust, 33
disturbance, 67
diversity, 5, 156, 168–170, 189
divination, 104
diving, 9, 100
document, 79, 100, 101, 131, 154, 158, 187
documentary, 12
documentation, 47, 88, 136, 138, 155, 189, 190, 209

dog, 55, 166
domain, 99
doom, 164
dose, 100, 104, 178, 194
doubt, 89, 190, 194
Dover, 1–6, 62, 69–71, 73, 76, 77, 79–83, 88, 89, 94, 95, 145, 192–194
Dover, 73
dowsing, 92, 104
dragon, 163
drawing, 65, 68, 83, 137
dread, 98
dreaming, 22
dwelling, 50, 168

Earth, 26–28, 70, 94, 126, 144, 145, 152, 189–191
ecology, 46, 47, 67
economy, 5, 6, 58, 166
ecosystem, 51, 67
education, 48, 92, 151, 159–162, 197, 202, 211–214
effect, 5
effectiveness, 30, 104
effort, 171
element, 125, 171
elusiveness, 54, 126
emergence, 41, 81
empathy, 186
encounter, 5, 10–12, 14, 20–22, 24, 25, 49, 59, 61, 69, 75, 85, 88, 128, 151, 198, 199
encryption, 204
energy, 13, 98, 102, 122, 123, 132
enforcement, 14, 53, 158
engagement, 3, 92, 151, 159–162, 202, 204, 211–213
England, 209

enlightenment, 20
Enrico Fermi, 9
entertainment, 43, 54, 167, 172, 173, 178, 187, 197
enthusiast, 43
entity, 72, 80, 98
entry, 124
environment, 17–19, 51, 53, 67, 71, 82, 98, 102, 103, 116, 126, 150, 169
environmentalism, 187
equation, 145
equipment, 66, 93, 100, 130, 132, 138, 147, 155
equivalent, 53
error, 138
essay, 31
establishment, 212
estate, 171
Etzel Cardeña, 103
evaluation, 4, 48, 80, 130, 139, 141, 151, 195, 196
evening, 7, 69, 73
event, 8, 10, 14, 24, 27, 32, 59, 60, 77, 97, 102, 128, 129, 209
evidence, 8, 13, 14, 17–21, 25, 27–29, 31–34, 37, 41, 43, 45, 47, 48, 50, 51, 53, 54, 56–67, 70–72, 74, 75, 77–80, 82–84, 86–95, 99–108, 112, 115, 117, 118, 120–122, 124–132, 135–137, 139–141, 145–150, 152, 154, 155, 157, 158, 160, 171, 173, 174, 178, 184–186, 189–197, 201–204, 209, 211–213
evolution, 47, 144, 179

exaggeration, 56, 103, 192
examination, 27, 43, 78–80, 85, 87, 91, 105, 107, 115, 132, 150, 189, 192–194
example, 24, 25, 29, 36–38, 50, 56, 63, 64, 66, 67, 83, 86, 88, 122, 128–130, 135–138, 145, 147, 148, 150, 155–158, 165, 168, 170, 171, 176, 178–182, 184–186, 197, 201, 202, 212
exception, 67
exchange, 5, 24, 25, 47, 92, 157, 159, 202, 212
excitement, 3, 192
exercise, 111, 112
exhibit, 56, 99
existence, 2, 3, 14, 21, 26, 27, 29, 30, 33, 36, 37, 41, 42, 47, 50–56, 58–67, 72, 75, 78, 79, 81–85, 89, 90, 94, 99, 112, 118, 121, 123, 125, 126, 128–130, 135, 136, 144–146, 150, 166, 170, 171, 175–179, 184, 190–192, 194–197, 209
expectation, 69, 81, 102
experience, 3, 10–12, 14, 20, 27, 76, 77, 81, 84, 102, 115, 124, 128, 165, 180, 182, 199, 212
experiment, 12, 82, 137, 138
experimentation, 3, 137, 157, 194
expert, 84, 141
expertise, 67, 91, 123, 151, 154, 155, 157, 159, 174, 191, 193, 195, 202, 204, 207
explanation, 8, 11, 12, 14, 21, 28, 30,

      53, 71, 77, 80, 83, 87, 89,
      108, 112, 116, 117, 123,
      124, 126, 137, 193
exploitation, 102, 180
exploration, 3, 5, 12, 19, 22, 28, 36,
      43, 44, 47, 49, 59, 73, 95,
      120, 127, 130, 143, 144,
      155–157, 160–162, 167,
      170, 174, 176, 187–189,
      194, 199–202, 207, 210,
      213, 214
explore, 1, 7, 10, 13, 17, 18, 22, 24,
      30, 34, 36, 44–46, 54, 57,
      59, 61, 62, 65, 70, 71, 78,
      80, 82, 83, 85, 86, 92, 94,
      97, 99–101, 104, 106, 112,
      113, 115, 117, 119,
      121–123, 125, 127, 130,
      132, 139, 141, 143, 144,
      147, 150–152, 157, 159,
      163, 165, 167, 170, 172,
      174–177, 179, 181, 183,
      186, 191, 192, 197, 198,
      200, 202, 205–207, 211,
      213
explorer, 43
exposure, 31, 56, 174, 184
expression, 175
extent, 30
eye, 4, 131, 139, 174
eyewitness, 2–4, 47, 50, 58–60, 62,
      66, 72, 75–77, 84, 88, 90,
      91, 94, 121, 122, 124, 129,
      130, 132, 135, 137–139,
      171, 180, 187, 190, 192,
      194, 195

fabric, 43, 179, 181
fabrication, 60, 103, 124

face, 5, 16, 69, 71, 102, 140, 166,
      199, 210
facet, 196
fact, 8, 65, 76, 88, 94, 108, 139, 174,
      179–181, 194, 196, 200,
      202, 211
factor, 63
faith, 182
fame, 88, 193
familiarity, 63, 154, 178
family, 98, 103, 177, 184
fantasy, 30, 180
fascination, 2–5, 14, 41, 43, 46,
      52–54, 73, 74, 81, 95, 97,
      99, 108, 121, 125, 165,
      167–169, 172, 174, 176,
      178, 184, 185, 197–199
fate, 165
fatigue, 87
favor, 66, 137, 158
fear, 3–5, 20, 39, 55, 73, 77, 81, 94,
      98, 116, 136, 165, 166,
      171, 184, 187, 192,
      198–200
feasibility, 146, 190
feature, 18, 53, 174
feedback, 140, 150
fiction, 31, 36, 65, 75, 94, 108, 139,
      170–172, 174, 177–179,
      181, 194, 196, 197, 200,
      202, 211
field, 2, 11, 14, 19, 20, 24, 25, 38, 41,
      43–49, 52, 54, 58, 61, 62,
      65–67, 71, 72, 74, 75, 77,
      90–94, 100, 118, 125, 132,
      133, 135, 138–144,
      146–156, 158, 159, 161,
      168, 170, 172, 174–177,
      179–181, 201–207, 209,

Index

210, 213
figment, 5
figure, 2, 42, 56, 58, 71, 73, 76, 197
film, 14, 63, 209
find, 94, 124, 136, 201
finding, 42, 192
fire, 163, 164
fish, 41, 51, 171, 201
Flatwoods, 71
flaw, 27
flexibility, 156
flood, 4
flurry, 1
flying, 8, 58, 108, 118
focus, 45, 80, 82, 101, 152, 184
fog, 87
foil, 8
folk, 41, 153, 176, 179, 180
folklore, 1, 36–38, 47, 51, 56–59, 63, 74, 85, 89, 94, 118, 121, 122, 155, 164–169, 176, 179, 180, 182, 185–188, 197, 198
food, 51
foot, 78
footage, 101, 102, 155, 202
footprint, 45, 54, 61, 72, 91, 118
forest, 13, 169, 209
form, 11, 37, 59, 80, 83, 89, 94, 98, 113, 123, 129, 145, 148, 149, 154, 158, 185, 186
formation, 37, 92, 130, 184–186, 200
formulation, 137, 194
fortune, 163
fossil, 171
Foster, 212
foster, 5, 49, 92, 105, 150, 154, 157, 198, 213

foundation, 42, 59, 113, 131, 144, 149, 150, 194
founding, 42
fraction, 145
frame, 209
framework, 11, 42, 142, 183, 184, 201, 202
Frank Drake, 144
freedom, 170
friend, 1, 76, 98
fringe, 65, 120, 149–151, 156
frustration, 57
funding, 46, 48, 66, 136, 155
funerary, 164
fur, 166
future, 45, 46, 49, 73, 95, 127, 144, 149, 159, 191, 204–206, 210

gain, 12, 14, 22, 30, 38, 39, 46, 47, 60, 61, 66, 74, 82, 85, 86, 91, 100, 115, 116, 125, 129, 130, 135, 153, 165, 168, 169, 186, 198, 200, 202, 204, 207, 212
gait, 69
galaxy, 145
gap, 49, 92, 95, 115, 123, 133, 143, 150, 151, 157, 159–162, 186, 191, 200, 202, 213, 214
gateway, 174, 176, 187
general, 3, 33, 53, 88, 93, 144, 148, 151, 159, 198, 203
generation, 166
genetic, 25, 56, 61, 67, 79, 81, 124, 203
genre, 177
geography, 71, 152

geology, 144
ghost, 29, 54, 97–99, 103, 121, 122, 148
giant, 164
Gibbons, 89
glance, 115
glimmer, 136
glimpse, 167, 180
glow, 64
glowing, 1, 2, 55, 57, 60, 64, 69–71, 73, 75, 76, 88, 93, 98, 116, 165, 192
goal, 61, 79, 131, 157
goat, 55, 165, 166
god, 170
government, 3, 7, 8, 21, 32–34, 190
ground, 153, 157, 177
groundbreaking, 48, 51, 149
groundwork, 137
group, 10, 25, 37, 81, 84, 129, 183, 185
growth, 41–43, 153
guardian, 38, 168
guidance, 98, 143, 156, 157, 182, 213
guide, 12, 65, 95, 137, 164

H.G. Wells', 197
H.P. Lovecraft, 177
H.P. Lovecraft's, 187
habit, 55, 165
habitat, 67, 122, 175, 203
hair, 52, 55, 61, 76, 79, 118, 122, 125, 190, 203
hallucination, 14, 192, 193
hand, 33, 64, 66, 94, 121–123, 131, 149, 157–159, 184, 189, 199
handling, 131, 203
harm, 67, 92, 136, 161
harmony, 175
haunting, 29, 98, 176, 178
head, 53, 57, 60, 69, 74, 76, 88, 140, 164, 166, 192
heart, 164
heat, 102, 131
height, 1
help, 10, 19, 22, 36, 39, 49, 59, 65–67, 72, 79, 85, 86, 91, 92, 107, 117, 129, 130, 132, 138, 145, 150, 152, 154, 158, 159, 184, 194, 202, 211
Hendersons, 177
heritage, 37, 38, 155, 165, 166, 169, 187
Heuvelmans, 42
hiding, 32, 73, 190
Himalayas, 168
history, 10, 24, 29, 30, 32, 41–43, 46, 50, 57, 63, 97, 108, 118, 163, 170, 175, 176, 197, 209, 212
hoax, 5, 13, 14, 50, 63, 70, 128, 139, 193, 209
hockey, 166
home, 1, 10, 13, 76
hope, 81, 90, 136
horse, 57, 74, 164, 166
hotspot, 5
hound, 171
house, 76, 103
hub, 47
Hugh Gray, 50
human, 8, 12, 21, 24–29, 38, 41, 57, 59, 63, 69, 70, 80, 81, 87, 94, 99, 100, 121, 124, 126, 136, 143, 164, 165,

Index 227

167–170, 182, 183, 186,
189, 192–195, 198, 200,
201, 204
humanity, 11, 19, 25, 26, 126, 127
humidity, 158
hunting, 89, 122, 148, 164, 180
hybridization, 25, 124
hypnosis, 10, 11, 24, 30, 31
hypnotist, 31
hypothesis, 8, 26–31, 51, 53, 66, 70,
71, 94, 137, 189–191
hysteria, 56–58, 64, 70, 87, 94

idea, 3, 4, 26, 29, 124, 144, 158
identification, 61, 204, 210
identity, 5, 6, 36, 37, 58, 59, 61, 82,
93, 166, 167, 180, 185,
186, 200
illness, 30
illusion, 70, 193
image, 36, 51, 53, 56, 78, 83
imagery, 58, 176
imagination, 3, 11, 25, 29, 31, 36, 38,
41, 42, 50, 57, 59, 70, 75,
83, 93, 99, 108, 121, 125,
127, 144, 158, 165, 167,
168, 171, 172, 175–178,
180, 187, 188, 197, 198
imaging, 61, 102, 131, 143, 147,
150, 158, 202
immersion, 176
immortality, 163
impact, 2–5, 10–12, 14, 20, 22, 36,
39, 60, 62, 67, 75, 77, 91,
92, 98, 102, 103, 116, 167,
174, 178–181, 183, 185,
186, 188, 197–200, 209,
211
implantation, 124

implausibility, 59
importance, 4, 47, 48, 56, 57, 59, 60,
62, 67, 87, 92, 104, 107,
112, 139, 144, 151, 160,
161, 170, 188, 194–196,
201, 202, 205, 211
impression, 2
improvement, 148
inception, 46
incident, 7, 8, 13, 14, 26, 28, 55, 209
inclusion, 43, 171, 211
increase, 5, 29, 129, 136, 138
individual, 83, 85–87, 113, 122,
183, 207, 210
industry, 5, 51, 178
influence, 4, 11, 13, 28, 30, 36–38,
43, 51, 60, 63, 81–85, 87,
94, 102, 129, 130, 140,
168–170, 172, 174,
176–185, 192, 193, 197
influx, 4
information, 3, 4, 9, 21, 22, 24, 29,
31, 33, 37, 46, 48, 49,
59–61, 64, 66, 67, 71, 72,
76–81, 84, 90, 92, 93, 101,
102, 106, 111, 128–132,
149, 156, 159, 172, 174,
184, 190, 192, 202–204,
211, 212
injury, 64
innovation, 154
inquiry, 4, 34, 48, 65, 101, 139, 146,
149, 151, 156, 158, 168,
171, 176, 178, 179, 183,
185, 188, 191, 194, 196,
201, 212, 213
insight, 61, 117, 198, 201
inspiration, 52, 167, 171, 172, 175,
176

instance, 30, 41, 63, 85, 129, 137, 151, 161, 168, 169, 171, 184, 192, 204
instill, 167
integration, 150, 213
integrity, 91, 93, 102, 131, 138, 139, 141, 143, 148, 161
intelligence, 9, 116, 126, 146, 190
interaction, 21, 24–26, 109, 175
interconnectedness, 115, 169
interest, 1, 3, 5, 10, 19, 25, 37, 42, 43, 46, 50, 52, 54, 74, 99, 112, 131, 137, 140, 151, 161, 173, 174, 176, 186, 211
internet, 33
interplay, 31, 39, 86, 125, 183
interpretation, 12, 13, 30, 31, 36, 81, 83–87, 89, 94, 102, 130, 140, 147, 148, 158, 169, 183, 185, 186, 195, 201
intersection, 59, 122, 123, 151, 159
intervention, 29
interview, 21, 72, 90, 91
intoxication, 87
intrigue, 2, 3, 5, 34, 97, 133, 171, 174, 175, 178
introduction, 154
investigation, 14, 15, 17, 19, 22, 27, 41, 43, 47, 49, 59, 60, 62, 65, 66, 71–74, 77, 78, 80, 82, 86, 87, 90–93, 99, 104, 125, 127, 130–133, 136, 146, 147, 150, 154–157, 159, 161, 162, 167, 176, 180, 185, 192–194, 196, 199, 200, 202, 205, 207, 209, 210
investigator, 10

involvement, 26, 27, 32, 46, 143, 156
isolation, 82, 199
issue, 180
Italy, 25
Ivan T. Sanderson, 43

J. Allen Hynek, 109
J.B. Rhine, 141
jackal, 164
Jacques Vallee, 83
Jerome Clark, 83
John Baxter, 1, 73, 88
John E. Mack, 83
John F. Kennedy, 32
John G. Fuller, 12
John Palmer, 103
journal, 48
journey, 10, 54, 95, 165
joy, 97
Julian Rotter, 129
Jupiter, 146

kangaroo, 166
kind, 17–22, 24, 25
knowledge, 19, 25, 27, 34, 41, 45–49, 54, 64, 69, 73, 92, 95, 101, 123, 137, 138, 150–159, 166, 167, 170, 172, 174, 180, 186–192, 194, 198, 200, 201, 204, 206, 207, 211, 213
kraken, 164

laboratory, 57, 91, 99
lack, 17, 25, 33, 45, 48, 53, 54, 58, 59, 63, 64, 66, 70, 82, 88, 90, 92, 94, 99, 102, 118, 120, 121, 125–127, 135, 136, 140, 145, 154, 155,

157, 190, 191, 197, 199, 203
lake, 50, 63, 67, 74, 166, 171
Lake Champlain, 63
land, 169
landing, 20
landscape, 73, 106
language, 77, 212
Latin America, 2, 71, 169
law, 14, 53, 158
layer, 4, 5, 9, 38, 89
layout, 131
lead, 29, 64, 66, 83, 84, 87, 129, 149, 153, 154, 158, 191, 192, 199, 200, 203
learning, 12, 184, 198, 204, 211, 213
Leeds, 57
legacy, 5, 6
legend, 36, 52, 54, 56–59, 103, 165, 166, 171, 179, 180
legitimacy, 89, 114, 153
length, 52
lens, 34, 94, 117, 127, 172, 182, 200, 205
Leon Festinger, 128
level, 30, 109, 116, 171, 197
levitation, 116
lie, 14, 70, 95, 188
life, 9, 14, 22, 26, 29–33, 50, 52, 84, 85, 94, 112, 117, 144–146, 150, 152, 164, 170–172, 174–177, 190, 197
lifespan, 145
light, 8, 10, 13, 14, 26, 27, 37, 38, 46, 56, 61, 62, 67, 70, 72, 80, 81, 83, 85, 86, 89, 95, 101, 120, 123, 125, 128, 130, 143, 147, 151, 155, 159, 165, 191, 194, 200, 201

lighting, 53, 56, 63, 78, 87, 103
lightning, 64
likelihood, 29, 65, 129, 132, 145, 152
limit, 66, 155, 191
limitation, 153
line, 87, 151, 164, 171
link, 38, 120, 124, 125
list, 159
literacy, 92, 198, 211, 213
literature, 31, 36, 43, 164, 167, 170–172, 177, 178, 186, 187
livestock, 38, 39, 55–57, 74, 165, 169, 179
living, 97, 98, 122, 171, 201
local, 2–5, 7, 10, 36–39, 51, 55, 58, 62, 63, 67, 75, 81, 89–91, 93, 103, 154, 155, 165–167, 169, 171, 179–181, 185–187, 199, 213
location, 1, 21, 61, 71, 73, 74, 91, 102, 103, 124, 131, 204
Loch Ness, 51
locomotion, 78, 89
logger, 13
London, 178
loop, 97
Loren Coleman, 83
Loren Coleman, 46
loss, 55, 115
Lutz, 103

mainstream, 34, 41, 45, 47–49, 81, 99, 115, 121–123, 133, 135, 141, 143, 149–151, 156, 173, 177, 187, 188, 197

maintenance, 129, 130
majority, 62, 124, 191
makeup, 79
man, 27–29, 118, 164
Mange, 55
mange, 55, 56
manifestation, 11
manipulation, 25, 78, 116, 124
manner, 84, 131, 137, 151, 161, 201, 213
map, 5
marginalization, 199
mark, 2, 54, 186, 187
marketing, 51
marriage, 11
Mary Shelley's, 170
mascot, 166
mass, 37, 50, 56–58, 64, 70, 87, 94
Massachusetts, 1, 3–5, 69, 73, 76, 88
material, 8, 61, 79, 130
matter, 150, 161, 201
Mazzocca, 76, 77
meaning, 38, 80, 98, 168, 183, 184
means, 20, 24, 97, 101, 112, 121, 166, 170, 195
measure, 79, 137, 142
measurement, 138
mechanism, 98, 184, 185, 187
media, 1–4, 10, 13, 28–31, 37, 42, 54, 56, 74, 75, 77, 81, 84, 85, 87, 167, 169, 174, 175, 179, 184, 185, 187, 193, 198, 212
meditation, 22, 24, 182
medium, 175
mediumship, 132, 133, 158
member, 98
membership, 46

memory, 10, 22, 30, 31, 60, 76, 77, 129, 195
mention, 99
merchandise, 5, 36, 197
merit, 140
metal, 176
method, 65–68, 104, 137–139, 151, 157, 194, 196
methodology, 75, 93, 137, 140, 143, 150, 159, 160, 180, 181, 195, 207, 208, 210
Mexico, 38, 55, 165
migration, 152
Mike Mazzocca, 69, 73, 76
military, 7, 8, 14, 27, 32, 108, 209
million, 41, 53
mind, 12, 13, 21, 22, 29, 63, 65, 90, 94, 99, 100, 104, 120, 122, 148, 172, 180, 193, 200, 201
mindedness, 104, 127, 150, 153, 157, 188
mindset, 33, 37, 56, 59, 105, 108, 178, 179, 201
misidentification, 50, 51, 56, 62, 70, 86–88, 192, 193
misinformation, 8, 33, 46, 178, 185, 200, 211
misinterpretation, 51, 57, 59, 64, 65, 81, 87, 124, 139, 148, 154, 191, 192, 203
misperception, 51, 63
misrepresentation, 174
mission, 146
mistrust, 33
mix, 54
mixture, 5
mold, 61
moment, 1

Index 231

monitoring, 49, 103, 158
monster, 36, 129, 164, 166, 180
moonlight, 87
morphology, 78, 209
moth, 165
Mothman, 2
motion, 61, 89, 203
motive, 32
movement, 91, 102
multitude, 190
multiverse, 126
murder, 14
music, 175, 176, 178, 186, 187, 197
mystery, 2, 3, 17, 50, 52, 56, 59, 73, 74, 94, 98, 171, 175, 176, 187
mystique, 171
myth, 38, 53, 56, 59, 65, 167
mythology, 29, 163–166, 168, 169, 175, 176, 197

name, 55, 58, 165
narrative, 4, 73, 75, 87, 89, 161, 171
nature, 3, 4, 8, 11, 12, 17, 19, 20, 22, 25, 27, 29, 30, 45, 53, 54, 58, 61, 64, 66, 67, 70, 72, 74, 75, 78–82, 86, 88, 91, 93, 94, 98, 99, 109, 111, 116, 117, 120, 122, 123, 138, 140, 141, 143, 151, 164, 165, 169, 175, 177, 178, 183, 187, 189, 198–201, 213
neck, 50, 74
need, 4, 38, 41, 45, 46, 62, 66, 72, 90, 94, 102, 103, 125, 150, 153, 158, 179, 187, 193
neighboring, 3
Neil Gemmell, 51

Nessie, 36, 50–52, 74
nest, 164
network, 154, 185
neuroscience, 85, 143
New Hampshire, 10
New Jersey, 57, 58, 74, 166, 197
New Mexico, 7, 26, 32, 108
New York, 103
news, 7, 8
newspaper, 47
Niagara Falls, 10
night, 1, 2, 10, 69, 73, 74, 76, 87
non, 20, 61, 62, 82, 86, 123, 154–156, 171
none, 82
nonexistence, 121
North America, 52, 53, 63, 74, 169
nose, 69
notion, 11, 177, 190, 191
notoriety, 14, 58, 60
novel, 154, 170, 171
number, 28, 78, 108, 145

object, 7, 8, 32, 83, 86, 108, 202
objective, 25, 47, 60, 79, 94, 137, 148, 158
objectivity, 72
observation, 17, 70, 137, 189, 194, 207
obstacle, 135, 136
occasion, 171
occurrence, 83, 84, 86, 132
ocean, 164
octopus, 164
odor, 52
off, 182, 201
offer, 19, 27, 45, 49, 65, 70, 72, 77, 86, 89, 99, 101, 123, 127, 143, 149, 151–153, 156,

167, 172, 183, 191, 200, 210
offering, 59, 71, 72, 123, 156, 165, 167, 179, 184, 185
official, 8
offspring, 25
Okanagan Lake, 166
one, 1, 2, 7, 10, 13, 14, 24, 27, 30, 50, 52, 54, 71, 75, 80, 81, 87, 94, 95, 98, 129, 135, 144, 146, 164–166, 168, 176, 195, 199, 209
openness, 151, 186
operation, 8
opinion, 4, 37, 185
opportunity, 19, 73, 140, 172, 213
orange, 1, 2, 60, 64, 69, 70, 73, 76
order, 21, 30, 65, 74, 88, 90, 118, 121, 130, 137, 157
organization, 46, 49
origin, 27, 58, 70, 72, 74, 98, 109, 118, 122, 144, 179, 189, 193, 203
other, 1–3, 12, 14, 15, 20–22, 24–26, 33, 36–38, 42, 43, 47, 59, 61, 64, 66, 71, 73–75, 78–80, 82, 83, 85–87, 89, 91, 94, 95, 98, 99, 102, 103, 115, 117, 118, 121–125, 130, 131, 137, 138, 143–147, 149, 150, 152, 156–159, 166, 175, 176, 184, 187, 189, 192, 193, 198, 199, 207, 212
otherworldliness, 176
outreach, 48, 49, 91, 93, 161, 162, 213
overlap, 119, 122, 191

overview, 100, 108, 146
ownership, 204, 212

panel, 83
panic, 13
paper, 139, 140
paradox, 145
parallel, 21, 126
paralysis, 11, 12, 14, 64, 70
paranoia, 32
paranormal, 1, 2, 4, 5, 29–31, 33, 38, 51, 54, 55, 59, 60, 74–77, 80, 82–95, 98–108, 115, 117, 121–123, 125, 127–133, 139–141, 143, 147–149, 151–162, 167, 172–174, 177, 178, 181–183, 185–187, 194–202, 207, 209–214
parapsychology, 91, 99, 141, 143, 144, 197
pareidolia, 51, 60, 63, 80, 83, 183
park, 53
parsimony, 196
part, 21, 37, 43, 70, 84, 89, 124, 139, 165–167, 169, 170, 181, 189, 193
participation, 151, 154, 159, 160, 212
passage, 8, 70, 74, 77
passion, 188, 201
past, 28, 33, 97, 127
pattern, 72
Patterson-Gimlin, 63
peace, 101
peer, 48, 84, 139–141, 150, 151, 195
people, 3–5, 29, 36, 39, 50, 52, 57, 63, 84, 98, 108, 112, 121, 128–130, 133, 154, 163,

167–169, 173, 177–180, 183, 184, 188, 197
percentage, 111, 112
perception, 4, 11, 23, 28–31, 36, 63, 64, 81, 82, 84, 85, 87, 89, 99, 124, 127, 130, 153, 169, 172, 174, 179, 181, 192, 194, 195
period, 1, 10, 13, 73, 75, 88, 124, 207
perpetuation, 37, 64, 84, 178, 179, 211
persistence, 57, 129
person, 70, 81, 85, 98, 128–130
personnel, 7, 27, 209
perspective, 9, 11, 12, 28–30, 58, 70, 72, 74, 80, 81, 84, 88, 94, 170, 185, 187, 188, 193, 194, 202, 211
Peter A. Sturrock, 28
phenomena, 2, 4, 11, 14, 16, 17, 19, 21, 22, 27–34, 36, 38, 43, 51, 54, 55, 59, 60, 62, 64–66, 71, 75–78, 80, 82–94, 98–104, 108, 109, 112, 114–118, 120–125, 127–132, 137–144, 147–149, 151–162, 167, 168, 172–174, 177–188, 191, 193–202, 205, 207, 209–214
phenomenon, 2, 5, 11, 22, 29, 36, 39, 51, 53, 56, 59, 63, 64, 74, 75, 77, 80, 81, 83, 87, 91, 97, 108, 112–117, 120, 122, 137, 148, 152, 159, 183, 186, 188, 193, 194, 202
Phoenix, 27

phoenix, 163, 164
photo, 103
photograph, 50, 103
photography, 67, 79
physicist, 9
physics, 19, 22, 26, 27, 100, 140, 151, 205
physique, 69
piece, 14, 75, 80, 83, 89, 95
place, 13, 23, 25, 58, 73, 127, 146, 166, 175, 178
plane, 121
planet, 24, 146, 173, 188–190
plaster, 53, 61
platform, 37, 46, 47, 171, 174, 176
plausibility, 25, 90, 145, 152, 178, 193
play, 8, 14, 30, 36, 37, 39, 46, 50, 51, 59, 76, 81, 84, 85, 92, 94, 101, 103, 104, 125, 129–131, 133, 136, 139, 150, 151, 154, 162, 166, 168, 169, 172, 176, 179, 181, 185, 186, 194, 200, 201, 205, 207, 211, 213
plesiosaur, 50, 51
point, 8, 11, 26, 29, 42, 77, 193
Point Pleasant, 71, 165
pollination, 43
poltergeist, 80, 98
polygraph, 14
pop, 164
popularity, 167, 169
popularization, 26, 198
population, 4, 49, 53, 58, 165
portrayal, 4, 178, 179, 181
Portsmouth, 10
posit, 81
position, 8

positive, 146, 169, 200
possibility, 14, 22, 31, 34, 41, 56, 57, 59, 63, 65, 70, 78, 79, 82, 84, 86, 87, 104, 117, 125, 145, 146, 150, 167, 171–173, 178, 185, 193
potential, 8, 9, 12, 19, 27, 29, 43, 46, 59–61, 66, 71, 72, 75, 77–79, 82, 87, 89–93, 100–103, 122–125, 131–133, 136–138, 140, 143–148, 150, 152, 153, 158, 159, 172, 175, 191, 194, 200, 202–204, 209
power, 38, 56, 59, 81, 87, 94, 102, 124, 161, 163, 167, 172, 175, 176, 184, 188, 203
practice, 180
prayer, 182
presence, 4, 17, 19, 21, 50, 53, 61, 69, 79, 83, 90, 98, 102, 116, 121, 140, 195, 202
presentation, 140
preservation, 131, 186, 187
press, 8
pressure, 84
prevalence, 65, 85
prey, 164
pride, 5, 58, 180
primate, 66
principle, 195
privacy, 67, 92, 102, 143, 161, 204, 205
problem, 153
process, 48, 65, 70, 92, 132, 139, 140, 147, 150, 151, 155, 195, 204
product, 57, 59, 135
production, 197
professional, 46, 148, 155, 157, 201, 213
profile, 42, 53, 94, 106, 108
program, 93
progress, 158, 214
project, 29, 51, 157
proliferation, 65, 112
prominence, 11, 43, 52
proneness, 30
proof, 27, 33, 50–53, 61, 62, 64, 79, 89, 94, 124, 135, 136
propensity, 85
proper, 42, 56, 68, 131, 165, 180, 211
property, 7, 204
proportion, 69
propulsion, 26, 27
protection, 182, 187
protector, 165
protocol, 90, 93
proximity, 73
pseudoscience, 45, 149, 188, 211
psychic, 92, 98, 99, 132, 133, 141, 143, 158
psychokinesis, 99
psychologist, 12
psychology, 8, 29, 60, 72, 77, 100, 143, 151–153, 193, 200, 205, 212
public, 1–4, 10, 11, 13, 28, 31, 36, 37, 42, 43, 46–49, 52, 54, 66, 67, 73, 74, 81, 84, 87, 92, 93, 125, 144, 148, 151, 159–162, 174, 185, 190, 196, 198, 202–204, 210–214
publication, 138
Puerto Rico, 38, 55, 74, 165, 169
puncture, 55, 74

purpose, 47, 116, 139, 182
pursuit, 46, 48, 137, 155, 198, 205
purview, 157
puzzle, 22, 74, 76, 80, 95

quality, 48, 78, 89, 139, 140, 154, 157, 195, 202, 205
quantity, 148, 202, 205
quest, 72, 100, 123, 183
question, 11, 19, 32, 34, 93, 94, 145, 160, 176, 177, 188, 192–194, 211, 212
questioning, 31, 91, 104, 106, 139, 171, 194, 201

race, 25
radar, 8
radio, 3, 4, 146
ranch, 7
rancher, 7
range, 3, 17, 20, 25, 51, 53, 65, 72, 75, 99, 101, 110, 141, 148, 151, 154, 183, 186, 187, 195, 198
rarity, 54
rationality, 85, 184
rationalization, 184
reach, 3, 26, 49, 144, 148, 212
reaction, 3, 4
reality, 3, 19, 23, 29, 30, 37, 59, 81, 87, 94, 117, 121, 123, 126, 143, 171, 178, 188
realm, 19, 54, 62, 70, 72, 80, 85, 93–95, 98, 101, 118, 122, 127, 149, 155–158, 160, 170, 171, 182, 188
reasoning, 92, 104, 105, 108, 137, 139, 140, 160, 185, 211
reassurance, 185

rebirth, 163
rebuttal, 86
recall, 10, 21, 59, 60
recognition, 38, 43, 45, 66, 72, 188
recollection, 77, 124
record, 131, 132
recording, 90, 103
refer, 17, 118, 123
reference, 11, 48, 203
referencing, 28, 60, 165
regard, 167
region, 28, 51, 55, 89, 176, 181
regression, 10, 21
reinforcement, 130, 184
rejection, 129
relation, 30, 61
relationship, 37, 118, 120, 121, 157, 169, 176
release, 8
reliability, 4, 11, 66, 80, 90, 91, 104, 131, 137–139, 141, 154–156, 158, 192, 193, 195, 203, 208
reliance, 191
religion, 146
remain, 62, 70, 72, 77, 93, 98, 111, 127, 140, 145, 149, 158, 189
reminder, 14, 29, 34, 52, 61, 73, 169
remote, 13, 24, 41, 45, 52, 58, 66, 92, 117, 121, 122, 136, 147, 173, 190, 202, 203
renewal, 163
report, 20, 24, 30, 84, 92, 103, 111, 116, 124, 154, 203
reporting, 4, 13, 71, 84, 143, 148, 155, 180, 203
representation, 161
reproducibility, 137, 138, 140, 191

reptile, 38, 50, 51, 55
reputation, 180
requirement, 195
research, 1, 7, 11, 12, 14, 19, 22, 25, 27, 30, 38, 43, 45–49, 54, 62, 65–68, 71, 72, 74, 75, 77, 80, 82, 85, 90–93, 95, 99, 100, 112, 114, 117, 120, 123, 125, 130–133, 136, 138–143, 147–151, 153–162, 166, 170–172, 174, 176, 187, 189, 191, 193–195, 199–202, 204, 205, 207, 208, 210–213
researcher, 66, 139, 140
resident, 57
resilience, 168
resolution, 147, 202
resource, 48
respect, 67, 92, 93, 157, 161, 169, 180, 183, 185
response, 8, 185, 199
result, 3, 5, 11, 14, 24, 31, 56, 58, 63, 64, 70, 80, 94, 117, 122–124, 135, 140, 192, 193, 197, 199, 200
revenue, 180
reverence, 187
review, 48, 66, 138–141, 150, 151, 195
Rich Newman, 103
Richard Wiseman, 83
richness, 170
ridge, 53
rigor, 48, 49, 71, 80, 120, 138, 140, 143, 147, 157, 160, 162, 203
rise, 3, 163, 183, 187
risk, 154

road, 13, 73, 76
robustness, 138
rock, 176
Roger Clarke, 103
role, 3, 4, 8, 11, 12, 29–31, 34, 36, 37, 39, 41–43, 46, 50, 51, 59, 61, 62, 65, 73, 76–78, 81, 84, 85, 87, 92, 94, 100, 101, 104, 122, 125, 129–131, 137, 139, 147, 150, 151, 154, 155, 159–162, 164, 166, 168–170, 172, 174, 176, 178, 179, 181, 183–185, 194, 195, 200, 201, 203, 205, 207, 211–213
room, 13, 94, 125, 136, 156
Roswell, 7, 26, 32, 108
rubber, 8

safety, 161
saliva, 61, 79, 203
sample, 57, 203
sampling, 67
Sanderson, 42
saucer, 8
scale, 155
scanning, 50, 67, 195
scarcity, 45, 48, 136
scenario, 87, 124
scene, 13
school, 1, 212
science, 31, 38, 41, 46, 48, 49, 65, 81, 85, 115, 118, 121–123, 127, 133, 143, 148–152, 154–157, 159–162, 186, 188, 197, 200, 201, 203–205, 211–213
scientist, 42, 137, 170

Index 237

scope, 46, 148, 155, 156, 160, 211
Scotland, 51, 67, 74, 168, 185, 197
scream, 57, 166
screen, 172, 174
scrutiny, 17, 28, 104, 120, 125, 135, 143, 147, 148, 150, 191, 195, 204
sculpture, 175
sea, 164, 186
search, 3, 9, 41, 50, 54, 59, 71, 129, 136, 144–146, 178, 194, 195, 202
second, 1, 17–19, 24, 25, 73
secrecy, 33, 190
section, 1, 7, 13, 17, 24, 36, 44, 46, 57, 59, 62, 78, 80, 82, 83, 86, 90, 93, 97, 104, 108, 112, 115, 121, 123, 125, 130, 139, 147, 151, 154, 160, 163, 165, 167, 168, 170, 172, 175, 177, 179, 181, 186, 194, 198, 202, 205, 207, 211
security, 33, 167
selection, 210
self, 145
sensation, 42
sensationalism, 102, 174, 178, 200
sense, 3–5, 20, 29, 36–38, 58, 70, 83, 85, 99, 101, 116, 167, 174–176, 178–180, 182–185, 187, 199, 200, 204, 212
sensing, 45, 117, 136, 202, 205
sensitivity, 143, 180, 181, 185
sensor, 61
series, 55, 65, 103, 209
serpent, 50, 163
session, 103
set, 24, 80, 122, 154
setting, 73, 164
shadow, 98
shape, 5, 6, 29, 36, 38, 56, 60, 61, 74, 78, 81, 83, 84, 86, 127, 129, 144, 153, 167, 169, 177, 179, 181, 183, 184, 186
share, 5, 15, 18, 46, 48, 74, 92, 113, 117, 154, 157, 158, 168, 174, 187, 213
sharing, 37, 49, 67, 91, 138, 155, 156, 158, 174, 185
sheep, 55
sheriff, 7
shift, 37, 150, 151, 199
show, 135
side, 73, 76, 131
sighting, 1, 2, 28, 50, 56, 57, 61, 65, 73, 75, 79, 81, 84, 85, 89, 91, 93, 111, 148
sign, 164
signal, 146
significance, 4, 12, 38, 39, 51, 52, 54, 57–59, 62, 66, 73, 74, 81, 89, 91, 94, 99, 123, 125, 127, 137, 148, 153, 154, 165, 167–170, 172, 174–177, 181, 182, 186–188, 198, 207, 210
silicon, 146
similarity, 77, 94, 116, 122
site, 8, 21, 47, 101
situation, 124, 130
size, 55, 61, 71, 78, 79, 166
skepticism, 4, 11, 16, 37, 49, 55–57, 72, 80, 86, 92, 94, 95, 100, 104, 106–108, 114, 120, 122, 124, 132, 133, 136,

139–141, 143, 144, 150, 158, 178, 184, 185, 195, 196, 199, 202, 211
skill, 106
skin, 10, 55, 56, 61, 69, 76, 116, 203
sky, 10, 13, 29, 108
sleep, 11, 12, 14, 64, 70
smartphone, 148
snout, 69
Snowman, 168
socialization, 84, 85, 184
society, 34, 36, 46–49, 146, 168, 177–179, 183, 185, 186, 198, 200
sociology, 151, 193, 200, 205
software, 147, 158
solace, 5, 38
solving, 153
sonar, 50, 67, 195
song, 178
sorrow, 97
sound, 152, 164, 195, 203
soundness, 140
source, 5, 52, 64, 77, 116, 168, 172, 175, 180
South Africa, 201
souvenir, 180
space, 19, 21
spacecraft, 9, 13, 29, 64
span, 1, 57
spark, 156, 161, 167, 176, 199
speaker, 159
species, 25, 26, 42, 48, 51, 53, 54, 56, 57, 61, 66, 67, 70, 72, 78, 79, 81, 82, 87, 89, 91, 94, 135–137, 145, 150, 152, 171, 189–193, 201, 203, 204
specimen, 94

speculation, 4, 27, 32, 70, 74, 81, 94, 99, 108, 109, 112, 122, 125, 137, 144, 166
speed, 26
spine, 177
spirit, 3, 104, 122, 131, 166, 169
spiritualism, 141
spirituality, 25, 183
spread, 8, 13, 33, 38, 52, 64, 129, 178, 211
spring, 1
squid, 164
stance, 62
standard, 161
standardization, 157
standpoint, 11, 59, 83
starting, 77
state, 13, 70, 81, 87, 99, 128, 158, 199
statement, 8, 137
statue, 165
status, 49, 136
step, 17, 66, 132, 137
Steve Alten, 177
Steven Spielberg's, 197
stigma, 66
stigmatization, 199
stone, 1, 73, 76, 88, 89
story, 2–4, 12–14, 30, 75, 83, 103, 164, 165, 170, 171, 178
storytelling, 4, 56, 161, 165, 167, 175
strain, 5
strength, 146, 168, 190
stress, 11, 59, 67, 87
student, 1
study, 2, 10, 11, 16, 21, 22, 25, 26, 31, 38, 41–47, 49, 51, 56, 58, 66, 68, 71, 75, 78, 79,

81, 90, 92, 94, 99, 101, 104, 106, 108, 111, 112, 118, 121–123, 125, 128, 135, 136, 138, 141, 143, 144, 150–153, 158–160, 162, 168–170, 172, 174, 175, 180, 183, 186, 187, 189, 192–198, 200, 202, 205
subject, 16, 21, 24, 25, 53, 63, 70, 74, 100, 112, 121, 124, 138, 150, 156, 161, 171, 175, 191, 195, 201
subset, 118
sucker, 55, 165
Suffolk, 209
suggestibility, 11, 13, 22, 30, 31, 77, 102, 195
suggestion, 25, 31, 77, 81, 82, 87, 88, 94, 102, 124, 192
summary, 5, 12, 205, 213
sun, 163
superstition, 183
supply, 51
support, 19, 27, 30, 51, 66, 71, 75, 77, 79, 92, 93, 98, 101, 120, 127, 129, 135, 141, 143, 156, 184, 185, 189, 190, 194, 195, 200
surrounding, 2–4, 7, 12, 14, 31–33, 38, 39, 48, 51, 52, 59, 73, 76, 77, 81, 86, 87, 89, 91, 99, 120, 123, 144, 152, 165, 167, 170, 176, 177, 180, 183, 185, 186, 190, 193, 195–197, 199, 200, 211
surveillance, 102
survey, 93, 202
survival, 42
suspense, 171
swimming, 50, 63
symbol, 51, 54, 58, 197
symbolism, 165, 168, 169
system, 109, 129, 141

t, 5, 9, 164
table, 150, 205
tail, 57, 74
tale, 164, 166
tapestry, 127, 167, 175, 183
task, 54, 148, 150
taxonomy, 61
team, 51, 62, 166
technique, 102
technology, 14, 22, 43, 45, 61, 62, 126, 133, 136, 143, 144, 147–150, 189, 202–205, 210
telepathy, 10, 20, 99, 141
television, 2–4, 13, 29, 37, 43, 54, 84, 112, 172, 174, 177, 178, 185, 197
temperature, 102, 132, 158
temptation, 164
tendency, 27, 30, 60, 63, 64, 85, 128, 140, 158, 184
tension, 2, 11
term, 5, 46, 49, 108, 117, 209, 210
terminology, 153
terrain, 54, 69
test, 65, 137, 138, 204
testability, 127, 139
testimony, 76, 88, 195
testing, 91, 125
Texas, 56, 165
texture, 69
the Appalachian Mountains, 53

the Great Lakes, 53
the Okanagan Valley, 166
the Pacific Northwest, 53
the Scottish Highlands, 50
the Travis Walton Alien Encounter, 13, 14
the United States, 11, 38, 169
theme, 74, 159
theory, 14, 21, 22, 29, 32, 37, 42, 51, 53, 80, 94, 123, 124, 126–129, 183, 193
therapy, 30
thinking, 4, 25, 28, 34, 36, 46, 48, 56, 65, 71, 85–87, 92, 93, 103, 104, 106–108, 111, 120, 124, 149, 158–160, 162, 167, 180, 184, 185, 194, 195, 198, 201, 202, 211–213
thought, 51, 82, 122, 127, 145, 170, 171, 201
thriller, 177
time, 1, 8, 10–12, 19, 21, 27, 31, 51, 70, 73–75, 77, 81, 88–90, 98, 115, 124, 127, 136, 148, 155, 187, 190, 207, 210
timeframe, 73
timeline, 127
timing, 73
tool, 11, 31, 65
top, 8, 89
topic, 74, 97, 108, 111, 112, 140, 144, 150
topography, 204
tourism, 5, 51, 166, 197
tourist, 181
town, 1–7, 73
trace, 80, 125
track, 91, 132, 202, 207
tradition, 81
trail, 136
training, 154, 156
transformation, 182
transition, 11, 118
transmission, 184
transparency, 66, 138, 143
trap, 75
trauma, 30, 197, 200
travel, 10, 21, 26, 27, 127, 178
Travis Walton, 13
Travis Walton Alien Encounter, 14
treasure, 163
tree, 63, 76
trip, 10
truck, 13
truth, 2, 8, 14, 21, 32–34, 52, 54, 57, 59, 70, 87, 90, 120, 157, 168, 171, 180, 183, 191, 200
turmoil, 98
turn, 175, 176
turning, 26
type, 19, 61, 62, 82, 98, 99, 122

U.S., 8, 32, 108
ufologist, 109
ufology, 11, 14, 20, 25, 72, 90, 91
uncertainty, 73, 184
understanding, 12, 14, 17, 19, 22, 23, 26, 27, 30, 34, 36–38, 41, 43–50, 59, 60, 65, 67, 68, 70–73, 76, 77, 80, 82, 83, 85–87, 90–92, 94, 95, 100, 101, 108, 113–117, 120, 121, 123, 125, 127, 130, 133, 138, 141, 143, 144, 146, 148–159, 161,

162, 165, 167–172, 174, 176, 179, 180, 183–188, 191, 193, 194, 196–202, 205–207, 209–214
underworld, 164
unease, 3, 4, 116, 199
unexplained, 3, 5, 27–29, 31, 32, 34, 62, 78, 80–82, 85, 89, 95, 98, 99, 101, 102, 104, 109, 111, 121, 127, 129–132, 157–159, 167, 174, 176, 177, 179, 182–184, 195, 199, 207
uniqueness, 3, 74
United States, 55
unity, 5
universality, 168
universe, 9, 23, 25, 27, 127, 144–146, 152
up, 3, 4, 7, 8, 13, 20, 21, 31–33, 48, 71, 147, 203
USA, 13
use, 4, 43, 60, 78, 92, 93, 124, 130, 147, 150, 158, 176, 184, 202
utilization, 26

vacation, 10
validate, 21, 37, 60, 82, 112, 131, 135, 136, 146, 190
validation, 92, 101, 138, 141, 154, 200
validity, 25, 65, 66, 68, 71, 83, 86, 88, 118, 137, 139, 148, 158, 183, 191, 193, 195, 200, 208
value, 150, 153, 155, 173, 178, 201, 209
vampire, 38, 56
variety, 4, 99, 142, 156, 195, 199
vastness, 9, 95, 188
vegetation, 20, 204
verification, 138
veterinarian, 56
vicinity, 88
video, 101, 103, 118, 155
view, 14, 32, 34, 129, 181
viewing, 24, 92, 187
vision, 98
visitation, 21, 26–28, 109
visitor, 73, 95
visual, 17, 51, 62, 64, 78, 88, 91, 102, 121, 147, 161, 178, 187
visualization, 205
voice, 5, 164
vulnerability, 77, 199

wakefulness, 11
wall, 1, 73, 76, 88
Walton, 13, 14
war, 97
Warren Zevon, 178
water, 50, 51, 67, 168, 182, 202
watermelon, 60, 76, 88
way, 5, 36, 46, 60, 64, 75, 80, 81, 84, 167, 172, 179, 186, 187
wealth, 60
weather, 8, 32, 90, 108, 109, 118
weathering, 193
weighing, 164
weight, 70, 78, 79, 89, 94
well, 5, 6, 10, 14, 18, 24, 27, 28, 30, 32, 50, 59, 63, 67, 68, 74, 86, 92, 102, 121, 143, 152, 161, 163, 169, 171, 174, 180, 182, 198, 200, 208, 209
West Virginia, 2, 71, 165, 177

whole, 51, 177, 198
wildcat, 58
wilderness, 54, 164, 169, 175
wildlife, 63, 161
will, 1, 7, 10, 13, 17, 24, 36, 44, 46, 54, 57, 59, 62, 64, 72, 78, 80, 82, 86, 90, 93, 97, 104, 108, 112, 113, 115, 121, 123, 125, 130, 139, 147, 149, 151, 153, 160, 163, 165, 170, 172, 175, 177, 179, 181, 186, 194, 198, 202, 205, 207, 211
William Blanchard, 8
William Brazel, 7
willingness, 29, 153, 180
wisdom, 34, 163, 164, 188
wisps, 64
witness, 8, 21, 22, 28, 53, 63, 72, 76, 77, 81, 87, 89, 98, 122, 135
wonder, 38, 52, 70, 167, 174, 175, 178, 187, 199, 200
work, 42, 44, 45, 60, 102, 135, 139, 144, 150, 157, 159, 176, 187, 196
working, 158
world, 1, 5, 29, 34, 36, 41, 45, 48, 50, 52, 54, 65, 68, 70, 73–75, 80, 83, 93, 95, 97, 100, 108, 118, 120–122, 125–127, 130, 137, 149, 151, 163, 165, 167–172, 175–177, 179, 182, 188, 190, 191, 193, 194, 197, 198, 200
worldview, 84, 85
writer, 42
writing, 98

year, 1, 2, 51, 73, 88
Yeti, 168, 203
Yowie, 169
Yowies, 169

zoology, 47, 67, 72, 146